Declarations of Independence

DECLARATIONS
of
INDEPENDENCE

Women and Political Power in Nineteenth-Century American Fiction

Barbara Bardes

AND

Suzanne Gossett

Rutgers University Press

NEW BRUNSWICK AND LONDON

Library of Congress Cataloging-in-Publication Data

Bardes, Barbara A.
    Declarations of independence : women and political power in
  nineteenth-century American fiction / Barbara Bardes and Suzanne
  Gossett.
      p.   cm.
  Bibliography: p.
  Includes index.
  ISBN 0-8135-1500-9 (cloth)—ISBN 0-8135-1501-7 (pbk.)
    1. American fiction—19th century—History and criticism.
2. Women in literature.   3. Politics in literature.   4. Women's
rights in literature.   5. Politics and literature.   I. Gossett,
Suzanne.   II. Title.
PS374.W6B37   1990
813'.309352042—dc20   89-36066
                                                                CIP

British Cataloging-in-Publication information available

Contents

Acknowledgments

The origins of this book are intertwined with the origins of the Women's Studies Program at Loyola University of Chicago, the first such program adopted by a Jesuit university. The authors, a professor of political science and an English professor, met at the very first meeting held to discuss instituting women's studies at Loyola, and women's studies immediately demonstrated its potential for bringing together scholars in different disciplines as we discovered common intellectual and personal interests. With the assistance of a Loyola Mellon grant for course development, we designed and taught a new course called, "The Century of Struggle: Women in Politics and Literature in Nineteenth-Century America." Out of research done for that course came our earlier articles and, finally, the plan for the book.

Loyola University of Chicago has assisted us in many ways. In addition to the Mellon grant which supported our earliest research efforts, the university granted us both research leaves to complete *Declarations of Independence*. The Women's Studies Program provided office support, requested resources for the university library, and brought together a network of friends and colleagues who encouraged our work. Our colleagues Judith Wittner of the Women's Studies Program, James Rocks and Joyce Wexler of the English department, and Thomas Engemen and Jean Yarbrough of the Political Science department supplied helpful ideas, advice, and support as the book developed. At the Loyola University library, we benefited from the assistance and interest of Yvonne Damien, Tara Fulton, and Lorna Newman.

Our efforts to locate nineteenth-century sources and to understand the political culture of the period were aided in great measure by the librarians at the University of Chicago's Regenstein Library, in particular Sandra

Applegate and Patricia Swanson. We have also worked in the library of Cincinnati and Hamilton County, the New York Public Library, the Library of Congress, the Newberry Library, and the Centro di Studi Americani in Rome. Thanks to the proximity of the Center for Research Libraries in Chicago, we obtained films of rare novels and journals with extraordinary expedition.

Many scholars outside of our own institution have offered advice and comments on our work, and we express our gratitude to them while exempting them from any responsibility for our conclusions. Special thanks go to Robert Ferguson, Elizabeth K. Helsinger, and William Veeder, who answered questions, read outlines, and shared books. Members of the Feminist Literary Criticism Group at the Newberry Library gave us constructive reactions to an early sketch of the book. Sections of chapters 1 and 5 were read to responsive audiences at National Women's Studies Association meetings in Seattle and Champaign. Finally, we owe particular thanks to Mary Kelley and Lucy Freibert for thoughtful comments and helpful suggestions on the entire manuscript.

Versions of chapters 1 and 3 of this book appeared in *Legacy* 2 (1985) and *American Quarterly* 32 (1980), and we thank the editors of those journals for permission to use these materials.

Not long after we embarked on the book-length manuscript, we were fortunate to meet Leslie Mitchner of Rutgers University Press, whose enthusiasm for the project has been unfailing. Our copyeditor, Kathryn Gohl, is to be credited for the final polishing of the text.

Since we met, at that first Women's Studies planning session, our research and teaching efforts have been greatly enriched by our personal friendship. Our lives and work have also been enriched by our husbands, Dale Bardes and Philip Gossett, and by the love, if not helpfulness, of our children, Cara Bardes and David and Jeffrey Gossett. To the five of them we dedicate this book.

Introduction:
Fiction and Political Culture

In *My Wife and I*, published in 1871, one of the young female characters proclaims: "They do not try to control me, or enslave me. Why? Because I made my declaration of independence, and planted my guns, and got ready for war. This is dreadfully unamiable, but it did the thing; it secured peace; I am let alone."[1] This strong statement of self-determination is offered by Ida, a young woman planning to study medicine. Harriet Beecher Stowe, who had announced her support for suffrage in 1869, created in Ida a model for the proper women's rights woman.[2] Although the young wife of the title finds her true vocation in domesticity, her sister Ida is one of two women in *My Wife and I* for whom Stowe thinks the choice of a career over marriage is appropriate. Furthermore, Stowe underscores her commitment to Ida's position by her use of a powerful political symbol, the Declaration of Independence.

Stowe's choice of the Declaration to signify Ida's self-control and liberty is but one example in a long tradition of such usage by authors of American fiction in the nineteenth century. As a symbol, the Declaration recalled the moment of the founding of the American republic. In contradistinction to the Constitution, which created institutions of political order, the Declaration symbolized the natural right of every individual to freedom from oppression. As a central concept in American political culture, the Declaration was used as a rallying cry by many groups to demand recognition of their natural rights.[3]

Authors such as Catharine Maria Sedgwick, Louisa May Alcott, and Harriet Beecher Stowe allow female characters to use the Declaration as a symbol of liberty for women to convey a complicated and radical message. Since women not only were excluded from voting and thus from direct participation in the political system, but were assigned a domestic and subordinate role within the household, for a woman to appropriate the Declaration of Independence to herself meant she was asserting her equality to men and her independence of male control.

Early feminists fully understood the power of the symbol in political discourse. Led by Elizabeth Cady Stanton, the women who gathered at Seneca Falls in 1848 used the Declaration as the model for their Declaration of Sentiments and Resolutions. They wrote:

> We hold these truths to be self-evident: that all men and women are created equal; that they are endowed by their Creator with certain inalienable rights; that among these are life, liberty, and the pursuit of happiness. . . . The history of mankind is a history of repeated injuries and usurpations on the part of man toward woman, having in direct object the establishment of an absolute tyranny over her.[4]

The women made their claims on the political system as daughters of the American Revolution. As Stanton announced, in her address to the New York legislature in 1854, "Yes, gentlemen, in republican America, in the nineteenth century, we, the daughters of the revolutionary heroes of '76, demand at your hands the redress of our grievances—a revision of your State Constitution—a new code of laws."[5]

Within a year of the Seneca Falls Convention, James Fenimore Cooper turned the symbol on its head to illustrate the dire consequences that would befall society if women were granted such revolutionary liberty. In *The Ways of the Hour*, written in 1849 and published in 1850, the central female character, Mary Monson, complains of man's absolute tyranny: "I can feel my own longings. They are all for independence. Men have not dealt fairly by women. Possessing the power, they have made all the laws."[6] Cooper calls up the same imagery as Stanton and Stowe, but to different ends. His independent woman, Mary Monson, is a wealthy, willful creature who has left her husband and is quite out of control, wreaking havoc within the community. She is a negative example of the natural right to liberty demanded by Stanton. Yet despite their differences, Cooper, Stanton, and Stowe all agree on the power of the Declaration of Independence as a cultural symbol, available to support or ridicule women's claim for a greater share of political power.

The Declaration is only one of many symbols and concepts that constitute American political culture in the nineteenth century. Confronting the political culture, which we understand to be the beliefs, cognitions, and attitudes that individuals hold toward the political institutions and processes of a society, is central to understanding women's status in the nineteenth century. It was the political culture that defined woman's role as a citizen and established the boundaries that kept women in the private sphere early in the century and out of the polls in the Gilded Age. Furthermore, since the division between what is public and what is private is always fundamentally political, the political culture reaches into the familial setting through both law and custom. In this book, we use works of fiction to examine the constraints that the political culture placed on woman's role in the American republic and to trace the century-long struggle over that role as it was conducted, in part, through American fiction.

According to contemporaries, free white women in the early nineteenth-century Republic were citizens with "equal rights," in theory rights equal to those of men, and they were expected to learn and to transmit the same political culture as were their husbands and fathers. This political culture espoused dual spheres of activities for the sexes; women were responsible for educating young children in the proper moral and patriotic virtues and for upholding those same virtues within the home,[7] while men represented the household in the external political world through discussion and voting. As early as 1797, Hannah Foster interrupts her sentimental novel, *The Coquette*, to explicate the division of political duties between men and women. Mrs. Richman, a model republican matron, explains,

> We think ourselves interested in the welfare and prosperity of our country; and, consequently, claim the right of inquiring into those affairs, which may conduce to, or interfere with the common weal. We shall not be called to the senate or the field to assert its privileges, and defend its rights, but we shall feel for the honor and safety of our friends and connections, who are thus employed. If the community flourish and enjoy health and freedom, shall we not share in the happy effects? if it be oppressed and disturbed, shall we not endure our proportion of the evil? Why then should the love of our country be a masculine passion only? Why should government, which involves the peace and order of the society, of which we are a part, be wholly excluded from our observation?[8]

Mrs. Richman here articulates a set of cultural limits and expectations. Although women were not to participate in public life by speaking, voting, or bearing arms, Foster proposes that they take an active, though private interest in affairs of state. Fiction here informs us about attitudes toward women's role in the Republic just before the beginning of the nineteenth century; Mrs. Richman's rhetorical questions, which suggest that others may hold beliefs contrary to hers, hint at the areas of tension about that role. Characteristically, fiction both confirms and enlarges historical knowledge gained from other sources.

In the century after Foster wrote, the range of opportunities for women to participate in the public sphere expanded dramatically. Cultural beliefs about the public roles appropriate for women and the personal resources, including education, property, and wages, they could control changed even more than did the actual rights and status of women. Although most female citizens did not gain the right to participate directly in the political system through suffrage until 1920, they did gain access to the political sphere through the platform, through petitions, and through local policy-making on issues like temperance and purity. Each of these opportunities for independent action—such as the right to speak in public, the right to control property, the right to become a professional, or the right to contract for wage work—is political, because such rights are granted or regulated by the political system.

The changes in the political culture that allowed the enhancement of woman's status were the result of debates that often lasted for generations and formed a major element in many works of nineteenth-century fiction. *The Coquette* is a forerunner of such novels: as Cathy Davidson notes, it is "ultimately about silence, subservience, stasis (the accepted attributes of women as traditionally defined) in contradistinction to conflicting impulses toward independence, action, and self-expression (the ideals of the new American nation)."[9] Faced with these conflicting impulses, American writers from Foster on took positions on the proper intersection between the issues of public life and woman's assigned roles in the private sphere. These novelists did not merely reflect public attitudes, but, through their acceptance of the dominant tenets of the political culture or by mounting a challenge to those values, participated in the battle over woman's access to power.

The novels we examine in this book both index the cultural debate about women and political power and take an activist role within that debate. Fiction impinges on history, just as history impinges on fiction. In the nineteenth-century United States, novels were widely understood to be agents of cultural transmission and, less passively, participants in cultural conflict. As the *Literary World* stated in 1850, "The novel is now almost recognized with the newspaper and the pamphlet as a legitimate mode of influencing public opinion."[10] Many novels defend or promulgate the prevailing concept of womanhood; others could be considered part of a "subversive" or "radical" tradition in American literature. Yet even such novels are, as Sacvan Bercovitch argues, "implicated in the society they resist, capable of overcoming the forces that compel their complicity, and nourished by the culture they often seem to subvert."[11] When early feminists demanded their natural rights as defined by the Declaration of Independence, they remained

within their political culture even while they challenged it to resolve its in-
ternal contradictions. Could a society that professed an individualistic liberal value system and attempted to inculcate it in every citizen deny access to
that set of values to women? This tension between the core principles of the
American ideology and the cultural constraints placed on women engaged
the attention of authors and readers throughout the century.

While we agree with Lennard Davis that "all novels are inherently ideological and in that sense are about the political and social world. . . . Even
overtly apolitical novels have embedded in their structure political statements about the world,"[12] we do not accept his premise that all novels, as
products of the capitalist marketplace, are reduced to one, fundamentally
conservative, position ultimately inscribed in the novel's form.[13] Nor do we
accept the more nuanced view of Terry Eagleton, who suggests that literature, although necessarily springing from the dominant ideology, is best understood as a tool with which we can understand and critique the illusion
that is "the ordinary ideological experience of men."[14] Instead, we understand the ideology of these novels to be, as Bercovitch proposes, a "system
of interlinked ideas, symbols and beliefs by which a culture . . . seeks to
justify and perpetuate itself." In this view, ideology is "basically conservative; but . . . not therefore static or simply repressive."[15] As Janet Todd
writes, "Literature inevitably colludes with ideology . . . but it does not
simply affirm, and it can expose and criticize as well as repeat."[16] The cultural debate that erupted over women's demands for the right to participate
in the political arena did take place within the dominant ideological consensus, but this ideology, like any other, developed through conflict and,
even after it achieved "dominance, it still [found] itself contending to one
degree or another with the ideologies of residual and emergent cultures
within the society."[17] The struggle for women's rights was, in our view, one
that challenged the residual English culture based on the law of *baron et
feme*, and sought to replace it with cultural norms consistent with the natu-
ral-rights assumptions of the Republic's founding.

Our work grows out of the feminist investigation of literature and history
that has taken place over the past two decades, but differs from it in our
close attention to the role that fiction played within the context of the political and legal situation in which it appeared. We respond to Janet Todd's call
for "more feminist literary history."[18] Nineteenth-century fiction provides
an extremely rich and complex set of sources for understanding the cultural
changes that brought women into the public sphere. Novels were, in their
own time, clearly understood to participate in the socialization of the population. Many took a strong political stance; the *North American Review*
noted in 1844 that "the novel has become an essay on morals, on political
economy, on the condition of women, on the vices and defects of social
life."[19] Nina Baym suggests that by 1850, the novel was "conscripted by the

reviewing establishment as an agent of social control," in which the class struggle is "less significant than the generational struggle and, above all, the gender struggle." [20] Examples of fiction that took explicit positions on this gender struggle abound.

The precise purposes of this fiction, beyond entertainment of the audience and monetary gain for the author, varied considerably. Advocacy could degenerate into propaganda: some of the late suffrage tracts are no more. Yet nineteenth-century reading audiences would hardly have accepted Davis's "cliché . . . that when novels become political they become boring." [21] In particular, fiction that addressed the gender struggle spoke to the central issue in many women's lives. Recognizing the potentially subversive nature of the novel, many early nineteenth-century commentators suggested severe limits on the subjects appropriate for female readers. The political position advanced by fiction, of course, was not always on the side of change; authors were as likely to defend the status quo as to attack it. Bayard Taylor, a well-known travel writer, uses his first novel, *Hannah Thurston* (1864), to try to persuade women that they will benefit themselves and their communities by remaining within the domestic sphere, and James Fenimore Cooper's *The Ways of the Hour* satirizes recent legal changes in New York in hopes of alienating readers from such political programs. But many novels more or less overtly attempt to influence their readers to demand modifications in political and legal structures affecting women; from Catharine Maria Sedgwick's *Hope Leslie* (1827) to Helen Gardener's *Pray You, Sir, Whose Daughter?* (1892), which concerns a proposal to lower the age of consent to ten in New York state, writers give graphic depictions of the necessity for women's participation in government. Sometimes novelists settle for the less ambitious goal of educating their readers about the laws. This is one of Cooper's aims; a striking example, discussed in chapter 3, is E.D.E.N. Southworth's novel *The Discarded Daughter* (1852).

Novels are an extremely potent source for interpreting the struggle for women's rights, because fiction, in contrast to public political discourse, which tended to exclude the demands of women from discussion, focused on the private sphere. Through structure, character, and comment, authors could take positions on power relationships between men and women without directly addressing the publicly sanctioned hierarchy of the sexes in the political sphere. Novels of the period thus provide striking evidence about the motives for opposing women's demands for political power, motives that remained unspoken or only hinted at on the floors of the legislatures or in the columns of newpapers.

Given our premise that virtually all novels are political in that they are written within the context of culture and ideology, which novels best reveal the cultural struggle? The battle for women's rights in the nineteenth-century United States can be viewed as a series of separate but interrelated demands for specific forms of empowerment. Women first demanded the right to speak their conscience on the public platform and then the right to control their own property. Later in the century, the cultural debate focused on the societal consequences of women engaging in wage work, becoming professionals, and taking direct political action. Some of these demands were resolved fairly quickly, while others spanned generations. As much as possible we examine novels that engaged directly in these debates, often novels that openly represent the terms and circumstances of conflict within the society. Thus, for example, although Hawthorne's *The Scarlet Letter* (1850) explores the place of woman within an oppressive community, implicitly examining the relationship between speech and sexuality, *The Blithedale Romance* (1852) is more pertinent to the major debate about woman's voice that took place from the late 1830s until the 1850s. This debate had to do with women's ability to answer the moral call to help others. It was a public debate about the public use of the female voice, and it was associated with social change, particularly abolition and women's rights. Hester Prynne's meditations on the need to tear down and rebuild the entire society are always private; thus it is Zenobia, member of a reform community, a woman who proclaims her intention to "lift up my own voice, in behalf of woman's wider liberty," [22] but instead is silenced, who concerns us here. Similarly, because we proceed by topic, we discuss Henry James's *The Bostonians* (1886) twice, once relating his picture of a homeopathic female doctor to the conflict about women professionals, and later analyzing the novel more generally in the context of the demand for political rights for women.

Evidence for the particular focus of the debate about women's power at any given moment is historical, based not just on the novels but on newspapers and political sources of the period. Against this background, the immediacy of many novels can be demonstrated. When Angelina Grimké and Fanny Wright shocked the nation by taking to the public lecture platform to argue their beliefs, the country engaged in a lengthy quarrel over the appropriateness of women exercising this form of political influence. A brief novel entitled *The Lecturess* (1839) did not fall into a historical void; neither did *The Bostonians*, responding almost fifty years later to women's demand for a different kind of political influence. Because the fundamental issue was always woman's power in the state, the same concerns and fears continually surfaced, even though the immediate questions changed. Each new debate in the society took place with the novels of the past as partial historical context. And partly through the novels the debate over women's political status escaped from the political platform and came directly into the home.

Often it is possible to trace the biographical underpinnings of a novelist's position. We find biography to be important when it provides concrete examples of the culture's impact on the individual. Like Sandra Gilbert and Susan Gubar, we believe that "texts are authored by people whose lives and minds are affected by the material conditions of [a knowable] history . . . the author [is] a gendered human being whose text reflects key cultural conditions." [23] Yet not all texts need to be explained from personal experience, and unlike Gilbert and Gubar we are not constructing a story of "gender strife." As is clear in the two chapters where we explore biography most extensively, chapters 1 and 3, not only do male and female authors differ on the basis of their life experience, but the women writers themselves differ on the extent to which women should have increased power within the state.

It is not our contention that biography and cultural conditions form an unbreakable vise, constricting the freedom of an author's imagination. [24] Despite Harriet Beecher Stowe's documentation of the abuses she describes in *Uncle Tom's Cabin* (1852), her novel results less from factual information than from her personal attitudes toward possibilities for slaves and women in the mid-century United States. Stowe's ideas were formed by her experiences as a Beecher, as a woman, and as a mother, but her personal moral and religious reflections on the codes of her culture also enter into her analysis. Similarly, in *Work* (1873) Louisa May Alcott remembers her attempts at supporting herself; she confines her heroine to jobs acceptable for women; but she concludes by presenting an idealized, imaginative picture of a multiracial, multigenerational community of working women which goes far beyond Fruitlands.

The discussion in fiction of women's rights which we trace cuts across any division of literature into "women's literature" and ordinary fiction, as well as any easy distinction between canonized and uncanonized work. [25] For instance, within a two-year period the leatherstocking author James Fenimore Cooper and the "scribbling woman" E.D.E.N. Southworth wrote novels taking opposing positions in the ongoing, state-by-state conflict over giving married women control of their own property. Similarly, the debate over according professional recognition to women doctors is found in novels by such diverse authors as William Dean Howells, Sarah Orne Jewett, Elizabeth Stuart Phelps, and Hamlin Garland, some in the literary canon, some not. Since these novelists most often wrote in full cognizance of each other's work, artificial separation of the works of women and men, or of canonical and noncanonical literature, obscures the full extent of public discussion.

Consequently, while many of the novels we analyze were written by "major," usually male, authors—James, Hawthorne, Cooper, Howells—others are by authors, usually female, who also reached and influenced large numbers of people—Hale, Stowe, Phelps, Freeman, Alcott. Occasionally we discuss at length a work, for instance Beverly Ellison Warner's *Troubled Waters* (1885), whose acceptance and impact at the time are uncertain. Even when a novel is not well known today, reviews in influential journals may demonstrate its contemporary significance, or, as in the case of Lillian Sommers's *For Her Daily Bread* (1887), an introduction by a notable political figure may suggest the public attention it received.

Our approach, though it is deeply indebted to feminist literary criticism of the last two decades, thus differs considerably from that of many critics whom we follow. For example, in *The Faces of Eve: Women in the Nineteenth-Century American Novel*,[26] the only female writer whose work Judith Fryer examines is Kate Chopin; in *Gender and the Writer's Imagination: From Cooper to Wharton*, Mary Suzanne Schriber examines only one woman author, Edith Wharton; only male authors figure in Judith Fetterley's *The Resisting Reader: A Feminist Approach to American Fiction*;[27] and Joyce W. Warren's *The American Narcissus: Individualism and Women in Nineteenth-Century American Fiction* includes only Margaret Fuller.[28] All of these books restrict their attention to recognized, major novelists. Conversely, Nina Baym's *Woman's Fiction: A Guide to Novels by and about Women in America, 1820–1870* is concerned only with female authors,[29] all usually considered minor or outside the canon.

Combining analysis of the culture and, often, the legal situation with analysis of texts, our work keeps its primary focus on the debate over women's power, rather than on a more exclusively literary reevaluation or examination of major authors. Depending on the historical shape that the debate took as it shifted from topic to topic, our chapters compare the writings of women (Sarah Josepha Hale and Catharine Maria Sedgwick) or of men and women (William Dean Howells and Elizabeth Stuart Phelps) or, more rarely, of men and men (Henry James and Hamlin Garland). Given the continuing nineteenth-century emphasis on the rhetorical function of fiction, our method is historically appropriate for a period when the *North American Review* could call the novel "one of the most effective . . . forms of composition, through which a comprehensive mind can communicate itself to the world."[30]

Although much of the "uncanonized" literature we examine is by women, it is important to note that not all female authors wrote "woman's fiction." Baym has defined the "single tale" such novels tell as "the story of a young girl who is deprived of the supports she had rightly or wrongly depended on to sustain her throughout life and is faced with the necessity of winning her own way in the world." Jewett's *A Country Doctor* (1884) does not fit this category, nor does Sedgwick's *Hope Leslie*, nor does Mary Wilkins Freeman's *A Portion of Labor* (1901), though all conclude with the "formation and assertion of a feminine ego."[31] Instead, these novels confront the obstacles facing a woman who receives the support she expects but who wishes to exercise her powers further, through political action, professional independence, or labor organizing. *Uncle Tom's Cabin*, which has been at the center of recent discussions of canon formation, also does not participate in the usual plot of domestic fiction.[32] Yet, this novel is a critical exploration of the limitations of women's power in the Republic. It forms part of a major debate over the ways in which women could or should act upon their moral convictions, given the cultural limitations on their action in the political sphere.

Recent examinations of the domestic novel have emphasized the effect of these novels on the individual reader. Nina Baym argues that one purpose of the repeated plot of midcentury women's fiction was to strengthen the ego of its female consumers.[33] Coming from a theoretical commitment to reader-response criticism, Jane Tompkins, in *Sensational Designs: The Cultural Work of American Fiction, 1790–1860*, asks her readers to see the sentimental novel "as a political enterprise, halfway between sermon and social-theory, that both codifies and attempts to mold the values of its time." She finds a political purpose in *Uncle Tom's Cabin* related to our concerns but more general: "to bring in the day when the meek—which is to say, women—will inherit the earth."[34] Tompkins, expecially in her analysis of "the institutionalization of literary value," compares the fortunes of male and female writers. While we share Tompkins's general orientation, we analyze a much broader range of novels to demonstrate the ways American fiction raised immediate political questions about women and the consequent importance of this fiction in the public sphere.

There are, nevertheless, limits—beyond obvious questions of space—on our ability to be comprehensive. Although Alcott was able to envision a community of women that cuts across racial and class lines, very few other novelists were willing to extend the debate over the political status of women outside of the white middle class. Native-born white women who had been socialized into the political culture of the Northeast and who had witnessed the democratization of the Jacksonian period, which extended voting rights to most of their male counterparts, were the most vocal advocates for increased rights for women.[35] Since the rising political activism of northern women occurred in the region where the publishing industry flourished, the early novels that take a position on women share a regional context. In the antebellum period, class distinctions rarely figure into fictional discussions of woman's place. Although novelists duly noted that many women had entered the factory labor force, they accepted the notion that such employment was temporary and rarely evidenced any idea of class consciousness. Similarly, antebellum novelists who were concerned with black women as slaves or sexual objects gave no attention to their loss of political rights as women.

After the Civil War, the consequences of industrialization and western expansion spill into the novels, adding new dimensions to the conflict over women's political power. Although a number of black women authors begin publishing, their primary concern is race rather than the political status of women.[36] Class issues, however, enter directly into a number of novels about the situation of women who work outside the home, whether the novelist addresses the conditions of factory labor, as in Phelps's *The Silent Partner* (1871), or the snobbery that keeps women of separate classes apart, portrayed by Howells in *A Woman's Reason* (1882). Similarly, the regional focus broadens. With the rise of a publishing industry in Chicago, novelists from the West provide examples of women who are truly independent and the "new men" who might be their partners. By the end of the nineteenth century, the fictional debate expands far beyond the eastern middle class.

As we examine the debate in nineteenth-century American fiction over women's power, three recurring themes emerge. The first is the inevitable intersection of the private sphere with the public realm. The culture provided a clearly defined set of duties and obligations for women within the domestic sphere. Yet the same responsibilities that the culture defined as domestic, and therefore nonpolitical, could force a woman into the public world. The intersection between the spheres is particularly evident in the case of the abolition movement. Obeying the cultural injunction that called on women to meet a higher standard of morality and spirituality, many women found themselves persuaded by the abolitionists that slavery was an abomination and that it was a sin to do nothing toward stopping it. Yet women soon learned that selling needlework at bazaars would have no effect on the plight of the slave; what was needed was political change. To effect such change women were moved to contest the limits of their sphere by joining mixed groups, circulating and signing petitions to Congress, and speaking in public for the cause.

Novelists writing about women inevitably breached the boundaries of the public sphere. Political import is obvious in *Uncle Tom's Cabin*, where even the women characters who accept their domestic roles become embroiled in the greatest controversy of the century. But it is equally present in such romantic novels as E.D.E.N. Southworth's *The Discarded Daughter*. Though this tale comes complete with the trappings of a Gothic—pirates, forced marriage, and children of unknown birth—Southworth requires long explanations of the laws governing married women's property in Maryland to justify the details of her domestic plot.

As the issue of abolition so clearly illustrates, women who felt morally called to take action faced severe limits on acceptable behavior for women. Since they were excluded from voting or other forms of active participation in the political sphere (and most women approved of that exclusion), the most effective form of influence remaining to them was persuasion. The power of the female voice is a second theme that appears in fiction throughout the century. Whether speaking for suffrage, as in Bayard Taylor's *Hannah Thurston*, or for the cause of labor, as in Mary Wilkins Freeman's

The Portion of Labor (1901), vocal women are powerful women. Like the larger society, authors repeatedly attempt to limit and control this power. Some, like Stowe, constrain the power of their female characters by keeping their voices within the household, while others restrict their women by separating voice from physical presence or from conscious control, as in the case of Hawthorne's Priscilla in *The Blithedale Romance*. Another way to contain the female voice is to confine it to acceptable subjects. In *The Silent Partner* the young factory worker Sip, radical, angry, and magnetic, concludes the novel by becoming a preacher, urging her audience of factory workers toward Christ rather than rebellion. These fictional strategies for controlling the female voice closely paralleled the historical attacks on the moral character of such women speakers as Frances Wright, the Grimké sisters, and Victoria Woodhull.

Fear of women's sexuality is the third recurrent theme in the debate over granting women more political power. The woman who spoke in public exercised power not only through her voice and words but simply through the presence of her body.[37] Critics of female speakers frequently assailed not their speeches but their femininity; they were chastised for being sexually exposed or else accused, conversely, of losing their sexual identity through their actions. In *The Blithedale Romance* Hawthorne counters Zenobia's obvious sexual power by silencing her. Similarly, in *The Bostonians*, as Verena speaks in a packed New York drawing room, Basil Ransom concludes that "she was meant for something divinely different—for privacy, for him, for love," and he succeeds in silencing her before she can "give [her]self" to the roaring crowd at the Music Hall.[38]

The fear and discomfort provoked by the publicly displayed female body permeated the entire society. One of the most powerful arguments for keeping women out of the industrial workplace was the potential effect of the daily mingling of men and women. Anticipating that women in wage work would be tempted to promiscuity, the economic novels of the later part of the century debate whether the workplace bears an obligation to protect women or whether women themselves are solely responsible for their own virtue. In Social Darwinian terms, the ability of a woman to control her sexuality in the workplace becomes a test of her character; the pure woman will be rewarded with a husband and her proper place in the domestic sphere, where, by definition, she will have only indirect political power.

The three themes—the intersection of the public and private spheres, the power of woman's voice, and the threat of the female body—are closely linked. If, in response to her conscience or faith, a woman tried to exert influence on public issues, she found it necessary to speak, usually outside the home. To enter the political debate on an equal footing with men, she had to participate in the public forum, where along with her words her sexuality would become an issue. This linkage between political action and sexuality is rarely spelled out in fiction but more frequently is implicit as novelists struggle with the cultural limits on female power.

The chapters that follow are arranged in roughly chronological order, paralleling historical shifts from topic to topic as Americans debated the limits on women's public power and novelists constructed conflicting models of public existence for women. The analysis begins with two novels published in 1827, the watershed year between the Era of Good Feelings and the Jacksonian period. Each of the novels presents a vision of the place of women in the republic of the Founders: *Northwood*, by Sarah Josepha Hale, idealizes woman's role in the perfect republican society, while *Hope Leslie*, by Catharine Maria Sedgwick, offers a critique of woman's place in the Republic under the guise of a historical novel set in Puritan times. These two works predate any public articulation of women's rights, except the controversial speeches of Frances Wright.

Yet soon women who had little sympathy with the radical ideas of Wright were following her example by speaking publicly, thus setting the stage for the first debate over women's participation in the political arena. As others have noted, the activities of women in the cause of abolition were a major source of the nineteenth-century women's movement.[39] Driven by a deep moral belief that they should do everything possible to aid the slave, many women sought to change the cultural prescription that forbade them the right to speak or exercise public influence outside their homes. By the late 1830s the question of how women could affect public affairs while remaining within traditional roles began to be argued in fiction. The quandary emerges in *The Lecturess*, where the heroine is forced to choose between the call of her conscience to speak on behalf of the slave and her duty to her husband and child. The contradiction between the didactic message of the novel and the management of sympathy toward the heroine epitomizes cultural tension about this new activity for women. Indeed, even the novel's anonymous publication may be an example of woman's uncertainty about raising her voice in public.

Social discomfort with women speaking in public extended far beyond dissension on the slavery question, though it was this issue that led women to claim the right to participate in public discourse and to attempt to sway those outside the family circle. Three novels of 1852, *Uncle Tom's Cabin*, *The Blithedale Romance*, and *Isa*, demonstrate the tension over woman's power expressed as the presence of her voice and body in the public sphere. Their attitude toward female discourse is always ambivalent: Hawthorne silences his two heroines, Chesebro' half damns hers, and even Stowe, who clearly expects salvation through women, suggests that the female language of moral obligation is ineffective and the speech of those without political rights is meaningless. The anxiety in these novels over woman's demand to be heard in public had both political and sexual sources; ultimately woman's attempt to be the subject rather than the object of discourse was a profound political gesture.

Another question that dominated the women's movement and public discussion before the Civil War was the right of married women to control their dowries or inherited property. Novels as early as Sedgwick's *Redwood* (1824) explored the implications of coverture and the transfer of all property from wife to husband. By the 1840s, a number of states had revised their laws to give married women more control over their own property, causing widespread debate about the potential consequences of this increase in female power. Two novels epitomize the debate. New York's legislation provoked Cooper to write *The Ways of the Hour* (1850), outlining his objections to the entire direction of the social order by showing how his heroine abuses the independence she gains from the Married Women's Property Act. Southworth's *The Discarded Daughter*, serialized the following year, defends a woman's need to have the power of property, while arguing that legal changes are limited in their effect by the personal relationship between husband and wife.

Only a small percentage of women had property to control, but as the century proceeded many more became wage earners. Shifting and uncertain attitudes toward the entry of women into the labor force paralleled divided attitudes toward unbridled economic development. Laissez-faire capitalism encouraged the use of whatever workers were most cheaply available, regardless of sex, and Social Darwinism gave a philosophical justification for not protecting women from industrial conditions. On the other hand, middle-class domesticity remained a basic social ideal affecting working women as well as those at home. A spate of post–Civil War novels reveals the spectrum of attitudes toward capitalism—from praise, through pleas for amelioration, to outright condemnation; as these novels analyze the impact of the capitalist economic system on social relations in the United States, they also argue the place of women within that system.

Despite differences in their economic views, the novels consistently raise the same questions regarding women at work. They consider whether a wage-earning woman must lose some inherent feminine quality; they meditate on the strength of sisterhood, asking whether it can survive class division; and they speculate on the results of having female sexuality in the workplace. As we shall see in *The Silent Partner* and *Troubled Waters*, no necessary connection existed between radical economic proposals and radical beliefs about working women. Yet these novelists all recognize that wage work will give women new kinds of power in their personal and political relations. The culmination of this fiction comes in a much-underrated novel of the turn of the century, Mary Wilkins Freeman's *The Portion of Labor*, which paints a revolutionary portrait of a working woman, a strike leader seen in her full complexity as a social, sexual, and economic being. Freeman, who takes up all the issues raised about working women in the preceding fiction, also explores these women's solidarity with male workers and their place in the confrontation of capital and labor.

The power that accompanied independent work was even more threatening when women attempted to enter professions. Although certain conservatives like Sarah Josepha Hale had justified a campaign for female doctors by arguing that women were needed to serve their own sex and preserve their modesty, the demand for access to traditionally male positions was more often viewed as an egotistical desire for independence. Once women had breached the medical or divinity schools they could claim professional status and a social recognition that not all of society was willing to yield. Those women who aspired to such professions as doctor, minister, lawyer, or scholar were usually assumed to have given up their claim to domestic life. But in answering William Dean Howells's *Dr. Breen's Practice* (1881), Elizabeth Stuart Phelps breaks with the prevailing code and concludes *Dr. Zay* (1882) with the Amazonian heroine's marriage.

Many early women physicians were doubly different, in that they were homeopaths as well as female. The novels play with this "irregularity," attacking and defending both the method and sex of these new professionals, and occasionally using objections to one as a screen for dislike of the other. The most progressive argument for female physicians, one which does not make women doctors the different other in a series of dichotomies, is presented by Hamlin Garland in the subplot of *Rose of Dutcher's Cooley* (1895).

From the very earliest days of the women's movement, some leaders, such as Elizabeth Cady Stanton and Susan B. Anthony, saw that women's interests could only be protected by direct political action, including suffrage. But after the Civil War it was women's indirect political action that commanded public attention. The success of women lobbyists gave rise to a series of novels that project Gilded Age disgust with political corruption onto these dangerous charmers. Exceptionally, in Henry Adams's *Democracy* (1880) it is not demonized woman who destroys the integrity of government: corruption of government threatens a pure woman. While these "lobbyist" novels dispute the inherent morality of woman's character, they agree that women exercise almost unlimited power over government, even without the benefit of formal rights.

Cultural limitations on the appropriate role for women were most strongly felt when it came to a request for direct political power, and the result was a series of extreme reactions. For Bayard Taylor in *Hannah Thurston* and Henry James in *The Bostonians*, political power for women is sublimated sexuality. Like Cooper they believe that such power will destroy woman's feminine nature and undermine the family and other social structures. But novels ranging from Hamlin Garland's *A Spoil of Office* (1892) to minor didactic narratives take the other side in the argument from biology, asserting that woman's direct participation in politics is necessary to enable her to protect the integrity of the family.

Ultimately the impact of fiction on the political culture is circumscribed. Although novels participate in the sequence of debates over what kinds of political and economic resources American women should control, they are unable to establish a viewpoint entirely independent of the prevailing ideology. Novelists like Cooper and Hale defend the residual norms even as the culture is changing, while others, including Sedgwick, Alcott, and Freeman, who create powerful, independent women acting in defiance of male control, still retreat from portraying women as exercising full political power, that is, authority over men in the public sphere. Not until 1915, only five years before women were given the vote, did a novel appear in which women ruled; Charlotte Perkins Gilman's *Herland*, a utopian fantasy, not only gave women political power but declared independence by eliminating men altogether. The inability of nineteenth-century American authors to envision a truly equal political society reflects not a weakness, but the strength of a political culture that, even in the late twentieth century, is not ready to accept women in the highest political offices in the nation.

1

Two Visions of the Republic

Six years before Tocqueville makes similar observations on the status of American women, Squire Romelee, the voice of wisdom in Sarah Josepha Hale's *Northwood*, comments:

> I presume you will not find, should you travel throughout the United States, scarcely a single female engaged in the labors of the field or any kind of out-door work as it is called. And the manner in which women are treated is allowed to be a good criterion by which to judge of the character and civilization of a people. Wherever they are oppressed, confined, or made to perform the drudgery, we may be sure the men are barbarians. But I do not believe there is now or ever was a nation which treated their women with such kindness and consideration, tenderness and respect, as we Americans do ours. Here they are educated to command esteem, and considered as they deserve to be, the guardians of domestic honor and happiness, friends and companions of man.[1]

Although Romelee's analysis of woman's role makes no mention of political rights or the state, the appropriate status of women is clearly enunciated: women are equal (not oppressed), respected, and educated for a special place in the social order. They are to be "guardians of domestic honor" and, within that sphere, "companions" of their spouses. This passage briefly summarizes a set of political and social beliefs about the relative contributions of men and women to the American polity. In a sense, what is missing from the passage—overt political references—is as telling as what is included. The world of political ideas, which is discussed at length in *Northwood*, is the world of men.

Northwood, along with Catharine Maria Sedgwick's *Hope Leslie*, also published in 1827, demonstrates how fiction expresses the political culture of a period. Both novels are particularly concerned with the place of women within the political community. Comparison of the novels reveals that while both support the existing political system, *Hope Leslie* questions women's subordination to authority, which *Northwood* defends as essential to the success of the political order.

The two novels were both popular in their time. *Northwood*, Hale's first published work of fiction, led to her assumption of the editorship of the *Ladies' Magazine* later in 1827. *Hope Leslie* was Sedgwick's third novel and her greatest critical success.[2] Despite its strong criticism of the Puritans' treatment of the local Indians, the novel's blend of historical fact and adventure made *Hope Leslie* the type of novel which was approved reading for young women. In the early nineteenth century, romantic novels were often attacked for increasing the susceptibility of these women to unsuitable or overly passionate relationships.[3] The reading of history was urged instead, and historical fiction that emphasized the proper virtues was an acceptable substitute. Similarly, *Northwood* met the demand for patriotic literature; as the *Boston Spectator and Ladies' Album* put it, "*Northwood* is strictly an American novel, and relates only to the common events of life which are daily passing in our country. . . . We venture to say the taste that is not gratified with such scenes and characters . . . must have grown morbid by feasting too much on foreign productions."[4]

Constructing the Political Culture

Through authorial comments, plots, approved characters, symbolism, and other devices, both of these early nineteenth-century novels participate in the dominant political culture of New England. In 1827, readers of Hale's fiction were likely to share certain tenets of that culture: reverence for the Founders, belief in the importance of the small property-owner, and the conviction that partisan politics was men's business. At the same time, certain subgroups within the society rejected aspects of the larger culture. For example, members of the flourishing Shaker communities practiced celibacy, held property in common, and subscribed to equality of the sexes.

The political culture of a society is maintained through the process of political socialization. Individuals "learn" the proper attitudes toward government and politics from several sources.[5] In the nineteenth century, novels such as *Northwood*, with its unqualified patriotism, functioned much as modern media do, as part of the socialization process.[6] Hale's statement of purpose reflects her understanding of this public role. In the opening to the first edition of *Northwood* she wishes the book's success to come from "the expression of sentiments which virtue will approve" (1:4). The epigraph reads, "He who loves not his country, can love nothing." Like other republican authors, Hale believed that the public good depended on private virtue. Neither Hale nor Sedgwick would have characterized herself as a political writer, yet their novels contribute to the political instruction of their readers. Both novels delineate the character traits necessary to sustain the Republic, praise the fundamental political structures of the societies they portray, and reinforce the political beliefs of the reader by recalling the principles on which the nation was founded. Both narratives respond to the many demands of the day for distinctively American novels.[7]

The rapid growth and economic development of the United States subjected the dominant political culture to tension and conflict. Economic and social changes were sweeping the country as the commercial sector flourished, the cities grew, the pace of western expansion quickened, and immigration lessened the homogeneity of the society. Increasing urbanization and the introduction of factories widened class differences, although the political rhetoric emphasized increased opportunity for all. The widespread acceptance of political equality for all white males brought its own set of questions and fears. Reluctant democrats like Cooper questioned whether the common man could exercise complete self-government, while the foreign observer Tocqueville noted that the leveling effects of equality encouraged private, material motives in the citizens.[8] Both Cooper and Tocqueville called attention to a fundamental dilemma of the Republic: whether increased individual equality is compatible with order in the community.

Neither Hale nor Sedgwick attempted to address the leading controversies of Jacksonian democracy. In an era when party politics was becoming increasingly a social activity for men, it would have been inappropriate for a female novelist to consider such specific political issues as tariffs in her novel.[9] Nevertheless, both women responded to the general atmosphere of political change in the nation. The primary goal of each author is to present a vision of the Republic in keeping with the widespread movement to "restore" the virtues of the past in an age of rapid economic and social change.[10]

Hale does this directly. Northwood, the ideal homogeneous New England village, composed of the "yeoman farmers" so dear to Jeffersonian thought and bound together by shared belief in the Republic, is very similar to the vision held by Jackson himself. Marvin Meyers summarizes Old Hickory's ideal as a recollection of the revolutionary days of 1776–1800: "Laissez-faire notions were embedded in a half-remembered, half-imagined way of life. When government governed least, society—made of the right republican materials—would realize its own natural moral discipline."[11] Hale's community functions in like manner: each household contributes to the common good, and there are no true divisions of interest within the village.

Sedgwick, by setting her novel in the colonial period, is apparently equally patriotic, but she concentrates on the actions of individuals rather than on the political structure of the community as a whole. She creates in her heroine, Hope Leslie, a character whose highest value is freedom of conscience. In contrast to Hale, Sedgwick emphasizes individual judgment and personal liberty rather than the common good. The most striking feature of Sedgwick's attempt to "restore the republic" is that she expresses her belief in individual liberty primarily through female characters.

For both authors, the family and the position of women within it are central to the political order. The family, which holds distinct roles for men and women, is the building block of the democratic republic. This model is explicitly presented in both *Northwood* and *Hope Leslie*. That Hale and Sedgwick differ in their primary values is revealed in their treatment of women. For Hale, women play an important role in the Republic, but only in subordination to community and family needs. Sedgwick, while not directly attacking society or the family, exhibits her choice of liberty as the primary value through the creation of strong independent characters who defy the community for conscience's sake. Furthermore, Sedgwick reveals her own ambivalence about the position of women in an egalitarian society by using females to illustrate the tension between the individual and the community.

Hale's Vision of the Republic

Northwood is Hale's vision of the American republic as it functions in the New England town. It is the Republic writ small. Such a political society was patterned after the eighteenth-century understanding of the Hellenic republics: small, homogeneous polities governed by all the free citizens. As Gordon Wood points out, eighteenth-century American patriots understood that the highest goal of such societies was to provide for the public good. The individual citizens were free and possessed certain natural rights, but the common welfare superseded any individual's private demands.[12] In *Northwood*, Hale re-creates such a society and introduces, as the ideal type, Squire Romelee, who acts as a model and explains the system to the foreign visitor.

In republics, both ancient and modern, government officials are amateurs; the citizens take turns fulfilling their obligation to the community by serving in public office. Mr. Romelee has held a minor civil position and has served twice in the legislature: "he considered every freeman under sacred obligations to serve his country whenever and in whatever manner she required his services; and the confidence of his own townsmen placed him, almost every year, in some office, which, had he consulted his inclination or interest, he would unhesitatingly have refused" (1:10).

Maintaining such devotion to the public good is one of the most formidable challenges faced by any republic. Wood notes that republics were dependent for their survival on the character and spirit of the people. Such character traits as "frugality, industry, temperance, and simplicity—the rustic traits of the sturdy yeoman—were the stuff that made a society strong." [13] Republics cannot depend on fear of the sovereign or an aristocratic class to elicit obedience to the laws, but as the Squire explains philosophically, the freemen of the United States are far more obedient to the laws than are the English masses. Every citizen holds himself "responsible for the execution of those wholesome regulations, he has either directly or indirectly contributed to make, and for the observance of the constitution" (1:164). The laws rest on popular sovereignty, and the citizens are active participants in the political process. The Squire describes all Americans, and Yankees in particular, as "fond of argument"; their debating skills are encouraged by frequent elections. Such public discourse is further enhanced by freedom of the press and the "circulation, too, of newspapers and other periodicals throughout every part of the country" (1:114). Widespread knowledge, public debate, and participation in elections make the citizens feel a greater commitment to the laws.

Every society must socialize its young into its values and cultural traditions; the means of doing so were widely discussed in the early years of the United States. *Northwood* addresses directly the question of how to sustain the character of the citizenry. Public education is seen as an important tool in creating democratic virtue. Romelee explains to the Englishman that "every child in the New England States has the privilege of attending our free schools," and little Mary has received the prize for being "at the head of my class" (1:142–143). The singling out of Mary reflects Hale's strong belief in the importance of female education, a crusade which she sustained in *Godey's* throughout her lifetime. Davidson, however, points out that female education was itself a form of socialization: "women . . . were a primary target of a conservative social message. They should be educated at public expense . . . but educated *to* a certain set of beliefs." [14]

The most important tool for inculcating virtue is the home. The Squire is teaching his children habits of prudence, love of literature and science, and "cherishing in their minds hopes of obtaining the highest honors and privileges their country could bestow" (1:167). The mother's role is to shape character. As Emma Willard said in 1819 in her request for support for a female seminary, the "prosperity [of the nation] will depend on the character of its citizens. The characters of these will be formed by their mothers; and it is through the mothers, that the government can control the character of its future citizens." [15]

This attention to the role of women in the Republic has been documented by a number of scholars. Mary Beth Norton described the changes in women's own political consciousness that resulted from the American Revolution. Their participation in the war effort took specifically domestic forms, including the boycotting of British products and managing the family farm or establishment while their husbands took up arms.[16] According to Linda Kerber, the war increased the salience of politics for many colonial women but did not grant them any increased independence. Instead, as the necessity of creating and preserving virtue in the citizenry became an important issue, women "claimed a significant political role, though [they] played it in the home."[17] The republican mother had to be well educated and politically aware, although her only participation in political decision-making would be through others—her husband and sons.

This attitude prevailed for many decades. In 1852 Hale wrote in her "Editors' Table":

> HOW AMERICAN WOMEN SHOULD VOTE: "I control seven votes, why should I desire to cast one myself?" said a lady who, if women went to the polls, would be acknowledged as a leader. This lady is a devoted, beloved wife, a faithful, tender mother; she has six sons. She *knows* her influence is paramount over the minds she has carefully trained. She *feels* her interests are safe confided to those her affection has made happy. She *trusts* her country will be nobly served by those whom her example has taught to believe in goodness, therefore she is proud to vote by her proxies. This is the way American women should vote, namely, by influencing rightly the votes of men.[18]

The implicit message of *Northwood* is the same. The Romelees' Thanksgiving feast exemplifies the way women are to support the political order. While at the table, the Squire and an English visitor discuss political topics: education, the self-sufficiency of the Republic, and relations with Great Britain. Mrs. Romelee and her daughters serve; their conversation is not reported. But their role is revealed when Frankford laughingly asks Romelee if he imagines that currant wine and ginger beer are connected to the preservation of liberty, and is sharply reminded of the place of tea in the Revolution. Everything at the feast has come from Romelee's farm and has been made by Mrs. Romelee and her daughters; thus, the women are fundamental to the political and economic independence of the United States, and their efforts allow men the luxury of political debate. They show their patriotism by carrying out their domestic duties.[19]

As the ideal of republican womanhood, Mrs. Romelee is far more important to Hale's novel than the romantic lead, Susan Redington. Mrs. Romelee's relationship to her husband exemplifies order in the family commonwealth. She is an intelligent woman, respected by her husband, but she does not consider disobeying him. When Mr. and Mrs. Brainard ask to adopt one of the Romelee children, Sidney, Hale shows us a model discussion between the Romelee parents, and then gives Mr. Romelee the last word. After that, "Mrs. Romelee wept; but she urged no more objections"

(1:40). Mr. Romelee's death in an accident reveals most about the position of women and the parameters of their freedom. Mr. Romelee is brought home wounded in a fall. When the doctor comes to examine him, Mr. Romelee urges his wife to leave the room, saying, "But you must . . . it will overcome you." She replies, "My husband . . . you must not bid me go; I cannot leave you" (2:117). In the phrase "you must not bid me go" is embodied a precise balance of her independent desires and her unwillingness to disobey her husband. When Romelee does succumb, almost his last words are "Sidney, be a father to these little ones, and protect your mother" (2:124). The father thus transfers protection of his wife to his eldest son, who will now represent the household. It is, in fact, the sons as a group who decide how to divide up the farm and care for the various family members.

Throughout *Northwood*, women left on their own have few resources. When Sidney, deceived by the villain's forged letters into believing that Susan has broken off their relationship, remains on his regained southern plantation, Susan promptly becomes ill and nearly dies. Another young woman, Zemira, when separated from her beloved, "seemed fast declining" (1:256). Susan's mother proudly supports her daughter for some years after her husband's death, but dies without really being able to provide for her. Mrs. Romelee requires her sons' assistance. Women are both praised and honored for their contribution to the Republic, but nowhere does Hale indicate any expectation of independence on their part.

Both the plot and the characters of *Northwood* are designed to show the contrast between the republican village and other ways of life. Like other commentators of the time, Hale believes that republics are threatened by heterogeneity, luxury, loss of virtue, and failure of equality—evils found in less fortunate places. To demonstrate, Hale sends her hero, Sidney Romelee, to the South as a young boy and gives Sidney an English friend who can be properly astonished at the virtues of New England life.

The slaveholding South is perceived as a threat to the achievements of northern society.[20] For example, Sidney, a promising scholar as a youth, once he reaches the South is idle. His southern family, a contrast to the Romelee household, does not teach him necessary virtues. Lydia Romelee, Sidney's aunt, is a negative example of womanhood. A beauty, Lydia was not taught self-government in her youth. Though she was engaged to a local farmer, on a trip to Boston she met Mr. Brainard, a plantation owner from South Carolina, and soon married him. Her jilted lover attributed her fickleness "more to her injudicious education than to her heart" (1:19). She is, indeed, rather ignorant: not only is she unaware that her husband is a Roman Catholic, but in the South she is startled to find herself surrounded in her household by Negroes for whom her husband feels responsibility. Childless, she and her husband drift apart. Their activities illustrate the absence of community. They go separately to church, and he keeps himself busy with theater and other mild forms of dissipation. Much later in the novel, when Brainard, now a widower, dies during Sidney's trip up North, there is an implicit contrast with the death of Sidney's father. Romelee dies surrounded by his wife and children; Brainard dies quite alone.

Young Sidney falls in love with a beautiful girl named Zemira, who exemplifies the weaknesses of untrained young womanhood. When Sidney declares himself, she startles him by announcing that she is already secretly married and begging for his help. In comparison to her New England sisters, Zemira has little personal freedom and has developed little strength of character. The Romelee girls, and Susan, are rational creatures who can appropriately choose their own husbands. Zemira, instead, acts impulsively and nearly destroys her own happiness and her family's. At the same time Hale guarantees Zemira's future by making her secret lover none other than her New England schoolmaster, a man who can train her properly.[21] Sidney reads Stuart's letters to Zemira and concludes:

> He is worthy of her. . . . He sought her not as a toy for the moment, but to make her his friend, his companion through life. . . . I am not worthy of Zemira, for I could not guide aright her gentle spirit. . . . Why am I thus inferior to Stuart? . . . Had I remained in New Hampshire and won my way from the plough to the honors of a college, I should not now be envying the superior acquirements of even Stuart. . . . But luxury has undone me. (2:6–7)

In fact, the restoration of Sidney's virtue is completed when, due to his uncle's death, he himself becomes for a season a simple New England schoolmaster.

To symbolize the interdependence of family and community, Hale dovetails her plot with public occasions: a wedding, a Thanksgiving, a church service, and a funeral. Even such apparently private concerns as landscaping and house furnishing become public and patriotic: though the Romelees had at first planted "Lombardy poplars, an exotic" around their house, they "had already discovered their error . . . this was evinced by the young elms and maples planted between the poplars" (1:71). The chief ornament of the sitting room is "over the mantel piece, the eagle . . . in his beak he held a scroll, on which was inscribed the talisman of American liberty—*E pluribus unum*" (1:73–74).

The relation of the individual and society is symbolized by Sidney's dream. As a child Sidney almost drowns, but is saved by his father. After his father's death, when he despairs because "I am nothing, for I can do nothing; I am neither educated for a profession, nor have I habits of industry to gain a subsistence by labor" (2:131), he dreams his father again comes to rescue him, telling him to "do your *duty*; then may you expect happiness"

(2:133). This dream implies that the individual can only become "something," rather than "nothing," by accepting his ties to his family and to the community values.

By drawing the parallel between Sidney's relation to his father and the central force of the community, Hale presents an essentially nostalgic vision of happiness. Virtue is seen as developing sequentially through the three levels of community organization—family, village, and country—and the basis of this virtue is family instruction. Women at home are essential to the whole system. The individual, male or female, supports the community and receives support in turn. The idealized village of Northwood is Hale's prescription for the concerns of the early Jacksonian era. If Americans would pay heed to her model household and village, the best features of the Republic could be preserved in the face of social and economic change.

Sedgwick's Exclusive Republic

Like *Northwood*, Sedgwick's historical novel *Hope Leslie* evokes patriotic feelings by retelling the story of the founding of the colonies. By contrasting oppression in England with the freedom of the colonists and the wisdom of American leaders, the author reminds her contemporary readers of the reasons the colonists came to this continent.

Hope Leslie also celebrates the personal virtues necessary to the Republic. The characters, male and female, are models of valor, self-sacrifice, individual commitment, and chastity. Like Hale, Sedgwick subscribes, at least overtly, to the principle that the public weal must take precedence over the individual will for the society to survive. When a young man rejects his father's suggestions about marriage, he is reminded that "our individual wishes must be surrendered to the public good. . . . We have laid the foundation of an edifice, and our children must be so coupled together, as to secure its progress and stability when the present builders are laid low." [22]

Sedgwick's recounting of American history and dedication to republican principles earned praise from her reviewers. Unlike the writers of romances set in Europe, Sedgwick is a "republican writer, in a department which has hitherto been devoted to glorifying the spirit of feudalism, and its consequent false views." Her novel diffuses "the light of our institutions over the whole surface of our society." This reviewer understands the role of fiction in teaching citizens their duties: Sedgwick "would have young men stimulated to the moral glory of patriotic duty by . . . mothers . . . and . . . sisters [such as appear in her novels]." Her talent is "a true genius for commencing a literature for the mass of the American people which shall bring up their moral tone to the spirit of their institutions. Her mind appreciates the peculiar dignity of republicanism." [23]

The place of family in the political order is understood similarly by Sedgwick and Hale: here again the husband is the leader of the household in which the wife and children have their places. The Winthrop family exemplifies the well-ordered Puritan household, demonstrating the proper attitude toward political, religious, and personal life. The governor is portrayed as a firm but kindly leader of impeccable moral character. When Hope refuses to disclose her activities after curfew, the governor chastises her as disobedient to his domestic authority, using language that highlights the parallel between rebellion in family and state: "thou dost take liberties unsuitable to thy youth, and in violation of that deference due to the rule and observances of my household" (176). Mrs. Winthrop serves as the model and mother that orphaned Hope has been without. The governor's wife

> recognised, and continually taught to matron and maiden, the duty of unqualified obedience from the wife to the husband, her appointed lord and master; . . . Madam Winthrop's matrimonial virtue never degenerated into the slavishness of fear, or the obsequiousness of servility. . . . Like a horse easy on the bit, she was guided by the slightest intimation from him who held the rein; indeed . . . it sometimes appeared as if the reins were dropped, and the inferior animal were left to the guidance of her own sagacity. (144–145)

Sedgwick's portrayal of the family is so orthodox that one reviewer notes that she sees the family as the "only earthly shrine which God's own hands did ever erect for man to worship in." [24]

Nevertheless, Hope Leslie, unlike Northwood, depicts the American polity as troubled. Where Northwood is a homogeneous village, virtually untouched by the outside world, the Massachusetts Bay colony contains religious and political differences and is surrounded by an alien indigenous culture. Hale's novel praises all things American, but a major theme of Sedgwick's narrative is Puritan oppression of the Indians. Mary Kelley writes that in its portrayal of American expansion and Indian dispossession, "Hope Leslie resounded with an unmistakable challenge to the morality of a nation." [25] Sedgwick equates a Pequod massacre of the colonists with a colonial attack on sleeping Indian women and children, rejects the idea that the native peoples are subhuman, and treats her two heroines, the English girl Hope Leslie and the Indian maiden Magawisca, as equals. Meeting with Hope at the Boston cemetery where both their mothers lie, Magawisca evokes their common humanity: "think ye not that the Great Spirit looks down on these sacred spots, where the good and the peaceful rest, with an equal eye; think ye not their children are His children, whether they are gathered in yonder temple where your people worship, or bow to Him beneath the green boughs of the forest?" (189).

For Sedgwick it is not the coexistence of differing peoples that endangers the spirit of the Republic. Instead, the country's greatest challenge is maintaining an equilibrium between the individual and the group. Mr. Fletcher, guardian of Hope Leslie, comes to the New World to pursue political and religious freedom. He gave up the woman he loved in England for his Puritan beliefs, which her father recognized as threatening to the established hierarchy. His son, Everell Fletcher, later explains why the colony's governors sympathize with the parliamentary party in the English Civil War: "they virtually broke the yoke of royal authority, when they left their native land, and shewed what value they set on liberty by sacrificing for it every temporal good" (126). Nevertheless, Sedgwick demonstrates that the same Puritans who came to America seeking freedom to practice their religious beliefs established a religious polity that punished those members who claimed liberty of conscience. Fletcher himself retreats to a frontier outpost when oppression recurs in the Puritan colony: "He was mortified at seeing power, which had been earned at so dear a rate, and which he had fondly hoped was to be applied to the advancement of man's happiness, sometimes perverted to purposes of oppression and personal aggrandizement" (16). Fletcher's actions serve as a touchstone for the remainder of the novel. Repeatedly characters must choose whether to act according to their personal principles or those upheld by the community.

Most of the story follows the affairs of four people: the heroine Hope Leslie, child of Fletcher's original beloved and sent to him as a ward after her mother's death; her sister Faith Leslie; Fletcher's own son Everell; and Magawisca, daughter of the Pequod chief Mononotto, captured in a general massacre of the Pequods and given, along with her brother Oneco, to the Fletchers as a servant. In this household Mrs. Fletcher represents the maternal ideal. Her kindness wins the affection of Magawisca, who is torn by conflicting loyalties once she becomes aware that her father is planning to revenge the death of Magawisca's older brother on the Fletcher family. In the attack, which occurs when Mr. Fletcher is away, Mrs. Fletcher and her younger children are killed. Faith Leslie is carried off by Oneco, and Everell is taken to be sacrificed in vengeance. Magawisca, back among the Pequods, is unable to dissuade her father from killing Everell. Instead, just as the ax descends toward his head, she interposes in an attempt to deflect the blow. Her arm is lopped off, and Everell escapes. Later Hope twice assists Indian captives of the Puritans. First she frees from imprisonment the Pequod herb woman Nelema, who has been condemned as a witch. Later, with the aid of Everell, she engineers the escape of Magawisca from the community jail.

The implicit theme of *Hope Leslie*, embodied in repeated action, is that a woman may be driven by her sense of political powerlessness to undertake civil disobedience. Reviewers of the day noted that Hope's actions were unconventional, but ascribed them to personality rather than confront their political significance. They accepted the surface explanation that Sedgwick herself offers: Hope's "disposition [is] rash and generous" (346). In the *North American Review* she is called "full of enthusiasm, affection, truth, and yet sparkling with gaiety and wit."[26] Hale considered that Hope's weaknesses were a result of her "womanishnesses."[27] In effect, her errors were dismissed as the typically impulsive mistakes of a woman who follows her heart rather than her head. Yet a closer examination of the novel reveals that Hope's "errors" occur precisely because as a woman she has no way to act within the system.

Mrs. Fletcher's history suggests the consequences of traditional female behavior. Though she had no desire to move to the wilderness, she followed uncomplainingly: "Abraham would as soon have remonstrated against the command that bade him go forth from his father's house into the land of the Chaldees, as she would have failed in passive obedience to the resolve of her husband" (16). Writing a long letter to her husband, who is in Boston, she mentions her fear of Indians in the neighborhood, but she will not leave the homestead without his express orders. Magawisca repeatedly characterizes Mrs. Fletcher as the "mother-bird that shelters the wanderer in her nest" (39). She begs her father not to kill the Fletchers because "they have spread the wing of love over us" (63), and later she berates him because "yonder roof . . . has sheltered thy children—the wing of the motherbird was spread over us" (74). But Mrs. Fletcher's "wing" is inadequate; she is unable to protect her loved ones.

By her subsequent action to save Everell, Magawisca loses her arm. The subtext here is dual. On the one hand, the mutilation is symbolic of her destruction as a complete female person. She has broken out of the restraints of womanhood by heroic action and is consequently reduced, no longer fully female. She will never marry. At the same time the action symbolizes her altruistic female nature and ties her to her benefactress, Mrs. Fletcher, the bird whose wing was broken while stretched over her children. Women suffer whether or not they submit to male direction. Mrs. Fletcher loses her life, and her children, through obedient passivity. Yet women can also expect to be punished for interfering with men and the political processes of society that men establish. This is the lesson learned by both Hope and Magawisca.

In the remainder of the novel Sedgwick draws a consistent structural parallel between Hope and Magawisca. Both women have lost their mothers; each is closely tied to her father (or in Hope's case, her substitute father) and through him to a society and a political system. Both fall in love with Everell in childhood; neither quite recognizes her own feelings. Both women make independent decisions, and each at some point directly challenges the rules or laws of her own culture. Contemporary reviewers were not all convinced by the portrait of Magawisca. The bluntest comment is

Timothy Flint's: Magawisca is "a very pretty fancy; but no . . . squaw."[28] In the *American Ladies Magazine* Hale finds Magawisca full of moral grandeur, but improbable as a representative of an "injured race."[29] Sedgwick, however, makes Magawisca if anything more thoughtful and admirable than Hope.[30] The bond of womanhood between the two is symbolized in the moment at the Boston cemetery. Hope thinks, "mysteriously have our destinies been interwoven. Our mothers brought from a far distance to rest together here—their children connected in indissoluble bonds!" (192).

The tension between the political order and the individual conscience is most extensively explored through the character of Hope. Less bigoted than others in the Puritan community, partly because of her ties to the Established Church, Hope "enjoyed the capacities of her nature, and permitted her mind to expand beyond the contracted boundaries of sectarian faith" (123). Most importantly, she takes "counsel only from her own heart, and that told her that the rights of innocence were paramount to all other rights" (120). It is this self-reliance that persistently leads her into trouble, and heroism.

In her first rebellious action, when Hope frees the Pequod woman Nelema, she is acting out of both gratitude and a sense of natural justice. She does not accept the decision of the Puritan magistrates that the old woman's gestures while administering a snakebite antidote indicate witchcraft. Thus she rejects the authority of the religious sect over her personal judgment. In this Hope stands for the author, who editorializes early in the book about her age's advance over that which "hanged quakers! . . . which condemned to death, as witches, innocent, unoffending old women!" (16). For her pains Hope is sent to Boston to be supervised by Mrs. Winthrop, while she learns more appropriate ways of behaving.

As Magawisca is Hope's parallel, Esther Downing, "the pattern maiden of the commonwealth" (272), is her opposite. She is devout, obedient, and quiet. Secretly in love with Everell, she does nothing about it. It is Hope who engineers an engagement between Everell and Esther. Esther's passivity is most clearly seen in the discussion of a trick Hope played to save herself after being abducted. Finding herself in a boat with an Italian sailor who takes her for his patron saint, the well-educated Hope speaks gently to him in Italian and has herself rowed to shore. Governor Winthrop thinks that Hope "didst err, lamentably, in permitting . . . the idol worship of that darkened papistical youth." Asked her opinion, Esther says that she would rather Hope "hadst trusted thyself wholly to . . . Providence" (271–272). To demonstrate the limitations of this passive conception of female perfection, Sedgwick places both Puritan young women in circumstances where obedience to religious strictures comes in conflict with conscience.

During the period when Esther is engaged to Everell, Magawisca is captured and jailed as a dangerous enemy to the community. This is a real crisis for Hope. Magawisca is taken while bringing Hope's long-lost sister to a secret meeting. Furthermore, Hope does not believe that Magawisca is stirring up the Pequods, but she does believe she owes her an eternal debt of gratitude for saving Everell. Her first attempt to save Magawisca is entirely conventional: she goes and pleads Magawisca's case with Governor Winthrop. The scene forms a precise verbal parallel to Magawisca's pleading with her father for Everell. Just as Mononotto refuses and denigrates feelings of personal love, Winthrop, though outwardly kinder, is equally unyielding: "it will be difficult to make a private benefit outweigh such a public crime." Hope realizes she is expected to "passively await the fate of Magawisca" (274–275). Instead, like Magawisca earlier, Hope searches for a way to act.

Esther has refused to participate in a plot to free Magawisca, explaining that "she thought they had not scripture warrant for interfering between the prisoner and the magistrates" (277–278). But Hope and Esther operate on different principles, only one of which is acceptable for women in the Puritan community. Esther's is submission to religious and community authority; Hope's is justice and individual freedom, which may require action outside the law. For the second time she frees from prison an Indian woman condemned by a jury of men.

The dilemmas faced by Hope and Magawisca allow Sedgwick to question the legitimacy of a political authority that excludes certain groups in the population, in this case women and American Indians. To the Puritan jury Magawisca says, "I am your prisoner, and ye may slay me, but I deny your right to judge me. My people have never passed under your yoke—not one of my race has ever acknowledged your authority" (286). Hope never speaks against male authority, but her actions demonstrate a similar sense of being exempt from its application. Of course she is a romantic projection, and her actions go unpunished because Sedgwick chooses that they shall. In 1827 Sedgwick could not assert that women are oppressed by their exclusion from the political process, but she designs her plot to drive the reader to this conclusion.

Despite its historical setting and overt patriotism, *Hope Leslie* is inherently seditious in meaning, since it sets conscience, innocence, and individual liberty against the needs of the community or the state. Sedgwick knew that her novel, and Hope's actions, made a political statement. This becomes explicit when Hope explains to the old family retainer, Digby, that she acts independently because "I like to have my own way." Digby moves the conversation from the specific to the general:

this having our own way, is what every body likes; it's the privilege we came to this wilderness world for. . . . I watch the motions of the straws—I know which way the wind blows. Thought and will are set

free.   Times are changed   there is a new spirit in the world—
chains are broken—fetters are knocked off—and the liberty set forth
in the blessed word, is now felt to be every man's birth-right. (225)[31]

In fact, Sedgwick implies, for women, even in the United States, "times"
are not changed. Women remain as good as imprisoned by social, religious,
or marital restrictions. The repeated plot emphasis on prisons gives them a
symbolic significance. Against women who take independent action looms
the threat, actual or symbolic, of further restriction. From their position
outside of the political system some women may defy male society; the potential consequences are, significantly, a greater loss of freedom. Yet *Hope
Leslie* nevertheless suggests that it is women, though only a select few, who
are willing to break the chains and truly seize the birthright of the free.

Other Sedgwick novels of the period reprise the major themes of *Hope
Leslie*. Civil disobedience against authority recurs in *The Linwoods* (1835),
which takes place during the revolutionary war. Once again this disobedience takes the form of a prison break arranged by the heroine of the novel,
Isabella Linwood. In another example of Sedgwick's tolerance, she makes
the operative person in this rescue Rose, a Negro servant, whose freedom
Isabella had won as a child. Now the favor is repaid. Once again the prisoner must disguise himself as a member of another sex and race: where
Magawisca was dressed as the white tutor Chadock, here Herbert Linwood
is transformed by Rose's clothes and wears a wig of *"nigger's wool."* Rose,
left in the prison, is visited by the jailor, whom she ties up and leaves with
the words, "remember, that you were strung up there by a 'd——n *nigger'*—a nigger *woman!*"[32]

Yet another rescue from imprisonment occurs in *Redwood* (1824). In
this case the prisoner is a young girl, Emily, who has joined the Shakers
under compulsion. Sedgwick admits that among the Shakers, "no one was
ever detained by physical force; but to a weak and irresolute mind there are
moral barriers that are as impassable as prison-walls."[33] The members of
Emily's family decide in conference to attempt a rescue. Leader of the expedition will be Aunt Debby, a "natural protector of the weak and oppressed"
(1:260). At the end of the revolutionary war Aunt Debby "was so imbued
with the independent spirit of the times, that she would not then consent
to the surrender of any of her rights" (1:32). It is for this reason that she
has not married. Again Sedgwick links female politics to American political
ideology.

By the time the expedition sets out, the leader of the Shakers has abducted Emily and shut her up in a hut under the guard of an Indian. The
imprisonment is thus doubly illegitimate, since neither religion nor man has
any right to constrain Emily and her conscience.[34] Sedgwick's fear of repressive religion came from her early experiences with orthodox Congre-

gationalism, which she later abjured; she displaces her feelings about this denomination onto Puritanism in *Hope Leslie* and onto the Shakers in *Redwood*, each time associating women with the necessary escape.

In Sedgwick's view the political system and the legal or religious authorities may be wrong. The individual must, therefore, retain the right to make judgments independent of the community. Sedgwick does not hesitate to extend this liberty of thought, and occasionally of action, to women. Comparing *Hope Leslie* to *Northwood* we see that Sedgwick cannot subscribe to the same vision of a homogeneous, cohesive political society that Hale posits as both ideal and existing.

Politics and Biography

Hale's and Sedgwick's contrasting expressions of the Jacksonian spirit parallel the conflict between the "collective and individualistic tendencies within republican ideology itself." To adapt Mary Beth Norton's formulations of these discordant tendencies, *Northwood* "looked to the past and preached the necessary sacrifice of the individual will to the good of the whole." Sedgwick's novel, instead, hints at the future of "unencumbered individualism." [35] Furthermore, Sedgwick's decision to portray independent, free-spirited heroines in virtually all of her novels reveals an understanding of the specific conflict that republicanism created for women.

Both Hale and Sedgwick accept the cultural prohibition against women taking public stands on specific political issues, and both expect their female readers to do likewise. But by looking at their lives we can perceive the sources of their implicit disagreement over the place of individual liberty in American society. This disagreement presages conflicts in the political culture that would persist for the rest of the century.

Sarah Josepha Hale and Catharine Maria Sedgwick were born little more than a year apart, Hale in 1788 and Sedgwick in 1789, but their backgrounds and their experiences by 1827 were notably different. Hale owed "my early predilection for literary pursuits to the teachings and example of my mother." [36] In Sedgwick's case, "my mother's life was eaten up with calamitous sicknesses," [37] in fact, periods of mental illness. Instead, Sedgwick's father Theodore, an important Federalist who rose to be Speaker of the House of Representatives, directed his daughter's reading and initiated her into political concepts. "My father had the habit of having his children always about him, and . . . there was no part of his life which we did not partake. I remember well looking upon a Democrat as an enemy to his country. . . . I heard my father's conversation with his political friends." [38] Hale remained at home until, at age eighteen, she began to teach school, still in New Hampshire. Sedgwick was sent away to various schools, and, beginning at the age of eleven, she spent her winters in the city, usually New York.

By 1813 the two women's lives diverged even more significantly. In that year Hale, who had been teaching for some time, married a rising young lawyer. She referred to the marriage as a period of "unbroken happiness."[39] But just before she gave birth to their fifth child, David Hale died suddenly of pneumonia. Left with a family to provide for, the young widow first failed at running a millinery shop and then turned her attention seriously to writing. By 1827 she had published a volume of verse and won a number of literary prizes for her submissions to various popular periodicals.[40] *North-wood*, however, was her first popular success.

For Sedgwick the year 1813 was notable for her father's death. As Mary Kelley writes:

> Her father was the great intellectual influence in her life. But by awak-ening his daughter's curiosity and anticipation he made it inevitable that she would later experience a sense of intense deprivation. . . . The father's example as an active and influential statesman bore little rela-tionship to any future role the daughter could play. . . . Unlike her four brothers, all of whom became lawyers with varying political interests, the female Sedgwick was not invited to follow her father's public path. Instead, despite her own early interest in politics, she would have to look to "my sisters" . . . as helpmeet to a husband.[41]

We can see the process of Sedgwick's disillusion in two comments from her letters. At fourteen Sedgwick writes to her father about election results, con-cluding, "thus you see . . . I have become quite a politician." By 1812, at the age of twenty-four, Sedgwick tells him instead that examining his life to find rules for her own is like turning "from the survey of a lofty palace . . . to find a model for [a] little dwelling. . . . You may benefit a nation, my dear papa, and I may improve the condition of a fellow-being."[42]

Despite this resolution, Sedgwick did not marry. Certainly the marriage of her parents did not encourage her, and she wrote to her niece in 1847 that "so many I have loved have made shipwreck of happiness in marriage or have found it a dreary joyless condition." At the same time her insistence that she never found her beau ideal suggests that she may have rejected candidates as unequal to her father, or perhaps to her brothers. To them she was extraordinarily attached; her letters use language that moderns do not associate with affection between siblings. Kelley, noting Sedgwick's "deep and lasting ambivalence . . . [toward] a destiny she could neither totally embrace nor totally reject," describes how Sedgwick formed "with Robert and Charles what were for her sacred unions beyond the sacred altars of matrimony."[43]

Still, her closest brothers both married and had lives apart from their sister. Kelley suggests "it was probably no coincidence that Sedgwick began writing when Robert became engaged in 1821."[44] Her brothers encouraged her both personally and practically; when *New England Tale* was a success they spurred her on to her next novel, *Redwood*. The author of *Hope Leslie* was not a literary novice.

In these same years Sedgwick, along with her brothers, converted to Unitarianism. In one sense she was again following her father. On his deathbed Theodore Sedgwick had made a conversion before the Reverend William Ellery Channing; his daughter joined Channing in the Unitarian church in 1821. But Sedgwick's conversion to a more open, less authoritarian religion can also be related to her political beliefs. Gradually she became a democrat, quite unlike her father's household where "we . . . thought the people presuming, impertinent, and stupid"; she accepted that "*their* time had come. . . . They did not, perhaps, use their freedom gracefully, but they enjoyed it, and it was theirs." By 1828 she could joke about her democratic attitudes, calling them "treason against my caste."[45] For her, oppressive religion and oppressive government were almost indistinguishable, as she shows in her portrait of the Puritans in *Hope Leslie*.

By 1827, then, Hale and Sedgwick, both New England women in their late thirties, had cause to view the world differently. *Northwood*'s nostalgia is Hale's idealized tribute to the life she had led with her husband. So far she had had little experience with the larger world of politics and cities. Her main goal in writing the book was not "to win fame, but a support for my little children."[46] With those children she would live for the remainder of her life, including the fifty years she served as editor of *Godey's Lady's Book*. After Hale moved to Boston to edit the *Ladies' Magazine,* she was exposed to the political debates of the time, but she chose deliberately to keep both her personal and editorial life isolated from political conflicts. Only on a handful of issues that directly affected women did she permit herself to take a political position. In the most extreme instance, she and Mr. Godey agreed that no mention of the Civil War would appear in *Godey's Lady's Book.*

Sedgwick, on the other hand, in 1827 was as usual closely in touch with the political world. At the time Sedgwick wrote *Hope Leslie,* she frequently spent her summers with her brother Theodore and his family in the old family home in Stockbridge, Massachusetts. Theodore had continued the family heritage of political activism; in 1826 he remained within the remnants of the old Federalist party of his father and represented his district in the state legislature. Although he supported the reelection of John Quincy Adams in 1828, by 1830 he was willing to approve Jackson's administration, and later to run on the Democratic ticket for U.S. Congress.[47] Sedgwick's novels do not reflect the specific political issues that may have been debated within the Stockbridge household. Instead, her fiction repeatedly emphasizes one overriding issue common to the political and personal realms—the need for liberty and independence—a need that was never completely fulfilled in her own life.

Despite the fact that in 1827 Sedgwick was a popular and experienced author, there are intimations that her writing was a means of warding off depression. *Hope Leslie* depicts a woman unable to participate openly in the vital political processes that occupy the men around her. Further, the novel joins other suggestions in the biography that Sedgwick never fully solved her problem of accepting authority. Like her heroine, Sedgwick laid claim to her autonomy, to "having her own way." In 1835 she describes in her journal her reaction to hearing a sea captain speak of his independence on a ship, where he snapped his fingers and three hundred men stood before him, ready to obey: "My sympathy was with the three hundred men that had to obey, not the *one* that could command." [48] Sedgwick was never led to the personal equivalent of civil disobedience, because she carefully avoided granting authority over herself to another person.

The repeated concern with prisons and imprisonment found in Sedgwick's novels had an interesting consequence in her later life. Sedgwick approved of various reform movements, especially abolition, but "the only organized movement in which she played an active role, however, was that of prison reform; from 1848 until her death she was 'first director' (president) of the Women's Prison Association in New York." [49] She had deferred her membership until the committee from the men's society stopped reminding the women that they were "but a department." [50] This organization "was engaged in reforming jails that held women"; Sedgwick also worked with a home that found work for women released from prison. [51]

Though the United States changed greatly in the decades after 1827, Sedgwick and Hale retained their fundamental attitudes toward woman's place in the political culture. Each woman published a novel a quarter of a century or more later than those examined here. In 1852 Hale issued a revised edition of *Northwood* as a response to *Uncle Tom's Cabin*, and Sedgwick tried to recover from her depression following the death of her last brother by writing *Married or Single* (1857). Each novel provides an epilogue on the author's favorite themes.

Northwood, in 1852, had its subtitle changed from *A Tale of New England* to *Life North and South: Showing the True Character of Both*. The main additions, apart from some name changes such as Romelee to Romilly and Susan to Annie, are a medial chapter entitled "The Destiny of America," largely concerned with slavery, and a final chapter that shows how Sidney assumes control of his plantation. Hale's position on slavery is quite clear: the best thing that can happen to the slave is to be converted to Christianity in the United States and then sent to Africa to establish a higher civilization. A year later, in a novel entitled *Liberia*, she again used fiction to give a fuller exposition of these views.

The 1852 additions are a natural extension of Hale's conviction that women must transmit the belief system of the community. Sidney instructs his new bride that she will be required to teach the slaves their religious duties. It is the job of woman to lead her husband and "her family on gently but surely to happiness and heaven." The Squire's posthumous journal, which Sidney and his bride read together, reminds them that "in this soul education pious women are the most efficient instructors."[52] The position of women in the South is thus an extension of the original concept of republican motherhood: women must inculcate the attitudes and beliefs of the larger culture in their slaves as in their children.

Strikingly, we never hear Annie's words on slavery or the duties assigned to her. The villain of the piece almost succeeds in breaking off the marriage by forging a letter from Annie in the North to Sidney in the South, in which Annie tells her fiancé that she could not go south and "be a partaker in the sin of slavery." When the trick is cleared up, Sidney gives Annie a letter containing "a full confession" of his position as a slaveholder and asks her to be "as frank in expressing your own views." But narrative summary substitutes for Annie's voice. "Annie's reply was brief, but warm with sympathy for his feelings, and assurances of her co-operations."[53] There is no expectation that the heroine will or should express individual conscience against husband or established social codes; such stubborn insubordination, in fact, was the destructive tactic of the forged letter. Furthermore, by 1852 Annie's silence was itself a political statement, aligning her with women powerless to overturn slavery or to change their own position in society.

In *Married or Single* Sedgwick reveals yet again her ambivalence about woman's usual destiny: having written the book to "drive away the smile . . . at the name of 'old maid,'" she concludes by marrying off her heroine.[54] Twice she reverts to her obsession with imprisonment, actual or potential. In a sharp contrast to Hale, Sedgwick recounts how her heroine assists a runaway slave, as usual by disguise, in an open act of civil disobedience. Sedgwick emphasizes her heroine's courage and the choice she has made by creating a replay of the disagreement between Hope and Esther in that between Grace and her stepmother. The older woman asserts, "I do particularly wish . . . to avoid involving myself in this inconvenient subject of slavery. . . . I do not approve of *any* interference with the laws. Women's duty is clear on that point" (2:17). In a second episode a young woman enters New York's Tombs prison to free her brother and is compelled to spend the night locked in a cell. Alice's heroism is rather undercut by her nightlong battle against mice, which Sedgwick apparently thinks reveals Alice's feminine nature. The reader instead finds here another symbol of Sedgwick's terror that following individual conscience will lead women to nightmarish enclosure.

Sedgwick and Hale were both products of the eighteenth century. Hale's ideas continued to be the norm in the nineteenth, during most of which women were expected to uphold the Republic from within the domestic sphere. But Sedgwick is a transitional figure. Like Harriet Beecher Stowe, twenty-two years younger, she proposes that civil disobedience may be necessary to assist groups excluded from the Republic, but unlike Elizabeth Cady Stanton, born twenty-six years later into family circumstances similar to Sedgwick's, she never directly demands rights for women. Instead Sedgwick's novels repeatedly limit themselves to exposing the political constraints on women. Thus the novels of Sedgwick and Hale, written at an early moment in the national literature, embody divergent positions on the balance between individual liberty and community, and on the place of women in the Republic, which persist in American fiction throughout the nineteenth century.

Finding a Voice
to Answer the Moral Call

The right of women to influence politics by speaking from the public platform became a heated issue during the 1830s and remained a source of tension in American culture until the Civil War. The question was not women's legal right to express their ideas on public issues, either in print or through speeches. Rather, women who attempted to express publicly their attitudes toward contemporary political questions challenged the prevailing norms of social conduct and the political role defined for women as republican mothers. *Northwood* provides the correct model: women were supposed to influence public affairs only through private moral influence on their immediate circle of relatives and friends. Activity outside the home was proscribed as deleterious to their families, to society, and to themselves.

The demand for the right to speak in public was not usually a demand to speak for women's rights. Most of the women who expressed their social and political views were responding to the "moral call" to reform some aspect of society. Many issues, including temperance, "purity," and educational improvement, motivated women to enter the public sphere. But the overriding moral question from the 1830s to the Civil War was slavery. For women who were convinced by the Garrisonian view that to do nothing to eradicate this evil was immoral, speaking against slavery was a matter of conscience. Yet regardless of the purity of their motives, women speakers were viewed with suspicion, and it was assumed that their goals were self-serving.

The severity of the attacks on women who lectured or wrote on public issues suggests profound sources of discomfort. In a society where women were acknowledged to have a special claim to the moral education of the nation, why were they denied the right to speak on moral issues? Why were some treatments of controversial questions, such as *Uncle Tom's Cabin*, acceptable, while women who spoke directly for abolition were attacked?

What forces influenced authors who created female characters with public voices to retreat from granting them full authority? Looking closely at some of the vocal women who appear in novels of the period, and placing them within a political context, suggests why women answering the moral call produced such strong reactions.

Important changes in the social and cultural life of American society encouraged and prepared women to express their views publicly on moral and political issues. Among the factors that increased women's ability to participate in public life were the growing opportunities for women to be educated.[1] Likewise, the transformation of the United States from a primarily rural, agricultural nation to one more urbanized and heterogeneous contributed to educate women in social and organizational skills. Middle-class women in particular acquired the self-confidence and ability necessary to participate in the public sphere.

Developments in the religious life of the nation also encouraged women to exercise their recognized moral influence for social change and reform. The religious revivals of the Second Great Awakening stressed the primacy of individual conscience and urged women to follow their own moral senses.[2] Women internalized the moral superiority regularly ascribed to them, and when numerous causes and societies dedicated to the reform of the American community were organized in the 1820s, many felt called to play an active role in that ferment, either as auxiliaries to their male leaders or on their own.[3]

The various types of reform activities that engaged the efforts of women we can envision as a set of concentric circles with the home at the center. Even though all of these reform movements were intended to improve public life, women's participation in those movements—such as temperance or Bible societies—that were most closely related to their domestic or religious duties excited little controversy, while activism on behalf of those movements that were the farthest from the traditional domestic sphere generated the strongest opposition. In addition, those reform efforts that could be accomplished through persuasion within the home tended to be less controversial. Those that required public activity, particularly writing or speaking, to seek changes in national policy, were considered unsuitable for women.

The earliest reform movements that women joined could be justified as natural extensions of their role as moral guardians of the home. As early as 1824 women were involved in Moral Reform Societies to aid prostitutes.[4] This type of reform could be accomplished by women helping women, while avoiding contact with the male world. Similarly, the Second Great Awakening encouraged women to form religious societies and to support missionary efforts. Here again, women were persuading only other women within the privacy of the prayer circle.

The early manifestations of the temperance movement also respected the conventional limits on woman's role in reform. Women were urged to take personal action by refusing to serve liquor to guests and by persuading their loved ones to give up alcohol.[5] None of these efforts required that women enter the public sphere. A short story by Harriet Beecher Stowe, "The Coral Ring" (first published in *The Christian Souvenir: An Offering for Christmas and the New Year* in 1843), establishes both the rationale and the acceptable boundaries for women's action. Young Florence Elmore is told by her uncle that she has no "sort of purpose or object in life," but that there is "a great field for a woman like you, Florence, in your influence over your associates." This influence comes from "the power which is given to you women to awe and restrain us in your presence."[6] He informs her that an acquaintance of hers is "considered as a lost man . . . Elliot has not self-control enough to prevent his becoming confirmed in intemperate habits" (168). Horrified, Florence agrees to "try her enchantments," though at twenty "the idea of influencing any one, for better or worse, by anything she ever said or did, had never occurred to her" (170–171). Teasingly she binds Elliot to her service, and later at a ball when she finds him with a glass of wine in his hand she whispers, "I forbid it; the cup is poisoned" (172). Struck that his friends recognize his weakness, Elliot tells her that "I have really felt that I needed help, but have been too proud to confess, even to myself, that I needed it. You, Miss Elmore, have done what, perhaps, no one else could have done" (174). Shortly thereafter he signs the temperance pledge.

Florence operates solely through female charm and religious conviction. She speaks to a man outside of her family, but not outside of her social circle; more to the point, she speaks to him privately, first in her home, then, when at the public ball, on a balcony away from others. She exercises power and influence, but no one need know it but the recipient. Whether in 1843 Stowe thought that short stories like this were themselves a form of public influence is unclear; ten years later the contradiction between Stowe's own public voice and the one she allowed other women became overt.

Stowe was just one of the women beginning to achieve success in the literary field through the publication of novels and short stories. In the 1820s and 1830s Sarah Josepha Hale was the best example of a woman who won personal fame by her writing. "Scribbling women" and lady editors were not perceived as challenging the social limits as long as they stayed within certain bounds. Female authors wrote at home, sometimes anonymously, and rarely accepted public credit for their work. The editors and writers of ladies' magazines, even when giving social advice, cast themselves as "speaking" from one woman to another, as if at home. Their voices remained essentially private, and such women never made public appearances.[7]

If remaining within the privacy of the domestic sphere formed one constraint on female writers, others were placed on their subject matter. Lydia

Maria Child, a widely read author of books about child raising, edited a successful magazine for children, the *Juvenile Miscellany*, from 1826 until 1834. But after Child published her personal attack on slavery, *An Appeal in Favor of That Class of Americans Called Africans*, she was ostracized from Boston society, and enough subscriptions to the children's magazine were cancelled to destroy that periodical. Child's experience suggests that the one thing a woman writer could not do was take on a topic identified as political—and therefore male.

Hale was the model of the acceptable female voice and the arbiter of what was socially appropriate for other middle-class women. Frequently warning her readers to avoid political subjects, she herself adopted numerous causes but deftly defined them as nonpolitical. Her lifetime of crusading began when she took over the *Ladies' Magazine* in 1827. Her first public campaign was an appeal to readers for funds to complete the Bunker Hill monument. Despite some public derision, Hale managed to raise $3,000. The cause was impeccably patriotic, and Hale was not forced to display herself publicly; nevertheless, the power to raise such a sum was rare for women, and the campaign prefigured Hale's long career of establishing her own limits both to the "political" and to acceptable female activity.

Hale's involvement with the Seaman's Aid Society of Boston is an excellent example of her ostensibly "nonpolitical" activism. Distressed by the exploitation of returning seamen and the resulting problems for their families, Hale founded the Seaman's Aid Society in 1833. This ladies' organization not only established schools in which seamen's daughters could learn the needle trades, but took the politically radical course of founding a sewing cooperative that paid higher wages and charged lower prices than competing establishments. The work of the society became even more controversial (but still, according to Hale, not political) when it established "temperance houses" where seamen could board. All of this philanthropy—with its economic implications—was reported by Hale in the Society's annual reports, in which she made casual references to "the exciting and sometimes violent clashes between the organization and the owners of the slop-shops" who opposed their work.[8]

In 1839, however, the society faced possible defeat of the temperance law in the legislature. Hale, by this time editor of *Godey's*, retreated from direct political action. Although she felt that the Seaman's Aid Society was an appropriate activity for the women of Boston, she advised the members that outright lobbying was wrong. Instead, she advised them to "pray in secret that the hearts of the friends of temperance may be kept steadfast."[9] This strategic retreat illustrates the dilemma for women who respected the cultural limits on their activity. The issue Hale supported was within women's purview, but she could countenance only certain methods as acceptable means of achieving her goal.

Even Hale was uncertain about the proper limits on women's activity. In 1839 she did not approve of direct attempts to influence the legislative vote on the temperance law, but she had not always unequivocally ruled out such activity. Three years earlier, writing about the Boston Ladies Peace Society in the *Ladies' Magazine*, she had tried to respond to ladies "inquiring what is proper for them to do." The atmosphere at the time was charged by congressional passage of the gag rule, which effectively removed the right to petition on the subject of slavery. In an editorial note, Hale attempts to establish guidelines based on the topic of the reform. First she gracefully accepts the social norms, but then she contradicts herself, suggesting that if the issue is one about which women are particularly knowledgeable or which applies to their own interests, they may petition the legislature anyway:

> We will take this opportunity of remarking, that we have never approved of ladies' allowing their names to appear on petitions, for the redress of public grievances; nor has our name ever been given to such a list. Not that in all cases we would discourage our sex from open and organized efforts to influence public opinion; but we think they should limit their exertions to those objects which may be attained without exciting political and civil dissentions in the nation. For instance, we think it would be perfectly proper for ladies to present a memorial to the State Legislature, or to Congress even, on the subject of Female Education . . . because this subject is one which our sex are more competent to feel and understand. . . . But, in regard to questions touching the government, or the physical prosperity of the Republic, women . . . ought not, publicly, to interfere. They cannot vote to amend the laws, nor have they strength to compel their execution. Whatever knowledge or influence they may possess, should be directed to promote righteous principles . . . among those men with whom they are connected in private life.[10]

Here, Hale counsels women against involvement in issues of national dissension, yet encourages them to organize for benefits for their own sex. Later Hale publicly supported female education, the training of female teachers, missionaries, and doctors, and the extension of property rights to women. Her efforts, including personally lobbying successive presidents of the United States by letter, led to the adoption of a national Thanksgiving Day. She thus proved successful in defining certain issues pertinent to women as extensions of the private sphere, justifying limited modes of female influence.

Hale's reference to topics "exciting political and civil dissention" was a veiled allusion to slavery, the chief issue of national debate in the United

States from the 1830s on. This issue could not be "redefined" as nonpolitical, not even when it was couched in moral terms. Yet inevitably the same forces—education, religious conviction, and the desire to improve society—that led women into temperance, missionary societies, and moral reform campaigns also led many of them to take up the cause of the slave.

Women who were moved to work for abolition faced a strategic dilemma. Not only was the subject matter considered taboo for females, but the most effective tactic for converting others to the cause—raising one's voice—violated social norms. Northern women could not directly aid slaves by talking within the prescribed domestic circle, since the problem existed in other regions, and a comprehensive remedy required legal action in the public sphere. Although the colonization movement argued for returning the slaves to Africa after voluntary emancipation or purchases of slaves financed through contributions, slavery was unlikely to disappear through private and voluntary action. Many women realized that what was necessary was to persuade their neighbors and all citizens of the North to pressure the Congress to end slavery.

Given the cultural definition of women's role in the 1820s and 1830s, slavery was probably the most inappropriate topic that women could address in public life. First recognized as a national problem at the Constitutional Convention of 1787, slavery was always discussed as a political, constitutional, and legal issue. The debate was conducted in a discourse foreign to the sphere assigned to women. Similarly, the language of the female sphere—moral, spiritual, familial—was not used in the halls of Congress and rarely in courts of law.

Almost all Americans agreed that slavery, as a concept, was morally deficient, but the rights of the slaveholder, the rights of the states, and, indeed, the welfare of an inferior race were seen as prior to any fundamental moral question. Thus, slavery and its possible expansion into the territories and the new states were established as problems requiring political solutions, solutions that were inappropriate for female discussion. Furthermore, the question of slavery impinged on property rights. Antislavery groups might harp on the slaves' personhood, but the national debate focused on their status as chattel in a political culture that asserted the right to hold property as inalienable. Since most women had no right to hold property themselves, their views on "human property" had little credence.

Slavery was also an acid test of the limits on the power of the federal government. At a time when political power was most trusted at the local and state level and frequently feared at the national level, the slavery question became the ultimate measure of local governance. The prevailing understanding of the federal system made it possible and, indeed, laudable for individual northern states to abolish slavery and give certain rights to free Negroes while the southern states upheld the rights of the slaveholder. The

constitutional division of power between the states and the national government, not the social and moral condition of the slaves, was the controversy
most often debated in Congress. Here again, the discourse of the debate,
with its focus on constitutional arrangements and the relative powers of
state and national institutions, excluded women from the discussion.

The sense of public outrage against women meddling not only in the male
sphere of politics but in such a difficult subject is clearly shown by the institution of the gag rule in Congress. The rule, which forbade the introduction
of antislavery petitions after 1836 through the device of automatically tab-
ling all such petitions received, was in part intended to deprive women of
one of their previously acceptable forms of participation—the signing of
petitions. Debates over the rule in the House of Representatives reveal the
degree to which women merely petitioning against slavery were perceived as
violating proper standards of conduct. Commenting on petitions opposing
the annexation of Texas as a slave state, Rep. Benjamin Howard of Maryland noted, "I consider it discreditable. I think that these females could have
sufficient field for the exercise of their duties to their fathers, their husbands,
or their children. . . . I feel sorry at this departure from their proper
sphere." [11] Member of Congress and former president John Quincy Adams,
who opposed the gag rule steadfastly until its repeal in 1844, responded,
"Was this from a son? Was it from a father? Was it from a husband that I
heard these words? . . . Are women to have no opinions or actions on subjects relating to the general welfare?" [12] Adams recognized that the gag rule
robbed women of citizenship and personhood by refusing them any voice in
the public debate.

Women who felt the call to work for the antislavery cause faced a severely limited arena in which to labor. As the abolition movement gained
strength in the United States, women's efforts were, at first, parallel to their
activities in other areas. They formed auxiliaries to the male antislavery
societies and held fairs and bazaars to raise money to combat slavery.
Prayer, discussions within the home or with other females, fund-raising,
and, until the gag rule was passed, petitions were their only tools. New
avenues for their efforts were opened by the radical abolitionist William
Lloyd Garrison. He and his followers were anti-institutionalists, denying the
authority of churches and political authorities to limit their efforts to free
the slaves. [13] Women who followed Garrison felt free to ignore the strictures
of church or society against speaking or writing for the slave. They could
also assert that the immorality of slavery outweighed the claims of the Constitution.

The entrance of women into the public debate over slavery was recognized as a new form of female political participation. Antislavery women
had to speak to men, whether through the print media or on the public
platform, in order to effect change. Furthermore, claiming the right to speak

implied not only women's power to persuade outside the personal circle of influence, but also their political equality with men.

The Fate of Lecturesses

Evidence of the social tension created by women speaking in public or on public issues is found throughout the literature of the antebellum period. Novelists mirror the reality of the female speaker, they distort and satirize her, or they suppress her where she might be found. The literary portrayal of the woman who gives voice to opinions about public issues is always ambivalent; the authors struggle with the fate that will befall their female speakers and convey contradictory attitudes toward her. A fairly simple example is found in one of the earliest works of fiction to treat the female speaker directly. *The Lecturess* was a novella published anonymously in 1839 and praised by Hale in *Godey's* in December of that year. It appears to be a straightforward example of didactic popular narrative, written to convey a warning about what will happen to the woman who violates cultural norms by speaking in public. Yet even *The Lecturess* is not as transparent a fiction, not as clear a message, as its author apparently intended.

As the title indicates, the novel concerns a woman who lectures publicly for various causes. When she marries a man who disapproves of any activities for women outside the home, however, Marian, the heroine, gives up lecturing. Later her desire to reenter public life brings crisis to the marriage, eventual separation, Marian's return to lecturing, and her early death. The book teaches women that their happiness lies within the domestic sphere rather than in public activities. The message is so obvious that Baym refers to *The Lecturess* as the "earliest anti-feminist fiction." [14] However, the argument of the book—and the reader's response—is undercut by the positive presentation of the heroine and her well-argued defense of women's activism.

Marian is first seen through the eyes of her future husband, William Forrester. After writing several treatises on "Female Education," Marian comes to Boston to lecture. Before seeing Marian, William articulates the usual bases for opposition to female speakers: Marian is a woman stepping from the "sphere allotted her by God" and entering an office "for which she has neither physical nor moral strength." [15] In fact, Marian lectures to support her widowed mother. As a child, Marian had seen her mother struggle to provide for her daughter and had questioned "the justice of those laws and regulations of society, which exclude women from honorable and lucrative employments" (16). Nevertheless Marian's mother tried to restrain her daughter from a career on the platform, because "she knew that woman, to be happy, must choose a humbler path than that of public life" (18).

On hearing Marian speak, William falls in love with her and soon proposes marriage. To his astonishment, she refuses, citing the "injustice of man towards woman" (37). She mocks woman's obligation to "bow her head meekly in acquiescence to her husband's will, be it ever so arbitrary or unreasonable" (39).

After she has refused William, Marian goes to Charleston to lecture on slavery. She stands before a threatening mob until there is "an alarm of fire," whereupon she loses her courage, flees, and collapses with brain fever. In her illness, she concludes that her desire to raise her sex was merely a rationalization of ambition and vanity. The author thus denigrates the efforts of women to speak in public as narcissistic and denies the possibility of genuinely philanthropic motivations. With her new insights, Marian gladly accepts William's proposal and settles into married life.

The theme of a married woman's obligations is carried out through the contrast between Marian and William, and Sophia and Edward, their closest friends. Sophia, the ideal wife and mother, describes the duties of women as "holy work." When Sophia declines to attend a lecture by a woman, because her husband disapproves, she defends her decision as based on love, not obedience. Marian instead disobeys her husband and attends the lecture. William does not speak to her until six months later, after the birth of their son.

The conflict between a woman's moral role and her desire to carry that role into public life by responding to a moral call becomes overt in the climactic episode. Marian's early lectures are identified only with women's status. In them she promises to spend her life "in the endeavor to raise woman to that equality with man which is her right by the divine law of nature, and of which oppression alone deprives her" (25). When she first refuses Forrester, she identifies herself as "a lecturess—a public defender of the rights of her sex" (36). In these speeches she offends those who opposed women's rights not only by her method—public speaking—but by her topic as well. However, when Marian speaks for other moral reforms, issue and method become more clearly distinguished.

Marian and Sophia are visited by representatives of a "society for the diffusion of knowledge among the blacks in the Southern states" who ask them both to join and beg Marian to become their president. Sophia immediately replies that she will send "money or clothing, to alleviate the sufferings of my fellow-beings; but I have two little creatures given to my especial care, and to them belong my time and instruction" (94–96). Marian, in contrast, willingly accepts the invitation. When William objects, Marian invokes public rather than private considerations: "Why, my dear William . . . where is your Philanthropy? I think it is a noble cause; my heart has often bled for the sufferings of the poor slaves" (97). With this critical question, the author ends the discussion. She is unable to find a response for

William that would supersede his wife's concern for the public good, yet cannot condone Marian's insubordination.

The end of the novel imposes a conventional resolution that satisfies societal norms. Marian returns to lecturing; William leaves her and then, coincidentally, loses his money. Marian dies in poverty and alone, articulating the ostensible moral:

> True pride, true independence in a woman, is to fill the place which her God assigns her; to make her husband's happiness her own; and to yield her will to his in all things, conformable to her duty to a higher power. By such conduct will a woman attain her *rights*— the affection of her husband, the respect of her children and the world, and the approval of Heaven. (120)

On the surface, then, *The Lecturess* is a moral tale warning against the sin of pride in both husbands and wives. It is unusual—unique in its time period—in casting that story as one in which the heroine openly challenges the limits of social and moral action for woman. The author reveals her own ambivalence toward Marian's public career and philanthropic urges by her inconsistent management of sympathy toward her heroine and her clear articulation of women's grievances. The conflict between duties to woman's sphere and to higher social needs remains unresolved.

The Lecturess offers a first inkling of the unacknowledged bases for objections to women speaking in public. Marian gives her early lectures when she is single and fatherless; no man controls her. Although she is notorious, she is not castigated as immoral or un-Christian. Her mother's struggles offer partial justification for Marian's behavior, though character flaws such as pride contribute as well. But later, when Marian joins the philanthropic organization and returns to the lecture circuit, she is much more severely criticized and punished accordingly. The difference now is that she is married. On the simplest level this means she has added disobedience to her husband to her other sins, has chosen a public duty (the slave) over a private one (the baby). But implicit in her condemnation is a further, unnamed sin: something like theft. It is no longer her own property she is displaying in public. Her voice and her body now belong to her husband and should be on view only in her home.

Differing public reaction to married and unmarried female speakers was a major factor in the careers of the two real women on whom Marian Gayland was modeled. The novel is a roman à clef, and anyone who read the eastern papers was furnished with the key. Marian's career and experience with marriage parallel, in many details, those of two prominent women lecturers, Frances Wright and Angelina Grimké.

Wright, a Scotchwoman, first became famous in the United States when she published *Views of Society and Manners in America* (1821), observations formed on her first trip to the New World. In 1824 she returned to the United States, founding the Nashoba colony, which provided training and education to freed slaves. By 1828, when she began to lecture, she was identified with the communal ideals of Robert Dale Owen, and the two were frequently accused of believing in "free love."[16] Her early lectures often focused on the need for equal education for women. When Marian Gayland describes her sex as "sleeping away their lives without a struggle, without an effort to free themselves from the state of mental degradation which their task-masters have assigned them" (24), her rhetoric resembles Wright's language in "Of Free Inquiry," where she describes the "mental chains" of women and their "subordination" through ignorance.[17]

For a brief period, Wright, like Marian Gayland, retired from public life to begin a family. She married William Phiquepal D'Arusmont, another reformer, though with characteristic disregard of traditional values she waited until after the death of their first child to do so. Their second daughter was born in 1832. By the spring of 1834 she was back on the lecture platform in England. Waterman summarizes a letter among the Wright manuscripts that suggests the plot of *The Lecturess*:

> [Her English trip] does not seem to have altogether pleased her husband, for in a long letter . . . he ends by threatening to come after her if her negligence continues. Phiquepal . . . does not seem to have looked with favor upon her returning to public life. . . . It was her insistence, a few years later, upon returning to the lecture platform that seems to have caused the first serious rift in the happiness of their married life.[18]

Returning to the United States in late 1835, Wright began lecturing on monopolies, slavery, and civilization. She was also involved in New York politics. Her personal life as well as her stage appearance furnished material to the New York papers. Typical of the reviews was that in the *New York Daily Express* of September 28, 1838: "Her acting was very fair. She was dressed in white—with an open bosom, as if habited for a Ball room . . . her performance would have answered well enough for an employ on some Theatrical boards, at fifty cents a night."[19] The references to dress and behavior underscore the inappropriateness of her actions: the newspaper concerns itself with wondering what a married woman is doing exhibiting herself on the stage. Her lecture topic is secondary.

A closer personal model for Marian was Angelina Grimké. Angelina and her sister Sarah, daughters of a Charleston judge and slaveholder, had become Quaker abolitionists in Philadelphia. They began speaking for the antislavery cause in 1836 and later were recruited by William Lloyd Garrison to go on a New England speaking tour. There they attracted "mixed" audiences and were rebuked in a pastoral letter of the General Association of Congregational Ministers. The letter warned that when woman "assumes the place and tone of man as a public reformer . . . she yields the power which God has given her for her protection, and her character becomes unnatural." [20]

Corresponding with Theodore Weld, who had trained her as an antislavery speaker, Angelina maintained the right of women to participate fully in the public debate over slavery. She made no distinction between the right of single and married women to speak and act in the public eye. On August 12, 1837, Angelina wrote to Weld that she could not see why a wife should be subject to her husband any more than to her sister. Otherwise, *she surrenders her moral responsibility, which no woman has a right to do.* [21]

In February of 1838, Weld and Grimké became engaged. The subject of her continued lecturing caused much comment from friends and relatives. Even Theodore admitted that many thought she would be "utterly spoiled for domestic life" by lecturing to "promiscuous" (mixed) audiences, that she would be held "up as a beacon to warn from such unnatural violations of constitutional instincts all other females." Angelina admitted to wondering if she should retreat from the lecture hall.[22] It had become an increasing strain for her. The previous fall she had ended a tour by falling gravely ill.

Angelina Grimké married Theodore Weld on May 14, 1838, one day before the opening of the Anti-Slavery Convention of American Women, where she was a featured speaker. Three days later, Pennsylvania Hall was burned by a mob angered by the mingling of blacks and whites at the convention. Angelina's speaking career was over. Despite imploring and sometimes scornful letters from other abolitionists, she devoted her efforts to family life. The reasons proposed to explain her retirement range from her reaction to the split in the abolition movement to the financial, physical, and emotional strains of childbearing and housewifery.[23] But it is noteworthy that the only time Angelina spoke as a married woman was the day after her wedding, and that what the papers stressed was the sexual anomaly: "The crazy abolitionists . . . have . . . gone on to Philadelphia, and thrown the firebrand into that peaceable community. Mrs. Angelica Grimke Weld [*sic*] . . . was one of the agitators. . . . This is rather a queer honeymoon for Angelica and Theodore, wedded on Monday, bedded on Tuesday, and setting Philadelphia on fire on Wednesday." [24]

The Lecturess was no doubt inspired by the extensive publicity accorded the Grimkés in the late 1830s. The story mentions "two ladies" from Charleston who open an academy after Marian's visit, suggesting the Grimkés' origins in that city. The threat of fire when Marian speaks parallels the Philadelphia burning of the hall, as Marian's brain fever recalls Angelina's illness. By the time *The Lecturess* was written, Angelina Grimké had been married seventeen months and was expecting her first child. She was proving, and continued to prove by staying home, that a woman speaker was not permanently "spoiled" for marriage. She thus avoided the almost contradictory criticism that had been leveled at Frances Wright, which implicitly attacked her as promiscuous for mingling the body that should be only her husband's with the public.

The Grimkés remained somewhat defensive about their decision to return to private life. Four years after the marriage, Sarah wrote to a friend that their retirement was an act of "living out of our antislavery principles in every day life," of asserting "our unchanged opinions as to the equality of the sexes at the family altar, around the social board and on all the occasions which may and do arise in domestic life." [25] Yet the Grimkés' earlier public actions had already convinced many women that they could not live out their principles in privacy and silence.

Public Voices at Midcentury

By 1852 the issues that had driven Angelina Grimké and Marian Gayland to speak were argued across the nation. Passage of the 1850 Fugitive Slave Law made it impossible to pretend that slavery was a purely southern problem. The moral call to assist in the freeing of other human beings was everywhere. Each woman had to decide what response she could offer.

Many forms of semipublic activity by women had gradually lost their stigma, if they had not become commonplace. In 1851 Anne Wales Abbot writes anonymously in the *North American Review*, "it has become a wonderfully common piece of temerity for a lady to make a book. . . . If she does not hear some gruff remarks upon misdirected talents, and the concocting of puddings being the appropriate sphere of feminine intellect, it will be because the time is gone by for that." [26] A good example of the extension— and limitation—of women's public activity is found in the career of Dorothea Dix. By the early 1840s Dix was surveying jails and almshouses, writing memorials to state legislatures, and conducting campaigns for construction of mental hospitals. Yet despite her temerity in traveling alone and confronting the public officials in charge of hospitals and asylums, her memorials were discreetly presented in the legislatures by men who were allied with her. Thus she managed almost singlehandedly to bring about major reform, but avoided speaking in public.

Mid-nineteenth-century women found a number of innovative ways to amplify their voices. Among the most interesting were Margaret Fuller's conversations, which were at first exclusively for women but in their last series included a few men. These conversations were paradoxical: they encouraged women to use their voices, to converse, but in the seclusion of the "conversation." Though Fuller avoided controversial subjects when she was conducting these discussions,[27] she gained self-confidence and built the foundation for her later career as an investigative reporter writing about such social ills as prisons and for her participation in the Italian revolution of 1848.

The conversations looked tame, however, compared to the 1848 Seneca Falls Convention, which was rapidly followed by other women's rights conventions, despite objections and mockery. Many of the women participating in these conventions were activist reformers whose attempts to solve social problems had taught them they could not work for temperance, for the slave, or for prison reform if they could not speak themselves. Elizabeth Cady Stanton wryly comments that "gentlemen were all quite willing that women should join their societies and churches, to do the drudgery, to work up the enthusiasm in fairs and revivals . . . to beg money for the church, circulate petitions from door to door, to visit saloons . . . and sit round the outskirts of a hall like so many wall flowers . . . ; but they would not allow them to sit on the platform, address the assembly, nor vote for men and measures." [28] Susan B. Anthony had herself been a delegate from the Daughters of Temperance to a mass meeting where she was "informed that the ladies were invited to listen, and not to take part in the proceedings." [29] These women believed that, as one delegate to the National Woman's Rights Convention at Syracuse, New York, in September 1852 put it, "There *is* no limit to personal responsibility. Our duties are as wide as the world." [30] Whether women could carry out these duties through public speech became a topic in three important novels—*Uncle Tom's Cabin, The Blithedale Romance*, and *Isa*, all published in 1852.

Stowe's Powerless Voices

In *Uncle Tom's Cabin* Stowe reveals her deeply conflicted feelings about cultural limitations on women's response to the moral call. Her situation was very much complicated because she was a member of one of the most important public families in the United States, the Beechers. Like all Lyman Beecher's children, she observed from early childhood her father's model response to moral need.

Lyman Beecher believed in acting on his conscience, but as a gradualist he believed reform should come about by modifying the institutions already in place. He disapproved Garrison's demand for immediate emancipation, reminding him that "great economic and political questions can't be solved so simply." [31] He joined the movement for colonization, worked against the abolitionists, and in 1835 convinced the Congregational churches of Connecticut and Massachusetts to close their pulpits to " 'itinerant agents and lecturers' who preached 'erroneous or questionable' sentiments, a euphemism for abolition." [32]

For the Beecher sons the set of expectations regarding the way they were to improve the world was very clear: they were to become ministers, like their father, and though a few attempted to escape this destiny, eventually all of the surviving sons followed their father into the pulpit. Life was more complicated for Beecher daughters. Harriet had two older sisters, who presented her with vastly different models of "what women could do." Mary married young and was the only member of the family to live an entirely private life. She was also the only one who did not spend some time in Cincinnati, the city that gave the Beechers their first real experiences with slavery. The other sister, Catharine, was eleven years older than Harriet and, after their mother's death when Harriet was five, became the person closest to her. As a young teenager Harriet was first placed under Catharine's official tutelage in the elder sister's school in Hartford and then, at Catharine's request, became her apprentice teacher in the classroom.

By middle life Catharine Beecher had become a well-known public educator and respected author, famous for her campaigns to improve teaching and her publications on moral philosophy and domestic cookery. Like her father, Catharine claimed the authority to tell other people—especially women—how they should live. The titles of her publications were typically admonitory: *An Essay on Slavery and Abolitionism, with Reference to the Duty of American Females* (1837); *The Duty of American Women to Their Country* (1845); *Letter to Benevolent Ladies in the United States* (1849); *The True Remedy for the Wrongs of Women* (1851). Yet in all of these works Catharine reiterated her position that women should remain within the confines of the private circle of influence when it came to political questions. Characteristically, although she herself traveled around the country to raise money for her school, she inveighed against female speakers in the cause of abolition.

In 1832, Lyman Beecher moved to Cincinnati to head the Lane Seminary. Daughters Catharine, Harriet, and Isabella accompanied him to the city, where Catharine opened the Western Female Seminary. The family was caught up in a conflict within the city and the seminary over the question of abolition. When Lyman sided with the more conservative trustees of the seminary and banned discussion of abolition, a majority of the students—including Theodore Weld—left to attend Oberlin. Catharine shared her father's doubts about the activist abolitionists. In 1837 she published *An Essay on Slavery* as an open letter to her former pupil, Angelina Grimké, upon hearing that Grimké was undertaking a speaking tour "for the purpose of exerting . . . influence to form Abolition Societies among ladies of the non-slave-holding States." [33] Carefully Catharine laid out principles for women's behavior that were logical extensions of Lyman's views. Woman, recognizing her natural subordination, must "win every thing by peace and love . . . in the domestic and social circle" (100–101). As for organizing, a woman may seek the aid of co operation and combination among her own sex, to assist her in her appropriate offices of piety, charity, maternal and domestic duty; but whatever, in any measure, throws a woman into the attitude of a combatant, either for herself or others . . . whatever obliges her in any way to exert coercive influences, throws her out of her appropriate sphere.(102)

In an atmosphere poisoned by the infamous gag rule, Catharine even excuses woman from coming forward on behalf of "a portion of her sex who are bound in cruel bondage" (103). She accepts the necessity for the rule and puts the onus for not disturbing the legislators on the women, who risk being counterproductive if they protest. She objects that "petitions from females will operate to exasperate. . . they will be deemed obtrusive, indecorous, and unwise . . . they will increase. . . the evil which it is wished to remove . . . they . . . will tend eventually to bring females as petitioners and partisans into every political measure that may tend to injure and oppress their sex" (103). Thus, she justifies silencing disturbing voices in the name of civil peace; her emphasis on decorum shows how such an attitude was employed to silence women.

Harriet's career as an author was deeply intertwined with Catharine's. Harriet's first book, a geography, appeared under Catharine's name, and her first collection, *The Mayflower*, had an introduction by Catharine because the elder sister had more name recognition. The role that Catharine had created for herself, as a well-known author and educator who nevertheless claimed the domestic sphere as her own, was understood and approved by her younger sister. Harriet had applauded Catharine's *Duty of American Women* in 1845 for its public impact, writing to her sister, "It is a stroke well aimed, well struck and must do good, well done Katy!"[34] Still, when Harriet began to consider herself an author, she justified her new public career because its monetary rewards would enhance her domestic life. As she writes to a friend in 1838, the money will allow her "to have my house kept in the best manner and yet to have time for reflection and that preparation for the education of my children which every mother needs."[35] During the writing of *Uncle Tom's Cabin*, Harriet was attempting to fulfill the Beecher ideal for a woman, writing on a topic of public concern while maintaining all of her duties as wife and mother. Catharine returned the support and approval Harriet had given her earlier by moving in to take over the superintendence of the Stowe household.

It was another woman who asked Harriet to use her writing as a "stroke" against slavery. Harriet's sister-in-law wrote to her after the passage of the Fugitive Slave Act in 1850: "Hattie, . . . if I could use a pen as you can, I would write something that will make this whole nation feel what an accursed thing slavery is." [36] Clearly Isabella Jones Beecher believed Harriet's words could be a power in the fight against slavery. But Harriet herself, in *Uncle Tom's Cabin*, shows that for women, words are weak and dubious weapons. At this time in her life she also revealed a deep uncertainty about the efficacy of private influence. The entire novel suggests that the disenfranchised and powerless must take covert action; words are not enough.

In *Uncle Tom's Cabin* the debate about political strategies for ending slavery takes the form of a debate about voice. Throughout the novel Stowe contrasts the uselessness of speech, particularly the discourse of moral, social, or religious obligation culturally appropriate for women, with the vitality and efficacy of action. The novel abounds in examples of ineffective talk. The first section carefully establishes that the speech of those without political rights is meaningless; here, as in many other places in the book, Stowe equates blacks and women. Mrs. Shelby has "talked with Eliza about her boy. . . . I have told her that one soul is worth more than all the money in the world; and how will she believe me when she sees us turn round and sell her child?" She is no more effective when she tries to persuade her husband not to sell Tom and Harry; his response, framed in economic rather than religious terms, silences her. [37]

Stowe casts her next example in a comic vein. Sam, one of the Shelby slaves, has "a native talent that might . . . have raised him to eminence in political life" (93). He delights in riding attendance on his master to political gatherings, where, after watching the orators, he does burlesques and imitations. "In fact, Sam considered oratory as his vocation" (94). But it is not Sam's talk—impotent talk since he is a Negro with no political rights—that assists Eliza in escaping Haley; it is, instead, his actions, from planting a nut under the horse's saddle to losing his hat opportunely, that give her invaluable time. In foiling Haley, who has gained perfectly legal title to his new property, Sam is engaging in the civil disobedience of the powerless. This is more effectual than any words could be.

Stowe's distrust of talk is put into the mouth of the most feminized man in the book, Augustine St. Clare, who ruefully admits to his cousin that "my forte lies in talking, and yours, cousin, lies in doing" (212). Miss Ophelia agrees: prophetically she warns her cousin, "now is the only time there ever is to do a thing in. . . . You may die, or fail, and then Topsy be hustled off to auction, spite of all I can do," and she arranges an immediate transfer of ownership (360). Ophelia's "doing" is, however, unusual for women, as is her success. Most women—like Simon Legree's mother praying over him— just talk, powerlessly and inconsequentially. Even little Eva, whose words seem to many critics the heart of the novel, may be Christlike, but she is ineffectual. [38] Despite her dying requests, her father does not free his slaves, and her mother's temper does not improve. In fact, when Eva once proposes that if she had the family diamonds she would "sell them, and buy a place in the free states, and take all our people there, and hire teachers, to teach them to read and write" (310), she comes much closer to a vision of useful action than any of her prayers could.

Throughout *Uncle Tom's Cabin* a woman who cannot communicate with words may communicate through her body, and if she cannot speak in life she may speak in death. A persistent representation of the voice from beyond the grave is a curl of hair. Little Eva distributes these on her death-bed, and Simon Legree's mother similarly sends him one, whose voice is more eloquent than she ever was; it haunts him, and when he sees the curl of Little Eva's hair that Tom is wearing he becomes distraught. The paradigmatic case of the silenced voice is that of Augustine St. Clare's fiancée. The young woman's guardian, trying to exercise customary patriarchal rights and arrange a marriage between his ward and his son, effectively smothered all speech. The woman wrote "time and again" to Augustine, but he heard nothing; Augustine's letters also "ceased to arrive" (184). Only after he has made a rapid marriage on the rebound does she discover her letters have been stopped. Thus when she writes to him again she has recovered her voice in vain. When Augustine dies, he is found to be wearing her miniature, with "under a crystal, a lock of dark hair" (372).

Black women are more frequently compelled to silent communication than white women. The woman whose child is taken from her by Haley on the riverboat expresses her grief by throwing herself in the river. And Cassie gains her point more by body language and voice substitutes than by her fluency in French and English.

Cassie's life has taught her Stowe's general lesson, that the voice of the powerless is ineffectual. Her speeches to Simon, like those to the lover whom she begged for marriage, or those to the men she begged not to take her son to the calaboose, have no consequences. To save herself she needs alternate ways of representing her messages. These include the mysterious sounds made by the bottle in the garret, her abrupt change of room, the white sheeted figure that glides through the house at night, and the stiletto she flashes before the eyes of the terrified Emmeline. In other words, Cassie is forced to find forms of symbolic action that can be undertaken by the silent and powerless. The alternative, which she also considers, is nonsymbolic action, that is, killing Legree.

Cassie, Gilbert and Gubar point out, is one of a line of nineteenth-century "mad women in the attic," the dark and angry side of silenced women characters and authors.[39] But her situation needs to be read politically as well as psychologically. On Simon Legree's plantation there is no social order. As Cassie states, no one can bear witness to Simon's destruction of

Tom, because no black person can testify—no black person can be heard—in court. Under the slave system, slaves were persons without public voices. Their discourse, like that of women, was entirely private.

In the absence of order, Cassie is in a sense freed of all controls on white women who live in a structured, if restrictive, society. The nature of Cassie's peculiar "freedom" is symbolized by her performance as a ghost. No limits, not even between this world and the next, control her.

Yet Cassie's goal is completely moral and socially acceptable: she is trying to save young Emmeline from repeating her own sexual history. Cassie is carefully modeled on Mary Magdalene. A repentant fallen woman, she goes out to Tom when he has been scourged and brings him ointment and comfort. Later, Tom dies for her sins: he knows where she is hiding but will not reveal it. But even if Cassie has a savior, she cannot regain her soul on the plantation or in the American political system. She lacks a fundamental form of speech. She tells Tom, "I can't pray. . . . I never have prayed since my children were sold!" (462) and only becomes "a devout and tender Christian" (500) when reunited with her daughter Eliza.

Two speaking women in *Uncle Tom's Cabin* apparently repeat the successful persuasion of young Florence Elmore in "The Coral Ring." However, by 1852 Stowe recognized the limitations of the kind of female influence she had advocated in that story. In both cases in *Uncle Tom's Cabin* where women articulate their beliefs in private, they encourage public civil disobedience rather than purely personal reform. Furthermore, it is never woman's speech alone that persuades, but the presence of other factors that dispose men to follow her lead.

In the scenes in the home of Ohio state senator and Mrs. Bird, Stowe reemphasizes the difference between male and female discourse when discussing slavery. The senator has just voted for a state version of the Fugitive Slave Law, which his wife condemns as "cruel and unchristian." The senator teases her that she is "getting to be a politician," but she insists the argument is purely moral and asserts that "it's a shameful, wicked, abominable law, and I'll break it, for one, the first time I get a chance." She dismisses the political and economic justification that "it's not a matter of private feeling,—there are great public interests involved," and takes womanly refuge in private morality: "I don't know anything about politics, but I can read my Bible" (99–100).

Mrs. Bird does break the law in sheltering Eliza: her husband has explained to her that giving runaway slaves "something comfortable to eat, and a few old clothes, and send[ing] them quietly about their business" would be "aiding and abetting" (99). But it is not, finally, his wife's speeches that convince the senator that he too should disobey the law he helped make and drive Eliza to a station on the underground railroad. Though "our senator was a stateman, and of course could not be expected to cry, like other mortals" (106), he is overwhelmed by "the magic of the real presence of distress," the recognition that "a fugitive might be a hapless mother, a defenceless child" (110). If there is any speech that counts with him, it is Eliza's question, "Ma'am . . . have you ever lost a child?" (105). To this he replies with action.

In a similar example of the power of action over words, Stowe takes us to the Quaker community led by Rachel Halliday, whose ability to make things happen while using few words is emphasized. The task of getting a "complicated and multiform" Indiana breakfast is entirely organized by Rachel's "gentle 'Thee had better,' or more gentle 'Had n't thee better?'. . . If there was any danger of friction or collision from the ill-regulated zeal of so many young operators, her gentle 'Come! come!'; or 'I would n't, now,' was quite sufficient to allay the difficulty" (169). Yet despite Stowe's insistence that this is an "anti-patriarchal" (169) community and her focus on Rachel as its central figure—Jane Tompkins refers to Rachel as "God in human form"[40]—it is not Rachel's moral authority alone that saves George and Eliza. It is the concerted actions of the Quaker men who organize their escape, even facing gunfire. Doing what their entire sect believes they are "conscience bound to do" (225), the men act rather than talk.

Although Mrs. Bird breaks the law she indignantly criticizes, she makes no demand to participate in changing that law. No woman in *Uncle Tom's Cabin* confronts her political disenfranchisement. The omission is striking because George, a male slave, fully articulates his legal disabilities. He asks Mr. Wilson, "What laws are there for us? We don't make them,—we don't consent to them,—we have nothing to do with them. . . . Don't you tell us . . . that governments derive their just power from the consent of the governed? . . . Do you call these the laws of *my* country? Sir, I have n't any country" (135, 137). Once in Ohio, he shouts down to Loker and Marks that "we don't own your laws; we don't own your country; we stand here as free, under God's sky, as you are, and . . . we'll fight for our liberty till we die." Stowe refers to this speech as his "declaration of independence" (232). She never states that the argument would hold equally for women, but the constant thwarting of women's desire to act for themselves or on behalf of the slave implicitly reveals women's need for a similar declaration. Two years later, in her "Appeal to the Women of the Free States" (published in the *Independent*), Stowe broke away from her sister's conservatism and called on women to petition Congress against slavery.[41] It was not, however, for ten more years that she would actually call for the vote for women.

The final chapters of *Uncle Tom's Cabin* are frustrating and unsatisfying to modern readers. A consistent theme of the book is the inadequacy of the customarily proposed solutions to the slave problem. In this regard Stowe, who nowhere calls for immediate emancipation, writes a novel like a mathematical proposition, proving that only such emancipation can be effective.

Trusting to kind owners will not work: like the Shelbys, they may lose their money and be forced to sell their slaves. Or like St. Clare, they may die, leaving their slaves to worse conditions. Buying out the slaves will not work: it is a slow process and, as in the case of Chloe's attempt to buy Tom, may conclude only once the object of the purchase is dead. Promises of later emancipation may not work: St. Clare dies after he has promised to free Tom, and the only slave in the entire establishment who does not suffer from St. Clare's death is Topsy. Yet the book offers no solution to the slavery problem. The plot climaxes by sending first George and Eliza and then Topsy off to Liberia, but this reflects Stowe's recognition of American racism rather than a belief in colonization. In her concluding remarks Stowe acknowledges that the provision of a refuge in Africa "is no reason why the church of Christ should throw off that responsibility to this outcast race which her profession demands of her" and points out the difficulties of filling up Liberia with an "ignorant, inexperienced, half-barbarized race, just escaped from the chains of slavery" (516).

And so, since she does not have the courage to take the radical anti-institutional position of calling for emancipation, the only thing Stowe can finally tell individuals is to "see to it that *they feel right*." She reminds the men and women of the North that "you can *pray*." On the face of it this is a typical Beecher answer. The idea that "an atmosphere of sympathetic influence encircles every human being; and the man or woman who *feels* strongly, healthily and justly, on the great interests of humanity, is a constant benefactor to the human race" (515), recalls Catharine Beecher telling Angelina Grimké in 1837 that "it is of the greatest concern . . . to every man, that his fellow-men should *believe right*, and one of his most sacred duties is to use all his influence to promote correct opinions." Women therefore must use their influence to promote "a spirit of candour, forbearance, charity, and peace." [42] But for Stowe to stop here is to renege on the thrust of her novel. The real message of the book is emphatically not quietist. The text, as opposed to the narrative voice of the last chapter, does not tell women to go pray; instead, it instructs them to go *act*—if necessary covertly, but to act.

Stowe's growing doubts about the power of female speech raise the ultimate paradox of *Uncle Tom's Cabin*. A book full of examples of powerless speech was itself one of the most powerful examples of verbal persuasion in the nineteenth-century United States. Stowe herself knew this; it frightened her so much that she disclaimed her own voice. She told Mrs. Howard that "I did not write that book. . . . I only put down what I saw," [43] and in the 1878 preface to the novel she explained in the third person that after the author's first vision of Uncle Tom's death (a vision that came from the outside), "from that time the story can less be said to have been composed by her than imposed upon her." [44] Her role was that of a prophetess through whom the voice of the Lord was speaking. Stowe could not admit she had written a novel calling for abolition and female activism.

The Silencing of Zenobia, Priscilla, and Isa

Two other novels of 1852 also intervene in the cultural debate over constituting a place for the voice of the articulate woman. Unlike the women in *Uncle Tom's Cabin*, the women in *Isa* and *The Blithedale Romance* have public voices. But in both cases the authors undermine their own assertions about the power of these voices. In *Blithedale* the two female speakers are eventually silenced. In *Isa* Chesebro' negates Isa's power by repeatedly implying that Isa's speech inverts the concept of the moral call, that her voice is used to harm rather than to improve the world. Both books take more notice of the "woman's rights agitation" than did *Uncle Tom's Cabin*; perhaps for this reason they convey more alarm about woman's place in the culture.

"Would that Miss Margaret Fuller might lose her tongue," wrote Nathaniel Hawthorne to his fiancée, Sophia Peabody, off to spend the day listening to Fuller.[45] This was a feeling he never lost, though he was only able to silence the celebrated conversationalist a decade later, and metaphorically, in *The Blithedale Romance*. The likeness of Zenobia to Fuller has been often analyzed, usually in terms of biographical similarities: both women write about women's rights, both are public figures, both are connected to reformist communities, both die by drowning. There is another, more resonant though less explicit, relation between *The Blithedale Romance* and Hawthorne's thinking about Margaret Fuller. Hawthorne recapitulates the historical woman's sexual unconventionality, Fuller's dubious tie, which may or may not have been marriage, to the Marquese Ossoli, in Zenobia's equally uncertain relationship with the mesmerist Westervelt.

Hawthorne, whose novels reveal a distrust of almost anyone with the power of speech, from Puritan authorities to such differing individuals as Dimmesdale and Westervelt, was particularly disturbed by women with "tongues" because he connected women's public speech with sexual exposure and expression. This was equally true in his fiction and in his life. In *The Scarlet Letter* the letter Hester wears is simultaneously her silenced voice and the revelation of her sexual activity. In his correspondence with Ticknor, Hawthorne amply demonstrates how the association of speech and sexuality created the nineteenth-century double bind on women's voices. He observes that "generally women write like emasculated men, and are only to be distinguished from male authors by greater feebleness and folly; but when they throw off the restraints of decency, and come before the public stark naked, as it were—then their books are sure to possess character and value." Female expression is either inadequate—castrated—or indecent.

Thus he comments that Julia Ward Howe ought to be "soundly whipt" for "making public what she ought to keep to herself—viz. her passions, emotions, and womanly weaknesses," but nevertheless he found "Passion Flowers" "delightful." It is no wonder that despite Hawthorne's praise of his wife's travel writings, "neither she nor I would like to see her name on your list of female authors." [46]

In *The Blithedale Romance* Hawthorne divides—or multiplies—woman's indecent voice between Zenobia, the brilliant writer, and Priscilla, the veiled lady, who prophesies when she is exhibited. The plot is constructed to show how similar these apparently unlike women are and to explore the connections between public voice, sexuality, and the possibility of independent female action for moral change. Ultimately both women learn to keep their passions to themselves and choose silence as woman's best mode of expression/repression.

Despite Zenobia's glorious womanhood and Priscilla's pale and shrinking New England maidenhood, the women are half-sisters, they love the same man, and they are both public performers. Hawthorne insists on the sexuality of both women. Coverdale cannot look long at Zenobia without imagining her in "Eve's earliest garment," [47] and he speculates graphically that there is "no folded petal, no latent dew-drop, in this perfectly developed rose!" but "a wife!" (672). Priscilla's specialty as a seamstress is the knitting of little Freudian purses, whose "peculiar excellence" is the difficulty of discovering "the aperture; although, to a practised touch, they would open as wide as charity or prodigality might wish" (661–662). Some critics find credible the suggestion that Priscilla has fallen into prostitution, a common sideline of seamstresses. [48] Although Hawthorne's verbal insistence on Priscilla's virginity ("her air . . . perfectly modest, delicate, and virginlike" [699]; "she had kept . . . her virgin reserve . . . throughout it all" [808–809]) makes this unlikely, he seems unconsciously to equate the two sisters' speech, the opening of their mouths, with sexual openness.

The women are silenced in different fashions. Zenobia is increasingly distanced by the novel's construction, a construction Hawthorne mediates through his thoroughly untrustworthy narrator, Coverdale. [49] When we first meet Zenobia, Coverdale presents her directly and emphasizes her power as a speaker. She welcomes the newcomers "in a fine, frank, mellow voice"; she immediately proposes "singing" Coverdale's verses (644); and she promptly discourses on the topic he associates with her, woman's role. When one member of the community asks, "have we our various parts assigned?" Zenobia replies "with a mellow, almost broad laugh":

Oh, we of the softer sex . . . we women . . . will take the domestic and indoor part of the business, as a matter of course. To bake, to boil, to roast, to fry, to stew—to wash, and iron, and scrub, and sweep, and,

at our idler intervals, to repose ourselves on knitting and sewing—
these, I suppose, must be feminine occupations for the present. By-
and-by, perhaps, when our individual adaptations begin to develop
themselves, it may be that some of us, who wear the petticoat, will go
afield, and leave the weaker brethren to take our places in the kitchen!
(645–646)

But never in Blithedale does the development of individual adaptations free
women or assign them new roles. Instead, Zenobia is the Eve or Pandora
(652) who brings about the fall of this paradise, and as it falls, her voice
disappears from the narrative. With the exception of the legend of the veiled
lady, a legend that itself annihilates a public female voice, the "speaker"
rarely speaks.

Up to the time of the novel's events Zenobia has been not a speaker but a
writer, a cross between Fuller, whose *Woman in the Nineteenth Century*
presumably is the model for Zenobia's writings about women, and the
scribbling women whom Hawthorne detested and envied.[50] Priscilla, Coverdale surmises, "had read some of Zenobia's stories, (as such literature goes
everywhere), or her tracts in defence of the sex" (659). Yet Coverdale himself comments that "her poor little stories and tracts never half did justice to
her intellect; it was only the lack of a fitter avenue that drove her to seek
development in literature. She was made . . . for a stump-oratress" (669).
Zenobia recognizes the social constraints upon her natural gift. At Eliot's
pulpit,

> she declaimed with great earnestness and passion . . . on the injustice
> which the world did to women, and equally to itself, by not allowing
> them . . . their natural utterance in public. "It shall not always be so!"
> cried she. "If I live another year, I will lift up my own voice, in behalf
> of woman's wider liberty. . . . It is my belief. . . that, when my sex shall
> achieve its rights, there will be ten eloquent women, where there is
> now one eloquent man. Thus far, no woman in the world has ever
> once spoken out her whole heart and her whole mind. The mistrust
> and disapproval of the vast bulk of society throttles us, as with two
> gigantic hands at our throats! We mumble a few weak words, and
> leave a thousand better ones unsaid. You let us write a little, it is true,
> on a limited range of subjects. But the pen is not for woman. Her
> power is too natural and immediate. It is with the living voice, alone,
> that she can compel the world to recognize the light of her intellect and
> the depth of her heart! (737–738)

Covering himself with Coverdale, a man who cannot make himself heard
as a writer, Hawthorne proceeds to "throttle" Zenobia, making her very

utterances inaudible, presenting the reader with only beginnings or endings of important speeches, and calling into question the possibility of interpretation. Just as in *The Scarlet Letter*, Hawthorne's narrator here is impelled by "unresolved conflicts about anger, authority, and female autonomy" that create "contradictions in his voice as well as his story."[51] Typically, Coverdale cannot hear Zenobia when she speaks, so that his unresolved conflicts emerge as gaps in the narrative. For example, shortly before the scene at Eliot's pulpit, Coverdale, hidden in his "hermitage," had attempted to eavesdrop on Westervelt and Zenobia, but "Zenobia's utterance was so hasty and broken, and Westervelt's so cool and low, that I hardly could make out an intelligible sentence" (722–723). Not surprisingly, though Zenobia tells Coverdale she has "been several times on the point of making you my confidant," she decides against it (756).

Soon after, in town, Coverdale looks through Zenobia's window, where he sees, played out as if in a shadow box, a dialogue between Zenobia and Westervelt of which he again cannot hear a word. Returning to Blithedale, he comes upon Hollingsworth, Zenobia, and Priscilla, too late, inevitably, to hear the critical speeches Zenobia gives when "on trial for my life," speeches that explain "all, no doubt . . . Zenobia's whole character and history; the true nature of her mysterious connection with Westervelt; her later purposes towards Hollingsworth, and, reciprocally, his in reference to her" (819–820). Finally left alone with Coverdale, Zenobia says, "Poor womanhood, with its rights and wrongs! Here will be new matter for my course of lectures" (829), but the only lecture she delivers is her final silent action, suicide. In death her message can only be spoken through her body, and even then Coverdale is unable to decipher it: looking at her corpse, he cannot decide whether she expresses penitence in her bent knees or defiance in her clenched hands.[52]

Priscilla, the veiled lady, is also heard less and less. As Zenobia explains, Priscilla is "the type of womanhood, such as man has spent centuries in making it," and she loves a man who believes that "all the separate action of woman is, and ever has been . . . foolish, vain, destructive . . . woman is a monster . . . without man, as her acknowledged principal" (739–740). Priscilla herself asserts that she has no "free-will" (781), and as the veiled lady she more than acknowledges man: she is under the absolute control of Westervelt, the devilish mesmerist. At these times she can be heard, but is effectively disconnected from her own voice.

Even as the veiled lady Priscilla's speech is a thing of the past: on the night before he leaves for Blithedale Coverdale does receive "a response . . . of the true Sibylline stamp" from the lady, but when Priscilla later appears on the stage of the village hall the single sound she makes is a "shriek" as Hollingsworth rescues her (809). In her time at Blithedale she rarely speaks, increasingly becoming an "empty sign."[53] At Eliot's pulpit she merely hopes that Coverdale's and Zenobia's opinions of woman may be untrue. Later she responds to all Zenobia has said about Hollingsworth's relation to the two women by the simple phrase, "we are sisters!" (823). By the time, years later, when Coverdale travels to see her with Hollingsworth, she says not a word. Twice she tries wordlessly to communicate with Coverdale, first with a "slight gesture which I could not help interpreting as an entreaty not to make myself known to Hollingsworth" and then, when Coverdale raises the question of the reformation of criminals, with "an upbraiding glance" (844). Neither time is she successful, for Coverdale ignores her silent entreaties and prods Hollingsworth about the past.

Unresolved conflicts about the autonomy and authority of the woman with a voice are replicated in the obscure legal and financial details of the plot of The Blithedale Romance. Just as Hawthorne suggests that Zenobia has a voice and then takes it away, he also makes Zenobia wealthy and then takes her money away. Money, like sexual attraction and public speech, is power; Zenobia begins with all of them, and loses them all.

The facts about Zenobia's financial status are embedded in a convoluted narrative strategy that hides as much as it reveals. Zenobia, we are told, is wealthy; she assumes so herself (821). This money comes from her rich uncle, who raised her and died intestate (797). From this point on, however, there is no certainty. For one thing, critics frequently imply that Hollingsworth transfers his affections to Priscilla because, Moodie having been found, the money will now revert to him and therefore go to Priscilla. Nina Baym argues that Hollingsworth selects Priscilla over Zenobia for purely economic reasons.[54] It is true that Moodie says "my brother's wealth . . . is legally my own" (799), but there is no justification for assuming that if Moodie claims his wealth Priscilla would replace Zenobia as heir. Zenobia speaks only of the "strange fact that threatens to make me poor" (821, italics added). In fact Moodie tells Zenobia, "Keep your wealth. . . . Keep it . . . with one condition, only. . . . Be kind—no less kind than sisters are—to my poor Priscilla" (799). The narrative structure removes even this apparent certainty, however, as Coverdale admits that "the details of the interview . . . being unknown to me . . . I shall attempt to sketch it, mainly from fancy" (798).

Of course it is possible that Moodie does not think Zenobia has been kind enough to Priscilla. But more importantly, given the legal status of married women before most northern states had passed Married Women's Property Acts (the action takes place "twelve or fifteen years ago" [635]), it seems extraordinary that Zenobia controls her own wealth if, as is the likeliest interpretation, she has been married to Westervelt. She herself suggests her married status by saying that Hollingsworth only bothered with her "as long as there was hope of my being available" (822). Upon marriage all property would be transferred to the husband, unless financial settlements were made. Such settlements were unlikely in this case, since everything suggests that Zenobia's marriage was secret and imprudent. As usual, we are offered contradictory information. In his earliest musings on Zenobia as a wife, Coverdale says that the idea that Zenobia had ever been married "was unauthorized by any circumstance or suggestion that had made its way to my ears" (671). Eventually, though, Moodie tells him—in the story within the story, again offered without confirmation—that "there were obscure passages in Zenobia's history. There were whispers of an attachment, and even a secret marriage, with a fascinating and accomplished, but unprincipled young man" (797). Such a marriage, we may surmise, was made to obtain Zenobia's money. Just as Zenobia's voice turns out to be a fiction, so does the power she wields through wealth.

At the conclusion of *The Scarlet Letter*, Hawthorne makes explicit the connection between Hester's silence and her acquiesence to the community's moral judgment: though she had once imagined herself the "destined prophetess" of a new relation between man and woman, she "had long since recognized the impossibility that any mission of divine and mysterious truth should be confided to a woman stained with sin." [55] Nevertheless Hester was, for the first time and privately, willing to talk to other women about the condition of women. By the end of *Blithedale*, written as the debate about women's public voices became more acute, both women are entirely silent, Priscilla clinging to Hollingsworth and Zenobia behind the black veil. Furthermore, Zenobia's speeches on the injustice done to women are revealed as rooted in selfish egotism rather than in an altruistic response to a moral call. Baym, who believes that "Hawthorne's prevailing attitude toward feminist ideas, in all four major romances, is strongly sympathetic," argues that Zenobia fails "not because she is a feminist, but because she is not feminist enough." But the treatment of women's voices in *The Blithedale Romance* seems instead to exemplify what T. Walter Herbert, Jr., calls "Hawthorne's unstable fusion of feminism and misogyny." [56] In either case ambivalence about articulate women prevails. Speech is an exposure, either inadequate or indecent, and philanthropy, as Coverdale reflects, is "perilous to the individual" (844). Priscilla's anxious, silent tending of Hollingsworth, with his distorted vision of imprisoning reform, becomes a final parody of what it means for vocal women to become involved in moral reform.

Isa, the heroine and title character of Caroline Chesebro's novel, resembles Zenobia in her natural intelligence, her striking beauty, and her willingness to be unconventional. Like Zenobia, Isa is deeply moved by society's oppression of women, and she speaks fervently, though again like Zenobia, privately, on the topic. Public recognition has come to both women for their writing; though Isa writes on many topics, some of her literary efforts, like Zenobia's, are on behalf of her sex. In contrast to Hawthorne, however, the author of *Isa, A Pilgrimage* cannot decide the fate of her opinionated heroine, whose radical ideas threaten widely held societal values. The author's uncertainty about her heroine leads not just to gaps in what the narrator tells the reader but to final incoherence of tone: Chesebro', in Isa, constructs a woman of whom she knows she should disappove, but who instead fascinates her.

As a small girl Isa is taken from the poorhouse to live with a devout mother and son. After a series of incidents within the household, Isa realizes that the often-absent father of the family, Mr. Duggane, is a drunkard. The suffering he brings to the family leads Isa to attack the marriage bond, asking, "How can it be said or thought, that all marriage vows are not virtually broken by such vicious indulgence? How can any mortal be even justified in enduring a show of union, when the marriage covenant is virtually annulled?" [57] The experience in the Duggane household, coupled with Isa's independent intellect, later leads her to reject the marriage bond both in principle and for her own life.

As Isa grows older, she evinces a special talent for writing. After publishing a number of stories she is offered a post as editor of a major newspaper. While still at home she has begun reading and speculating freely, asking such questions as "why is not will God?" (51), and has been deeply affected by a book that Weare Duggane, the son of the house, calls blasphemy, immorality, sophistry. Increasingly Isa develops great "pride of intellect"(63) and has "no faith whatever, except in the faithlessness of all things" (112). Taking up her editorial position, she discovers that the author of the freethinking book is Alanthus Stuart, her coeditor, to whom she is more and more drawn. Eventually Isa abandons the morality and religion that she has been taught. She and Stuart live together without benefit of marriage, both giving public witness to their radical views through their writing.

The shape of the plot suggests that Chesebro' intends to present Isa as a negative example. She uses two ambiguous dreams to suggest that Isa may be damned for her beliefs. In the first, early dream Isa is on a ship. They meet an iceberg on which stands a man-angel who laughs as the ship is hit. His laugh runs through Isa "like electricity, and in a perfect ecstacy of joy," she laughs too (183). Unlike the other passengers, Isa does not call on God. When she relates the dream, her adopted mother questions this omission. She replies, "it was a weakness of the multitude—it did not save them— they perished; I was saved!" (183). Hearing of the dream, Duggane predicts that that "destroying angel, will come down to her from the rock! he will float away with her on that frail spar—she will be lost! SHE WILL BE LOST" (183). Just before Isa dies she dreams again of the ship hit by an iceberg. Again all the passengers but she cry "God," and are lost; she does not and is drawn up on the iceberg next to the figure on the top, who is now identified as Stuart. When she reports the dream Stuart asks, "you ascended from the waters to the throne beside me?" and she answers, "Yes, I was saved by you" (312).

At this point Duggane arrives at Isa's deathbed, begging Stuart to "speak to her now the name of God." Stuart's face "worked as in convulsion. Perchance God's spirit was proclaiming to him then an awful truth, and making for him there a dreadful revelation. But his human pride supported him" (318), and he says nothing. Chesebro's indecision about Isa is carried through the final passages: as Stuart is telling her that they will "never be separated after that reunion [beyond the veil]," Isa rallies and, looking at Duggane, cries out, "GOD!" (318–319). In light of Isa's dreams, where all who call on God drown, this may represent Isa's eternal damnation. The two men argue her fate. Stuart claims that she is dwelling in him, while Duggane accuses Stuart of damning her for all time. The last line of the novel is, "DUGGANE HAD DEPARTED FROM ISA LEE'S PRESENCE FOR EVER" (320).

In the subplot Chesebro' repeats her strategy of dividing the characters into the conventionally holy (Weare and his mother) and the unbelievers (Isa and Stuart), and once again her message is ambiguous. Mary Irving dies rather than violate her belief in the indissolubility of marriage, demonstrating true piety by trusting in God to help her resist the importunities of her newly reappeared girlhood lover. Isa, who urges Mary to divorce and to self-dependence, represents freethinking and the rejection of Christianity. Yet the apparently clear dualistic construction of the novel is undercut by the admiration that Chesebro' conveys for her heroine. Isa is not only beautiful and brilliant, but she has intellectual success. She finds lifelong love and companionship with Stuart, and when their baby dies there is no suggestion that this common nineteenth-century tragedy is a punishment. The contrast between Isa's joyous relationship with Stuart and Mary Irving's conventional marriage, where Mary, according to Isa, is a "slave wife," encourages the reader to favor Isa's unhallowed love.[58]

Isa's independence is identified with women's rights. At her first party in the city she hears people talking of a "woman's rights convention," and because "she had seen what women's wrongs were, and knew how they were borne" she felt "compelled to reply." An elderly general asks her what her "convictions in regard to this subject lead you *to do*?" When she replies mildly, "my duty, I trust," he rejoins, "Good! You will become no public lecturer; no ridiculous, ranting." But another person points out that "She does not need to be a lecturer. Miss Lee wields a pen!" (143).

Isa is a peculiar example of the consequences that befall the vocal woman. Although Chesebro' limits Isa to the pen rather than putting her on a platform, Isa speaks, strongly and clearly, throughout the novel. Rather than being driven by a religious moral call, Isa responds to her conscience as it is informed by reason. She justifies her attitude toward marriage by saying, "We are progressive. The institution was well enough for the people of past ages . . . it is . . . now become a bond too galling, too oppressive. In ninety-nine cases out of a hundred, people assuming matrimonial vows, especially women, sell their birthright of freedom for a mess of pottage. In its present state . . . marriage is not a holy thing—it is an abomination" (169). Unable to find any proof of the existence of the Divine Being, she disparages prayer as "nothing more or less than the longing of weak hearts in the midst of self-desertion, to give vent, voice to that weakness. . . . That is all" (208). Rejecting God, she finds her "ALL IN ALL" in Stuart (219).

Isa, gifted, brilliant, atheistic, is too radical a character even for Chesebro', who cannot decide her heroine's fate. Isa dies, but is she punished? Her voice is silenced, but is it for her role as a public figure, is it because she embraced an immoral life-style, or is it a consequence of her dangerous ideas? Chesebro' gives us no clear answer. A review in the *American Whig Review* (1852) shows that contemporary readers noticed the ambiguities and contradictions of the novelist's position:

> Amid all the trumpery about "Woman's Rights" and the reorganization of society on a superior marital basis, we can hardly discern what the authoress would teach us. Whether it were better for us to "dissolve the marriage contract," to repudiate all connections but those founded on desire . . . or whether it were better that we should continue to "marry, and be given in marriage," is left almost wholly in the dark. . . . What displeases most our ideas of propriety is, that evil doing does not meet with its reward. . . . The fault of the book . . . lies in these two things: Isa makes of her self-will, her intellectual progress, and her ambition, a threefold deity; and she unites herself to a man as his wife, yet while she is not so, and is happy in the union! . . . Perhaps Miss Chesebro' intended to show that the course of Isa, that her choice in life, was wrong; but it is only by very roundabout and unsatisfactory reasoning that we arrive at this conclusion." [59]

The reviewer's comments reproduce the reaction of the society to a woman like Isa. Chesebro' is faulted because she does not punish Isa severely enough for violating cultural and religious norms. More importantly, the reviewer links Isa's radical ideas and behavior with the "trumpery of Woman's Rights." By 1852, women with voices, women with pens, free love and women's rights were elements that together threatened to destroy the American social fabric.

The Veiled Lady

The multiple sources of authorial and social conflicts over "lecturesses" are symbolized in Zenobia's legend of the veiled lady. One critical function of the woman under the veil is to serve as a screen onto which men can project their fantasies and fears about women: "Some upheld, that the veil covered the most beautiful countenance in the world; others . . . that . . . it was the face of a corpse; it was the head of a skeleton; it was a monstrous visage" (728). This projection is possible because the veil conceals the woman's body; she exists only as a voice.

The absence of the body has political meaning. The invisible woman behind the veil is literally a *feme covert*, a woman under the control of a man (as indeed Priscilla is). Though she speaks, the relation of this voice to her self is shifting and ambiguous. When Theodore is given the choice of taking the lady unseen, or raising the veil and losing her, the choice has differing significance to him and to her. For the lady, to be accepted sight unseen means that her voice becomes her essence. The narrative is constructed so that this voice is heard only by Theodore. The veiled lady, in the legend, has a low voice "conveying her Sibylline responses" (729), but we do not hear her. Instead, she speaks privately to Theodore backstage, in the personal and typically enclosed space of woman. But Theodore does not choose the lady unseen: for him, the self of a woman is identical to her body, and he fears to kiss her lest, as once again he projects an increasing series of fears, "he should salute the lips of a dead girl, or the jaws of a skeleton, or the grinning cavity of a monster's mouth!" (731).

When the lady is not chosen for her voice, which represents her invisible personhood, she disappears and then becomes the mesmerist's "bond-slave, forever more!" (733). The tale of the veiled lady is told by Zenobia, and though Priscilla takes it to refer to her own career—she actually faints with anxiety at the conclusion—the tale applies as well to its narrator. Like the veiled lady, Zenobia wants to be accepted for her voice, rather than for her body. Furthermore, as a woman with a mysterious past, she wants to be accepted without further investigation. When the veil of her past is lifted, she, like the veiled lady, disappears, and indirectly becomes a bondslave to her feelings about one man. Finally, when her body is found, rather than being an answer to the enigma of her self, it offers contradictory, sibylline messages to those who try to "read" it.

Uncle Tom's Cabin, The Blithedale Romance, and *Isa* suggest three explanations for midcentury anxiety regarding women who demanded the right to speak. The first explanation is political and direct. A woman on the platform was implicitly asserting her rights as a citizen. Even if she claimed to be motivated by conscience, and spoke only on behalf of others, her very appearance on the platform, in a place where men exercised their rights as citizens, symbolized her independence. Opponents' fears of such demands for the rights of citizenship were strengthened by the calling of the Seneca Falls Convention and the rash of women's rights conventions that followed. And in fact, the women who consistently claimed a moral call to speak, the female abolitionists, confirmed suspicions that they were interested in their own rights as well as those of the slave: Abby Kelley actually spoke for the slave certain days and women other days.

The second explanation is more complex. Female lecturers created disproportionate anxiety because their voices could not be separated from their bodies. The sexuality of such women was unveiled as they spoke. A deeply sexual fear of having women on the platform emerges in the ambiguous and contradictory things that were said about the speakers. On the one hand, a woman on the platform, out of her sphere, was "desexed"—less than a woman or not a woman. It was partly to disprove this calumny that Angelina Grimké, once married, stayed home. On the other hand, the attacks on Frances Wright and the descriptions of Zenobia suggest that a woman speaker was not unsexed, but rather had a promiscuous relationship with her audience. Her voice, and the presence of her body, was a sexual provocation; nothing she might say could undo this fact. She was always "speaking woman's body."

Finally, by speaking, a woman was claiming her place as *subject* rather than *object*, as self rather than other. In this view, discourse is both power and the possibility of generating power; it is a political gesture even more important than a demand for voting rights. Though phrased in modern terms, this theory merely restates the opinion of the nineteenth-century opponents of the women lecturers. They believed that no matter what moral and altruistic reasons were given for speaking, speaking itself was a manifestation of female ego—Isa's "will"—and a threat to male dominance. All of the novels we have looked at, even *Uncle Tom's Cabin*, which glorifies Rachel's few words as equal to the "cestus of Venus" (169), confront this attitude, however obliquely. Women speaking were dangerous. They were political. And there was no telling what they would demand next.

3

Women and Property Rights

Male hegemony in the public sphere was threatened by the growing belief that women should control their own economic resources, whether in the form of property brought to a marriage or wages earned after marriage. The question of married women's property rights arose simultaneously with the debate over whether women might speak on behalf of abolition. Giving married women a measure of economic independence threatened to increase their legal power and to weaken the authority of their husbands. Yet tensions between the inherited English legal system and the fluid economic and social conditions of the young nation led many men, as well as women, to call for change.

Men and women of the American republic understood the legal relationship between husband and wife as one that allotted powers and responsibilities between the spouses. Even though the ideal marriage was envisioned as a companionate, even affectionate, partnership, the legal relationship remained that defined by Blackstone in the eighteenth century. His interpretation, which was derived from the common law practices of feudal England, became the foundation of American family law. Husband and wife, in this formulation, were one; this unity of the spouses, which was well understood to be a convenient legal fiction, placed the woman and her children, as well as all of her material assets, whether inherited or earned, under the husband's power.

The status of married women in Jacksonian America evolved from the Norman feudal relationship of *baron et feme*.[1] Once a woman contracted to accept the protection of her husband, she was, as Blackstone put it, "civilly dead." She could not control real property or convey it to anyone else, though by English common law if her husband predeceased her and there were no children, the real property returned to her estate.[2] She could not prepare a will or contract for debt. She could not act in trade, whether to buy the family's groceries or to sell butter and eggs, except as the legal agent of her husband. This status granted certain benefits, including not being subject to suit, not testifying for her husband in court, and not being liable for debt. Further, she was assured of a dower interest for life, usually amounting to one-third of her husband's estate, if he died before her. Such a life interest was intended to provide a subsistence for widows, thus freeing society from concern for their welfare.[3]

Most lawyers, jurists, and legislators believed that the doctrine of coverture that Blackstone elaborated was mutually beneficial for husbands and wives, and, given the "natural" characteristics of women—physical, mental, and emotional—was a necessary protection for wives. The legal relationship between husband and wife, which vested all legal power in the male, meshed well with the prevailing societal view of domestic relationships.

Although coverture apparently kept married women totally dependent on their spouses' good will and sense of justice, the legal disabilities of English wives could be relieved through a number of devices, including active trusts, prenuptial settlements, and suits through the equity courts. In the United States, all these devices were adopted along with the English common law, and most were in wide use during the early nineteenth century. Advice books for lawyers and the general public as well as books of the appropriate legal forms were available to help parents protect a daughter's property after marriage. The chancery courts of many states heard cases in equity that upheld the right of a woman to a share of her own property when the husband was negligent.[4]

In addition to undermining the rule of coverture, trusts, prenuptial agreements and the equity courts were in conflict with the changing economic and political situation in the United States. The two-tiered legal system, in which one set of practices, such as coverture, was enforced on the mass of the citizenry, while wealthier citizens could afford to sue for relief in the equity courts, came under attack as undemocratic, and a strong movement to abolish the equity system began. Furthermore, legal practice in the United States was less formal and class-oriented than in Europe, with a premium placed on simpler, more efficient legal practices. In a society where the sale and exchange of property was a common act, it became necessary to simplify the laws that kept women from conveying property so that business could be transacted. Thus, English forms and practices, many of which worked to restrain married women, were eroded by the exigencies of American life.

The enormous economic growth and instability of the Jacksonian era also created pressure for change. If a man's business went bankrupt because of a failure in the marketplace, not only did he lose his assets, but he could be forced to use his wife's property to satisfy his liability. The specter of the unlucky or untrustworthy son-in-law haunted many wealthy men, who therefore attempted to set up trusts for their daughters. A few states, particularly those in which land was the principal source of wealth, began to consider legislation to solve the problem.

Property in Fiction

Marriage settlements and the domestic effects of the property laws were common plot elements for early American novelists; as political concern and legal debate about property laws intensified toward the middle of the nineteenth century, the specifics of that debate spilled over into novels, whose plots and characters were constructed to express and influence opinion on these laws. A standard treatment of property issues occurs in two of Catharine Maria Sedgwick's novels, *Redwood* (1824) and *Clarence* (1830). In both there is great fear that rich heiresses will be pursued by "fortune hunters." This fear is realized conventionally enough in *Redwood*; the wealthy heiress does not recognize the value of the disinterested American hero and foolishly elopes with an English younger son who is in search of wealth. In *Clarence*, Sedgwick reverses the situation: Gertrude Clarence is systematically avoided by the worthy hero, who has "a sort of natural antipathy against a *fortune*—that I believe is the technical term for a prize-lady."[5] Romance flourishes only when Gertrude contrives to conceal her identity during accidental meetings.

In both of these novels, as was typical early in the century, the thrust of discussion about property tends to be moral. Wealth was regarded as a potential source of corruption in the Republic. Sedgwick is thus concerned to analyze the effects of large amounts of money on the character of the heroine, or of the hero who will gain control of her money through marriage. Her moral ideal is spelled out in *Clarence,* a novel in which the elder Clarence learns the limitations of wealth's power through his son's death. On the day of his daughter Gertrude's wedding to Gerald Roscoe—the only suitor indifferent to her fortune—Clarence gives him "papers which transferred to him the half of his fortune," and after Gerald has pointed out that the true gift is Gertrude herself, a friend comments that "this was a manner of giving and receiving, becoming rational and elevated beings, and he could not but contrast it with the usual quarrels about settlements—with the jealousy and parsimony towards sons-in-law on the one side, and on the other, the anxious reckoning of the father's wealth, and calculation of the chances of his life" (512). The emphasis is on the ethics and psychology of the individuals involved; the laws that "transfer" the woman's estate directly from father to son-in-law are not criticized.

Nevertheless the reading public was alert to the specific ramifications of those property laws. In *Redwood* the plot turns on the theft, by the wealthy southern belle Caroline Redwood, of evidence that a mysterious young girl, Ellen Bruce, is also Redwood's daughter by a previous marriage. When Caroline is confronted, she justifies her behavior by objecting to one of the consequences of the husband's total control of his wife's property. Caroline assumes that if the truth comes out, Redwood will divide his money between his two daughters; she says to Ellen, 'Your rights acknowledged, your fortune would be equal to mine, and that I could not but think very unfair, as nearly all papa's fortune came from my mother, and yours, you know, was quite pennyless.'[6]

No novelist was more interested in property, in its social, economic, political, and personal consequences, than James Fenimore Cooper. Novels written throughout his career—for instance, *The Pioneers* (1823), *Home as Found* (1838), and *The Redskins* (1846)—turn on property and its relation to political and familial structures. In properly arranged marriages between the people Cooper admires—the natural gentry who, without possessing "aristocratic" political rights, lead society by virtue of their culture, intelligence, and breeding—money is always an overt subject of discussion at the time of a wedding. Consolidation of assets is the confirming symbol of marital union; it is the assurance of class perpetuation. Cooper's novels repeatedly spell out the proper financial arrangements for a "happy ending."

The Pioneers (1823) is a complex analysis of the many implications of property ownership in a new country. "Indian, dispossessed Tory, present holder of the deed and squatter" all have claims to the land.[7] Natty Bumppo moves westward at the end of the novel, but his dispossession will inevitably recur there. The claims of Tory and deed holder are more simply solved by marriage. Judge Temple tells the newly revealed Oliver Effingham, "One half of my estates shall be thine as soon as they can be conveyed to thee; and if what my suspicions tell me, be true, I suppose the other must follow speedily."[8]

In this early work Cooper has Temple say nothing more explicit about the disposition of the inheritance between his daughter Elizabeth and his future son-in-law. If we read the sentence according to the law of 1823, Oliver, as Elizabeth's husband, will receive the second half of the estates when Judge Temple dies, for no separate provision or settlement is made for Elizabeth. This novel bears out Nina Baym's contention that "marriage . . . is shown in Cooper's Leatherstocking stories as a transaction between males, where the giving away of women creates a rhetoric of group membership and exclusion."[9]

Fifteen years later Cooper wrote *Home as Found* as a distillation of his opinions of the United States. His immediate concern for the rightful disposition of property at Three Mile Point carries over to the fictional love story. Eve Effingham, heiress to the Effingham estates of *The Pioneers*, is the epitome of perfect female breeding; she is in love, however, with a man whose parentage is uncertain. When Paul Powis turns out to be the son of Eve's father's cousin— and thus an Effingham—not only can Eve marry within her class, but she can keep the estates within the family. Yet for Cooper this is not enough. The day after the wedding Paul explains financial arrangements to his bride:

> We are each other's natural heirs. Of the name and blood of Effingham, neither has a relative nearer than the other. . . . Now your father proposes that his estates be valued, and that my father settle on you a sum of equal amount . . . and that I become the possessor, in reversion, of the land that would otherwise have been yours.[10]

In a classic nineteenth-century articulation of woman's proper attitude, Eve protests that she does not see the point: "You possess me, my heart, my affections, my duty; of what account is money after this!" Paul replies, "I perceive that you are so much and so truly woman, Eve, that we must arrange all this without consulting you at all" (470). Cooper here spells out what was only implicit in *The Pioneers*: Eve can be protected by monetary settlements, but Paul must be the owner of the real estate. Even in a time when the law gave the husband complete control over his wife's property, Cooper was worried about the possibility of the land reverting to her estate, should Paul die first.

The last of the Anti-Rent trilogy, *The Redskins*, is a novel entirely about property and its protection. Its central target is the 1846 New York state law permitting tenants, on the death of a landlord, to convert leases into mortgages. But by 1846 Cooper was also becoming aware of another challenge to customary social and property arrangements. When the hero, Hugh Littlepage, returns from Europe to protect his estates from the antirenters who disguise as "Injins" and attempt to achieve their goals by arson, he also encounters the chief Injin's sister, Miss Opportunity Newcome. Seneca Newcome menaces the social fabric by his contempt for Hugh's claim to his own property and by his criminal actions; his sister menaces that fabric by her personal and legal machinations to win Hugh and his fortune for herself. Once Opportunity realizes that her soft references to their childhood acquaintance do not move Hugh, and that in fact he is going to marry the clergyman's daughter, Mary Warren, she threatens a suit for breach of promise.

Hugh's somewhat cryptic reaction, "the quackery of Legislatures has set the ladies at work in earnest, and he will soon be a fortunate youth who can pass through his days of celibacy without some desperate assault, legal or moral, from the other sex," is Cooper's first comment on the growing demand for a New York law guaranteeing women the right to control their own property.[11] To demonstrate that a woman's economic independence can be adequately protected after marriage under the existing laws, Cooper has the hero's benevolent uncle settle money on Mary "without any rights to her future husband, let him turn out to be whom he may" (436). In specifying the limitations on Mary's husband, Cooper is even more explicit than in describing the settlements made for Eve Effingham. The arrangement here constitutes a response to contemporary proposals to change the laws and, implicitly, the legal and personal relations between men and women. Cooper would have a fuller response to this particular legislative "quackery" in *The Ways of the Hour*. To understand that novel requires an understanding of changes in the legal regulation of married women's property at midcentury.

Married Women's Property Laws

By the time Cooper wrote *The Ways of the Hour*, seventeen states had revised their laws regarding the degree of control married women could exercise over their real estate and other property. Although state legislatures occasionally copied their proposed bills from laws passed by other states, each assembly added refinements or provisions fitting the local situation. The debates over the issue reflected each state's legal history, economic needs, and prevailing cultural view of the family. Not only did the dimensions of the debate vary from state to state, but, as Elizabeth Warbasse suggests in her analysis of this legislation, so did "the precipitating factors which brought about the enactment of the early married women's property acts." [12]

It may seem surprising that the earliest legislation to change married women's property laws was passed not in an economically advanced state like New York, but in the frontier state of Mississippi. Because of the relatively undeveloped economic system of that state and extensive speculation in land, the panic of 1837 had more serious effects in Mississippi than in many other states. Families lost heavily mortgaged farms, and many investors in the local banks lost most of their fortunes. The common wisdom holds that the senator who introduced the first married women's property act into the legislature in 1839 was a wealthy man who, being deeply in debt after the panic, was seeking a way to keep the property of his fiancée free from his debts. [13] Senator T.B.J. Hadley's bill was extremely liberal in its provisions: the property that a woman brought to her marriage remained in her separate estate, and she could dispose of it as if she were single. The proposed law also protected any profits she made from her property or from her labor, an unusual provision for that time. Hadley's bill was defeated in the state senate on a very close vote. Immediately afterward, a committee began work on a revised version of the legislation, which passed within a week. The final legislation was more conservative than Senator Hadley's bill in several respects: although it gave a woman control of her landed estates, it did not protect her earnings, it did not clearly specify that she could dispose of her real property by her will, and it forbade the husband from transferring his property to her in order to avoid creditors. The law focused on the woman's property in slaves, exempting them from the husband's debts.

The primary goal of the Mississippi bill was to protect the wife's property from liability for the husband's debts in a period of extreme economic instability.[14] The principal objection to the bill was economic—that it would injure the rights of creditors—although some legislators also feared the effects of the legislation on family life. Supporters, on the other hand, thought it would provide economic stability in hard times and thus strengthen family life. There can be no doubt that the women of Mississippi understood both the intent and the legal effect of the legislation. Newspaper accounts noted that many women attended the debates and that the representative who cast the deciding vote in favor of the bill was lionized by the female population of the city after the victory.[15]

Four years after the passage of the Mississippi bill, the second married women's property law in the United States was passed, again by a southern state. Maryland, like Mississippi, faced an economic crisis; in this case, the state's involvement in the Chesapeake and Ohio canal project had bankrupted the state treasury and weakened the state's economy. During the last weeks of the session, while the legislature wrestled with the canal problem, a bill was introduced to allow married women to hold property. Mr. Causin's bill was an exact copy of the Mississippi legislation except that it omitted personal property other than slaves from the wife's control. Like the Mississippi law, the principal sections of the bill were concerned with protecting the wife's slaves from her husband's creditors.[16] The Judiciary Committee added a last section that also allowed the wife control of up to one thousand dollars that she earned through "skill, industry, or personal labor."[17] The Maryland law passed on March 10, 1843, with little public debate. A third southern state, Arkansas, passed an amended version of the Mississippi law in 1846.

All three southern versions of the married women's property law had common origins: economic instability in the state, concern for the protection of property from the husband's creditors, and a belief that the family could be protected through the law. Yet another factor contributed to the actions taken by Mississippi, Maryland, and Arkansas. Although these states had established a set of equity courts, these courts had little authority and were regarded as ineffective. With poor or weak equity procedures, trusts, which might be set up before marriage to protect a woman's property, were not easily enforced. Several of the other southern states, namely North Carolina, South Carolina, and Delaware, which had well-established equity systems, did not pass married women's property laws until after the Civil War.[18]

In the 1840s, virtually every northern state attempted to find legal remedics for the economic situation of married women, but the economic argument for protecting the family property was complicated by more open debate on the concept of coverture, by early feminist demands for more political power for women, and by the movement to reform the common law system.[19] Opponents to increased rights for women assumed that new laws would have deleterious effects on the institution of marriage. As one representative to the Rhode Island state legislature put it, "I have no desire, sir, to see man and wife separated unless by divorce. This bill has that effect. It separates the husband from his wife, and we should pass laws making their interests one and inseparable, instead of doing aught to sunder them."[20] On the other hand, Timothy Walker, a Cincinnati law professor, maintained that "the whole theory is a slavish one. . . . I do not hesitate to say, by way of arousing your attention to the subject, that the law of husband and wife, as you gather it from the books, is a disgrace to any civilized nation."[21] In his *Introduction to American Law*, first published in 1837 and one of the most popular law school texts of the era, Walker urged parents to create trusts for their daughters and deplored "the entire helplessness of a married woman, when her husband becomes a prodigal or spendthrift."[22]

Walker, like other male proponents of the legal changes, steadfastly opposed any extension of women's political rights. But early feminists made the connection between the economic and political situation of women. In Vermont, Clarina I. Howard Nichols, editor of the *Windham County Democrat*, successfully editorialized for new property rights, which she called "the first breath of a legal civil existence to Vermont wives" in 1847, and within two years she was speaking in the statehouse for women's rights. She explained that she could not "demand the suffrage before convicting men of legal robbery."[23] Also in 1847 Jane Swisshelm penned a series of extremely sarcastic letters to a Pittsburgh newspaper on the topic. She attacks the civil death of married women: "marriage no[w] reduces a woman to an enigma—a mathematical problem that has never yet been solved! She is dead in law, but can be punished for any breach of it. She becomes a dignified mistress of a family, occupying a lower place in the laws of the country than her coachman."[24] Swisshelm was a personal friend of the man who became the next governor of Pennsylvania, and the fruit of her letter-writing campaign may have been his support of a Pennsylvania property bill in 1848. The most far-reaching set of feminist demands was the Declaration of Sentiments written by Elizabeth Cady Stanton for the Seneca Falls Convention in 1848. The declaration objected that man "has taken from her all right in property, even to the wages she earns." The list of resolutions approved by the assembly demanded that women be elevated to a status equal to men, but did not call for immediate action on the property question, perhaps because New York had passed a married women's property law two months earlier.

On the issue of married women's property rights feminist and conservative women could agree. Beginning in 1837, Sarah Josepha Hale supported property rights for women. In 1852 she reaffirmed her position by publishing an article by an anonymous Boston lawyer attacking the common law disposition of property. "Marcellus" contends that where "unity of interest [between married persons] subsists, there will be no difference of opinion about the use of the property belonging to either party, and, where it is unhappily wanting, no circumstance tends more to widen the division than the law." [25] The essayist recalls occasions on which he has seen the widow's wedding gifts and "Canary bird" sold for payment of the husband's debts, or the deceased wife's property conveyed to the children of the husband's second marriage. He suggests that the proposed property law will have a positive effect on marriage by ending the preference of the law for one partner over the other. Mrs. Hale introduces the article by noting that Pennsylvania has already passed a married women's property law while "Massachusetts is yet groping in the dark ages on this important point." Expressing her own support for the legislation, the editor reveals how a conservative could do so: "The advance of popular opinion is on the side of justice. Men must secure to women their *rights*, and then, we trust, our sex will be intent only on performing their own duties." [26]

In 1848, New York passed a married women's property law that was among the most liberal in the nation. It specified that married women could keep for their own use any real or personal property that they brought to the marriage. The rights of women who were married at the time of the enactment were also assured, as long as the property had not already been made liable for the husband's debts. The history of the New York law recapitulates all of the elements that contributed to such legislation in the pre-Civil War years. Up to the 1840s the law in New York had followed the English doctrine of *feme-covert*: all personal property brought to the union by the woman or wages earned during marriage were controlled by the husband and became part of his estate to be awarded to his heirs only. If he died intestate, the widow could legally retain a specific list of items, including all spinning wheels, the family Bible, ten sheep, one cow, two swine, necessary apparel, beds and bedding, a widow's clothing, one table, six chairs, six knives and forks, six teacups and saucers, one sugar dish, one milkpot, and six spoons.[27]

The first legislation proposed to change these laws was introduced to the New York state legislature by Judge Thomas Herttell in 1837, the year of the Mississippi law. The judge's bill proposed extensive reforms that would grant married women sole legal control over their own property and earnings and grant a dower interest for widows in the husband's estate equal to that of widowers in the estate of the wife. Judge Herttell argued for the bill on moral, constitutional, and social grounds. In a pamphlet that reprinted

his views, Herttell noted that single women were treated as being as competent as men in handling property.[28] Therefore, depriving a woman of property simply as a result of a change in marital status was constitutionally
wrong, because it discriminated against citizens in their right to enjoy life,
liberty, and property under the law. The judge argued that society would be
affected positively by reform of these laws. The new law would prevent
"pauperism," help "educate the children," improve "public morals," and
generally increase the happiness of society.[29]

Herttell's proposal was reintroduced several times but never seriously
considered by the lawmakers, although such feminists as Ernestine Rose and
Paulina Wright began collecting signatures on petitions in support of the bill
from women throughout New York.[30] By 1842, another property law was
reported out of the Judiciary Committee of the New York State Assembly,
but did not reach a vote. Elizabeth Cady Stanton, with her children in tow,
personally lobbied the legislature for property rights in 1844, 1845, and
1846.[31] The rights of women were again debated at the Constitutional Convention of 1846, but a decision was deferred. The prolonged discussion of
reform in the property laws eventually produced near consensus on the need
for change. In 1848 the legislature overwhelmingly passed the Married
Women's Property Act, which secured legal ownership of property to married women, although it excluded earnings.[32]

According to recent legal research, the final passage of the property law
represented the closing of several loopholes in New York law that were
widely recognized as unfair to holders of real estate. The law was not passed
as a response to feminist pressure but as a matter of legal tidiness.[33] During
the first half of the nineteenth century, the legal profession in New York was
engaged in debate over legal reform. The major issue was the proposed
adoption of a legal code, similar to that adopted in France, to replace the
English common law system.[34] The codification movement aimed at establishing a system of laws that would guide the courts, in place of the "legal
fictions" like *feme-covert* and other remnants of feudal society that had
authority under common law. Furthermore, the legal reformers wanted to
end the appeal that could be made under the common law procedure to
"equity" or "fairness" outside of written law. Many reformers regarded
"equity" courts as the courts of the privileged classes and as unsuitable for a
democratic nation.

As Rabkin points out, while married women in New York were considered "civilly dead" and unable to hold property under the common law, the
equity courts permitted a woman to appeal for a just share of her husband's
estate or to enforce the proper administration of property held in trust for
her.[35] Parents would set up a trust to hold and administer property for their
daughter after her marriage (as was done for Eve Effingham). If the conditions of the trust were violated, she had recourse to the equity courts. In

effect, equity disregarded the fictional unity of husband and wife and condoned the writing of contracts or the extension of loans between spouses.

As part of the drive to write and adopt a legal code for New York, the Revised Statutes of 1836 abolished trusts in regard to real estate since they were "legal fictions." The "equitable" owner or beneficiary of a trust was to become the statutory owner. However, under New York law, married women could not legally control property, so the abolition of trusts made it impossible for property to be protected for women. Apparently, the revisers overlooked the use of trusts for "the purpose of keeping a married woman's property separate from her husband." [36]

As a result of this legislative omission, the advocates of married women's property rights were able to gain support from those legislators concerned with establishing protective devices for their daughters' estates. The debate over the solution to the legal dilemma, and over the effect on the family of granting such rights to married women, was carried on at length in the Constitutional Convention of 1846. Some proponents of women's rights argued that the oppression of women related to feudalism. Typical objections were raised by an elderly bachelor lawyer, Charles O'Conor, who argued that giving property rights to women would cause "controversies" to arise: "husband and wife would become armed against each other to the utter destruction of the sentiments which they should entertain towards each other." [37]

The proposal to incorporate the provision establishing property rights for women in the new constitution was defeated. At the same time, to complete the legal reforms of the 1830s, the new constitution abolished the equity court that was responsible for creating and supervising trusts. Two years later, the legislature passed a law sponsored by the conservative Judge John Fine, who, according to the recollections published in *History of Woman Suffrage*, had tried to keep his wife's property separate and had "found much difficulty, growing out of the old laws, in this effort to protect his wife's interests." [38]

The campaign for a married women's property law in New York continued for two decades and, in its final stages, was the subject of extensive public debate. Final passage of the Married Women's Property Act in 1848 attracted special attention, partly because New York was the most populous state in the nation. It also had one of the most advanced court systems, and changes there foreshadowed changes in other states. The same characteristics that gave the law a claim to historical attention were among those that drove Cooper to make it a central theme in his last novel.

Cooper's Last Word on Property

The Ways of the Hour, published in 1850, has usually been read as Cooper's final word on the judicial system. [39] This analysis oversimplifies: it also ignores the plot and characters that Cooper constructed to dramatize his opinions about law and politics. One can easily understand why: the plot is appallingly improbable, and the novel is so repetitious that it has always been contemptuously dismissed.[40] As a result, Cooper's principal target, the disaster he foresaw in economic freedom for women, has been missed, and the relationship between the plot, the judges and juries, and the attacks on the new Civil Code and New York State Constitution has never been explained.

The much-maligned action of the book centers on the murder trial of a beautiful, accomplished, but apparently friendless young woman who gives her name as Mary Monson. She admits this is an alias, yet stubbornly refuses to reveal her true identity. Mary was boarding in a country cottage when it burned down; she escaped, but two skeletons, with their heads smashed by a heavy object, were found in the owner's bed. The bodies are presumed to be those of the Goodwins, owners of the cottage. A stocking stuffed with gold by the avaricious Mrs. Goodwin is missing, and Mary, who seems to have unlimited money and whose purse contains a peculiarly notched coin belonging to Mrs. Goodwin, is indicted for the murder. Although she is defended by a famous Manhattan lawyer named Dunscomb, as well as by a local hack well versed in methods of jury tampering, and in spite of a physician's testimony that he believes the skeletons both to be female, Mary is convicted of murdering the Goodwins.

At this point she produces the presumably dead husband from the local tavern and solves the mystery by triumphantly cross-examining a neighbor woman until she confesses to stealing Mrs. Goodwin's gold and placing the unique coin in Mary's purse. Mary finally admits what her friends and counselors had suspected: she has deserted her interfering and obnoxious French husband because the new Married Women's Property Act enables her to control her own fortune.

Cooper's anger at Mary, which grows throughout the novel, is remarkable. After all, if the point of the book is only to show how juries are corrupted, elected judges are intimidated by the voters, and justice is travestied, Cooper could give us a falsely accused heroine who is entirely innocent, deserving of our sympathy, and finally rewarded with a husband and happiness. Instead, the accused woman seems to be innocent of the crime but guilty of other grievous errors in thought and action, and Cooper finally condemns her to madness. Furthermore, discussion of the proper duties of women and wives is omnipresent. Like his hero Dunscomb, Cooper is worried about what the world is coming to and knows that all the changes he sees are interrelated: " 'Coming to?' repeated Dunscomb. 'Do you mean the new code, or the "Woman-hold-the-Purse Law," as I call it? I don't believe you look far enough ahead to foresee all the damnable consequences of an elective judiciary' " (29).[41]

Cooper attacked the Married Women's Property Act of 1848 and the legal changes associated with it because he feared their effect on fundamental social structures. He intentionally obscured the logical and historical links between the passage of what he called the "cup and saucer" law and other judicial reforms, treating them for artistic and argumentative purposes as unrelated examples of "social evil." But he was just as worried about changing the property rights of women as he was about the venality of elected judges and partisan juries.

Comparing Cooper's treatment of the new property law with its legal history, we find inaccuracy and deliberate distortion. In *The Ways of the Hour* Cooper suggests through his approved character Anna that prenuptial agreements to secure the wife's interest (like those in *The Redskins*) offer more than adequate protection. He never alludes to the abolition of trusts in 1836 nor to any possibility that a woman's interest could not be protected in court. Furthermore, the property arrangements Cooper considered suitable for marriage were applicable solely to upper-class families such as those described in his novels. These legal settlements, appeals to equity court, and questions of estates were not a part of the lives of ordinary citizens.

Cooper weakens his novel—and argument—by obscuring the links between the financial independence of women and the philosophical and political roots of the new legal reforms. Attempts to broaden the economic rights of women as well as the abolition of equity courts were expressions of egalitarianism. Some reformers equated these legal changes with the ending of all feudalistic tendencies in the United States, including the hierarchical relationship between husband and wife. It is not coincidental that Cooper's headstrong heroine, Mary Monson, has been brought up in France, where the Bible is "very little read" (484) and where a married woman "under an air of great seeming propriety . . . does very much as she sees fit" (488). The codification movement was strongly influenced by the Civil Code adopted in France. Philosophically the movement expressed faith in logic, scientific reasoning, and the ability of the legislators as representatives of the people to make law. If the laws governing civil and criminal procedure were spelled out in organized, clearly stated principles approved by the legislature, the source of law would be the people rather than the judges. The codification movement was thus anti–common law, anti-British, and antiaristocratic. In the Jacksonian period of New York history, the extension of the franchise, the "antirent" movement to break up the great estates, and the abolition of equity courts and trusts were closely associated with the codification movement.

The opponents of these reforms—Anglophiles and social conservatives—found "codes" to be rigid, inferior, and likely to be unduly influenced by popular opinion. The argument against the women's property law sometimes used the immorality of French women as an illustration of the degradation that might result from such legislation.[42] Opponents of popular law-making defended the ability of judges to understand the social culture of the times and to adjust the common law to the needs of society and the claims of justice. In their view, no new legal structures were needed to reflect the more democratic notions of rights. As Lawrence Friedman notes, the claim that the law must evolve gradually was also used to oppose progressive economic and social legislation in this period.[43]

In *The Ways of the Hour*, Dunscomb, "'emphatically' a common-law lawyer" (13), attacks the new code and criticizes the new wave of popular government. In an oblique reference to the debate over codification, Dunscomb specifies how much power should be given to the people: "all power that they can intelligently and usefully use; but not to the extent of permitting them to make the laws, to execute the laws, and to interpret the laws" (86). Dunscomb's distinction here exemplifies Cooper's uneasy relationship with the Jacksonians, who endorsed the extension of the vote to all white male citizens based on the belief that the people could make political decisions directly. To the extent that this movement stood for a restoration of an ideal community of yeoman farmers, Cooper had supported its aims. After his stay in Europe, Cooper—like Hugh Littlepage in *The Redskins*—returned home to find that mass democracy was, in effect, leveling all distinctions, social and political. Thus, Marvin Meyers, in *The Jacksonian Persuasion*, argues that Cooper changed from a true Jacksonian democrat in the 1820s to a more disillusioned critic of that party's aims in the 1830s, although he never changed his party allegiance.[44] In *The Ways of the Hour*, the town of Biberry, which has no gentry, represents American life, and the trial that takes place there exhibits all that has gone wrong with the political system.

The novel opens with Dunscomb and Jack, his nephew and law clerk, discussing the recent legal changes in New York state. The older attorney attacks the new code, whose "forms of pleadings are infernal" (14); the new power of jurors, "fast becoming judges" (18); the constitutional convention, whose "object is to push principles into impracticable extremes, under the silly pretension of progress" (22); and the new state constitution. When his good friend Dr. McBrain enters we learn that Dunscomb is also against the Married Women's Property Act. McBrain, a widower, is about to marry again, but this time no marriage settlements are necessary because, as McBrain reminds Dunscomb, "the new law gives a woman the entire control of all her property . . . and I suppose she will not expect the control of mine." The lawyer immediately expresses his disapproval of the "one-sided" woman-hold-the-purse law and his own determination to remain single (27–29).

Dunscomb is drafted to defend Mary Monson without any notion that the case will bear out all of his worst fears about the consequences of the new law. Mary is introduced as an attractive young woman whose expression is a "mixture of intelligence, softness, spirit, and feminine innocence" (60–61). Her person, manners, and obvious wealth become frequent topics of conversation. In a discussion between Jack Wilmeter and Anna Updyke, daughter of McBrain's new wife, Jack hypothesizes that Miss Monson must be of age since the law now gives every woman "full command of all her property" after she comes of age. Cooper then opens discussion of the "tea-cup" law by having Jack quote Dunscomb's view that such legislation "will set the women above their husbands, and create two sets of interests where there ought to be but one" (202). Anna McBrain at once begins to play out her role as the ideal feminine type. Though she believes that marriage settlements should be openly made to provide for an "evil day," she prefers to see all income pass under the control of the husband. To Jack's delight, she announces (echoing Eve Effingham), "it is what every woman, who has a true woman's heart, could wish, and would do. For myself, I would marry no man whom I did not respect and look up to in most things; and surely, if I gave him my heart and my hand, I could wish to give him as much control over my means as circumstances would at all allow" (203).

As the history of Mary Monson is revealed, Cooper's characters trace her problems back to the newly increased economic rights of married women. Anna learns that Mary is married, and Dunscomb, sounding like the New York legislator Charles O'Conor, immediately blames her entire predicament on the new law: "there are runaway wives enough, at this moment, roaming up and down the land, setting the laws of God and man at defiance, and jingling their purses, when they happen to have money, under their lawful husbands' noses." The inherent fickleness of women is given legal backing by their control of their own property:

> But this damnable Code will uphold them, in some shape or other. . . .
> One can't endure her husband because he smokes; another finds fault
> with his not going to church but once a day; another quarrels with him
> for going three times. . . . All these ladies, forgetful as they are of their
> highest earthly duties, forgetful as they are of woman's very nature,
> are the models of divine virtues, and lay claim to the sympathies of
> mankind. (275)

According to Dunscomb the final consequence of the new order will be the most serious. The social innovation called "the liberty of woman" causes the disruption of marriages, fickleness of affections, encouragement of errant wives, and finally the next step in the "dissolution of civilized society"(491)—the licentiousness of women. Thus the new "cup and saucer" law is not only unnecessary, since marriage settlements can solve the problem of spendthrift or luckless husbands, but it is dangerous to the structure of society and the morality of all women. The constant switching from the lawyer's voice to the author's reveals that Cooper is in substantial agreement with his character. For instance, when Dunscomb fears that Jack may abandon Anna for Mary, he warns Jack about rich women:

> If they happen to unite moneyed independence with moral independence . . . their tyranny is . . . worse than that of Nero. A tyrannical woman is worse than a tyrannical man, because she is apt to be capricious. . . . At one time she will give, at the next clutch back her gifts. . . . No, no Jack, marry a *woman*; which means a kind, gentle, affectionate, thoughtful creature, whose heart is so full of *you*, that there is no room in it for herself. (350)

The authorial voice similarly bemoans:

> Alas! that women should ever so mistake their natural means to influence and guide, as to have recourse to the exercise of agents that they rarely wield with effect; and ever with a sacrifice of womanly character and womanly grace. The person who would draw the sex from the quiet scenes that they so much embellish, to mingle in the strifes of the world; who would place them in stations that nature has obviously intended men should occupy, is not their real friend. . . . The Creator intended woman for a "helpmeet." (406)

Mary also enlightens those who might disagree with Dunscomb. For instance, at first Dr. McBrain does not object to the new marriage law: "For my part, Tom, I'm disposed to leave a woman mistress of her own. The experiment is worth the trial, if it be only to see the use she will make of her money" (27). Here at the beginning Cooper seems to step back from Dunscomb, but in light of the entire story, where we see Mary Monson led into the greatest foolishness because she controls her own money, there is no contest: the few perfect women, like Anna and her mother Mrs. McBrain, will live as they should regardless of the laws of man, but other women will be tempted into error.

Structurally, the entire plot of *The Ways of the Hour* turns on women, who may be roughly divided into active and passive groups. In the first group is Mrs. Goodwin, greedy owner of the cottage, who proudly displays her gold, arousing envy in her neighbors. Mary says she is "managing, dictatorial, and sordidly covetous." Although Peter Goodwin "used every shilling he could obtain, for the purchase of liquors," Mary feels so sorry for him that she gives him money to live apart from his wife until she "might repent of her treatment of him" (460). The fire that occurs as soon as Mrs. Goodwin's treatment has driven her husband out effectively suggests she is responsible for her fate and ought to have satisfied her husband's desires, even if it meant giving him money for drink. She is unquestionably responsible for the greed aroused in Sarah Burton, the next-door neighbor who actually took the money Mary is accused of stealing.

Another active woman is Mrs. Gott, the sheriff's wife. Cooper was distressed that the position of sheriff had deteriorated until it was little more than jail-keeper and denigrates the position by showing that it is really Mrs. Gott who keeps the jail. Mary Monson is able to obtain copies of her keys and slip out whenever she wishes. Despite Mrs. Gott's warm heart and kindness to Mary, she is an unsatisfactory public servant. Cooper is careful to place only indirect blame on the sheriff. Mrs. Gott says that Mary's habit of quitting the jail gave her "a good fright the first time I heard of it, but use reconciles us to all things. I never let Gott into the secret, though he's responsible, as he calls it, for all his prisoners" (478). A parallel situation exists at the local tavern, where Mrs. Horton reigns. During the trial she is paid by Mary to secret Peter Goodwin, crazed by drink, in one of her spare rooms; money suffices to keep her from producing this piece of essential evidence until ordered to by Mary. In all four families we are told there are husbands, but Mr. Gott and Mr. Horton never appear, Mr. Burton says nothing, and Peter Goodwin's wife "ruled the roast" (239). These cases all imply that married women ought to be subject to their husbands, lest the women encourage vice and disorder or even, like Sarah Burton, commit crimes.[45]

The perfect and passive woman is best exemplified by Anna, who articulates her submission to the rightful role of women. Since Cooper would not want Anna to show too much unfeminine reasoning, he sometimes resorts to having her quote Dunscomb: "He said that most family misunderstandings grew out of money; and he thought it unwise to set it up as a bone of contention between man and wife" (202–203).

As she approaches marriage with Jack, Anna becomes more and more perfect. In a final conversation with Mary she affirms, "I see nothing humiliating or depressing in a woman's submission to her husband. It is the law of nature . . . [and] the bible" (484). Anna in this late novel once again embodies Baym's finding that in the Leatherstocking Tales, "no woman . . . belongs to herself." Instead, women are "the chief signs, the language of social communication between males; in the exchange of women among themselves men create ties and bonds."[46] Though Anna has been raised by her widowed mother, and bears her dead father's name, when she bursts into court upon hearing of Mary's conviction she identifies herself in the following ways: "I am Anna Updyke—Dr. McBrain's daughter, now, and uncle Tom's niece" (453). This last is a purely honorary connection, as Anna is not related to Dunscomb; her wedding to Jack will give legal status to the friendship between the two older men.

Mary, who has neither father nor uncle and has left her husband, represents a basic threat to the hierarchical organization of the ideal society. (Her assumed name, Monson, suggests monster or monsoon.) Everyone who sees Mary agrees that she is a lady: she speaks four languages, plays the harp, moves and dresses in the most cultivated way. While Cooper uses the town's instant distrust of her ladylike accomplishments as evidence for the people's tendency to attack as "aristocratic" anyone more refined than they are, his own anger at Mary is magnified, because she comes from the group of gentry about whom he cares most and threatens his value system from within.

Mary herself tells Sarah and Anna that it would have been better for her not to be rich (450) and confesses that "wilfulness has ever been my greatest enemy. It has been fed by perfect independence and too much money" (307). More often she defends herself: she has abandoned her husband because he wished "to advise and direct, and, in some measure, to control" her fortune (318). Her feelings are "all for independence. Men have not dealt fairly by women. Possessing the power, they have made all the laws, fashioned all the opinions of the world, in their own favour" (308). We are not surprised, in light of Dunscomb's mockery of the absurd reasons women give for leaving their husbands, that Mary's profound disgust with the vicomte grew from his habit of taking snuff.

Late in the novel, when the trial is over, Dunscomb tells Mary that licentiousness is the inevitable result of the liberty of women (491). While Mary herself has not given the slightest indication of sexual laxity, her freedom has made her into a sexual object. Suspicion rests on her because she is rescued from the fire by two men, in actuality her own agents. Almost all the unattached men are assumed to be in love with her. The most serious case is that of Jack Wilmeter, for he is briefly tempted away from the perfect Anna. In addition, Dr. McBrain is teased about being diverted from his upcoming marriage, Dunscomb is thought to defend Mary for love, and Timms, the country lawyer, proposes marriage to Mary and tries to obtain a divorce for her when he discovers her situation. Mary thus comes close to bearing out Dunscomb's prophecy that no "woman can throw off the most sacred of all her earthly duties . . . and escape from the doom of her sex" (491). Yet she is not herself guilty.

As *The Ways of the Hour* progresses, Cooper's anger increasingly shifts from the inadequate judicial system to its victim. Finally he reveals that Mary is insane, marked at least periodically by an inherited streak of madness. This is more a libel than a character trait, for Cooper does not bother either to prove Mary's insanity or to demonstrate it. Throughout the trial Mary has taken a serious interest in her defense and in the law, much to the amazement of both lawyers and rather to the disgust of Dunscomb. Anna, the ideal, told John that "surely, no woman . . . would bother herself about law"; Mary, by contrast, has a "strange predilection for law" (207). She is "cool" (256, 154) and "sharp" (196). Most frequently of all she is called "cunning" (253, 258, 269, 461, 481). That Cooper makes this adjective indicate insanity is shown when Peter Goodwin is accidentally noticed in the tavern by Dunscomb's party. They do not know who he is, but "Mrs. Horton had pretty plainly intimated [he] was out of his mind. . . . A look of cunning left very little doubt of the nature of [his] malady" (384).

Apparently Mary's madness consists in her ability to manage her own financial affairs, her interest in law, and her desire for independence. At the end Cooper simply announces that she "was in a state that left no doubt of her infirmity. The lucid intervals were long, however, and at such times her mind seemed clear enough on all subjects but one. Divorce was her 'ruling passion'" (493). He specifies that she continues to handle her money well during her madness. Her recovery coincides with Anna teaching her the New Testament— and her husband's departure for France.

Throughout *The Ways of the Hour* Cooper looks with horror toward the future of the United States. Fundamental property rights are threatened, new codes and constitutions endanger the law, and the educated gentry is being replaced by a mob that, as Timms the country lawyer demonstrates, does not constitute a meritocracy; as Mary says, "look around you, and see how everybody, almost everything, is becoming independent, our sex included" (489). It is important to realize, however, that not everyone in the United States of 1850 thought that giving women control over their property would lead inevitably to chaos and licentiousness. Within a year a popular female novelist, E.D.E.N. Southworth, had written a novel to express the opposite view.

Choosing Love over Money

Southworth's *The Discarded Daughter* appeared serially in the *Saturday Evening Post* from October 1851 until April 1852. This novel is full of wildly improbable plots and melodramatic characters, yet the entire tale turns on the hard facts of the disposition of property, specifically a great estate in Maryland called Mount Calm. Unlike Cooper, Southworth believes that giving women legal control of their property will preserve rather than destroy estates and families; however, she also believes that in marriage, the intimate relationship between husband and wife usually takes precedence over any legal arrangements. Thus while Cooper, writing in a framework of typically male discourse, sees the law as instrumental, the cause of an inevitable effect, Southworth, from a female point of view, sees any law as just one element affecting the marital relationship. To attack New York's Married Women's Property Act Cooper takes as a central figure a woman who values money over marriage; to show that no property law alone can empower women, Southworth follows a number of women, all of whom value marriage over money.

Alice Chester, heroine of the novel, is engaged to the local minister when her two brothers are killed in the revolutionary war. Her father immediately breaks her engagement—"there is a vast difference . . . between the position and privileges of a moderately dowered girl, and a young lady who is to inherit such an estate as Mount Calm." He chooses for his son-in-law General Garnet, who "has no fortune, but a name among the most glorious in the land."[47] Alice is forced to yield, though Garnet, a man whose hair contains "threads of fire," whose eyes beam "lurid fire," and who combines "the utmost inflexibility and even cruelty of purpose" with "urbanity of manner" (29), repels her.

The miseries of Alice's married life climax when it is time for her only child, a second Alice known as Elsie, to marry. Garnet is interested only in an alliance of property, and he has engaged Elsie to Magnus Hardcastle, nephew and heir to the adjoining estate. As the young people are in love, this arrangement is agreeable to all until the Hardcastle son Lionel, presumed lost at sea, reappears. Garnet then attempts to repeat his father-in-law's action and force Elsie to marry Lionel. He explains that he cares nothing for

> all the miserable, contemptible love sentiment in the world; I never *did*! . . . But that which I *want*, and that which I *will have*, is the union of these two joining estates, Mount Calm and Hemlock Hollow. . . . The young man who was to inherit the estate was to have the bride. It mattered nothing to me whether that were Magnus or Lionel; *but* the hand of my *heiress* was to be bestowed upon the *heir* of Hemlock Hollow. *That* was the treaty. (176–177)

He locks Elsie in the attic, but for the first time in her unhappy married life Alice revolts, assisting Magnus and Elsie to elope.

At this point Southworth begins her exploration of the property law and its limitations. Conveniently, Alice has a friend, Judge Wylie, who is able to explain her position to her (and the reader). Wylie comes to see Alice shortly after Elsie's departure, and his comments demonstrate how novels were used to educate readers and implicitly to influence their political attitudes. Although the novel is set earlier in the century, Wylie's advice is based on the Maryland law of 1843:

> "You know something, I presume, of the Maryland laws of property, of inheritance, and of marriage?"
>
> "No—no—I know nothing about it."
>
> "At least you know that when a girl marries, all the personal property she may be possessed of at the time of her marriage, or may afterwards inherit, becomes the property of her husband?"

"Yes, of course I know that."

"Yes—but—*listen*. All the LANDED property she possesses at the time of her marriage, or afterwards inherits, is *hers*—hers *alone*. Her husband can neither alienate it during his life, or will it at his death. He cannot mortgage it, nor assign it—nor can it be taken for his debts. It is *hers*, and hers *alone*. She alone has the disposal of it."

"Yes. Well?"

" . . . All the LANDED property, consisting of six thousand acres of the best land on the Western Shore, which you inherited from your father, is *yours, your own*, and at your death it is your *daughter's*, if she survive you, and unless you choose to will it to some one else. General Garnet can make no disposition of it either during your life or at your death. . . . Your daughter Elsie has, by her marriage, grievously offended her father. He may or may not pardon her. He may discard her. *Do not put it in his power to disinherit her.*" . . .

"Why do you say that to me?" . . .

"Because . . . it is said that women can always be kissed or kicked out of any right of property they *may* happen to possess. Now don't you, my little Alice, be kissed out of your six thousand acres. . . . For it makes you independent and of great importance. Don't you be kissed out of it, Alice, for you can leave it to your beloved daughter, who will need it." (205–206)

Everything Judge Wylie warns against, Alice promptly does. No Maryland law giving her her landed property can protect her from her own sense of marital duty and her husband's compulsion. Garnet has already felled her with "a heavy blow" as she attempted to free Elsie and then, when she sought a reconciliation after assisting the elopement, "pressed a passionate kiss upon her lips . . . the first kiss of many many years" (200). Both kicked and kissed, Alice is easily persuaded to "prove my love and respect, and confidence in him" by signing anything her husband requires. When Garnet comes with an "angelic smile," complaining to his wife that he is "the nominal master of Mount Calm only . . . a poor man" and asking her to prove her affection by signing a "deed of assignment" whereby she conveys all her "right, title and interest in the landed property" to her husband, Alice obediently does so (206–207).

That night, his angelic smile replaced by eyes flashing "lurid demoniac fire" (212), Garnet enacts the worst fears of the fathers of wealthy daughters. He tells his wife that he extracted the deed to punish her and Elsie, but that is not all:

And now comes the very best of the argument, which, like a good orator, I have saved for the very last. . . . You have disappointed me in my first plan for uniting two great estates. Before I have done, I will make you *regret* that,—the estates shall be united yet. You have taught your daughter to disobey me—very well—you have bereft her of her birthright for a caress, to your *shame* be it remembered,—and I have discarded and disowned her. But, listen: I have ANOTHER DAUGH- TER—the child of my love! —ha!—are you pale with *jealousy*? Listen, farther yet: all the broad lands of Mount Calm that came by you, and should descend to your child, and enrich her, will I bestow upon the child of my love; and her hand will I bestow upon Lionel Hardcastle. (216)

Alice swoons, appears to die, and is placed in the family vault, from which Elsie and Magnus, returning too late for the funeral, rescue her. Her returning consciousness is accompanied by thoughts of her legal position. Lying in her shroud Alice seems much better informed about marital prop- erty rights than she had been when visited by Judge Wylie. She contemplates going home, but "alas! it is not *my* home any longer! I do not own an interest there—not even a wife's interest in the homestead which I should have had, even had the estate come by General Garnet, for I have signed even *that* away—'*all* right, title, and interest'" (241). Her awareness of the law is, unlike Mary Monson's, forced on her by men. Despairingly, she agrees to go west with Magnus and Elsie.

Much of the rest of the novel is devoted to "the child of [Garnet's] love," Garnet Seabright, known as Nettie. The General is determined that Nettie, who is his granddaughter from an early, secret marriage (though he conceals this fact even from the girl), shall inherit Mount Calm. As he contemplates marrying again, he tries to make a will in her favor. His conversation with his lawyer reveals that it is not only about property laws that Southworth disagrees with Cooper: she also doubts the incompetence of juries and the malevolent leveling tendencies of the masses. Garnet's lawyer assumes that the child is the General's illegitimate daughter and warns Garnet that his "will might be *successfully* contested. . . . I give it, sir, as my best di- gested legal opinion, that in the event of your death . . . scarce a jury could be found to give a verdict against your *legal* daughter—a Chester— and in favour of your—, —I beg your pardon—*adopted* daughter—a stranger and an alien." Furthermore, "such are the prejudices in favour of wealth, rank, hereditary descent, and . . . *justice*" that the estate will prob- ably be awarded to "Alice Chester Hardcastle, the only living represen- tative of the old Chester family, who have held the land from the first settle- ment of the country to the present time—upwards of two hundred years" (304).

Even when juries are equitable and favor direct inheritance, Southworth shows that a man can twist property away from its rightful female owner.

General Garnet finds another strategy to ensure the alienation of the Chester land:

> I have it, now!—*a deed!* To-morrow morning, the first thing I do will be to have drawn up, sign, seal and record *a deed of conveyance*, giving the whole of this estate to Garnet Seabright, and retaining only a life interest in it myself. Yes! *a deed!* There will be no contesting or setting aside *that.* . . . Yes! I *must* revenge myself upon Hardcastle. I *must* punish that ungrateful daughter—true scion of the stubborn Chesters. And by all means, by *any* means—I *must*—WILL! elevate and aggrandize Nettie—my child, my darling. (305)

As soon as he has safely conveyed the estate to Nettie, the General dies of a heart attack.

The history of Nettie's relation to her property may be usefully compared to the histories of Alice Chester and Mary Monson. Nettie is nothing like Alice and Elsie; she resembles General Garnet in her "inflexibility of will" (315), the "rings of crimson fire" in her hair, and the "unquenchable light that half terrifies" in her eyes" (317). Much of her story is built on a dichotomy between her diabolic inheritance and her pure inclinations. Before she was taken home by the General she lived in extreme poverty on an island along with Hugh Hutton, a boy whom Magnus and Elsie eventually raise. The General's will has appointed Lionel Hardcastle as her guardian and directed (though not compelled) her to marry Lionel when she is of age, but Nettie is determined to find a "noble, aspiring, elevated nature such as that to which . . . my whole being . . . instinctively tends," who will "direct me aright in the faithful stewardship of my wealth and power" (320). Since the property is Nettie's, she is not under economic pressure to heed the General's wishes.

Lionel, though heir to the neighboring estate, is morally corrupt; Nettie recognizes that his true goal in the marriage is to gain control of her lands. Lionel attempts to terrify her into marrying him: he points out that her reputation will be destoyed if she refuses because she has traveled with him as his ward, and later he attempts to rape her on a visit to her childhood island, saying, "*To-day* you reject my hand with scorn. *To-morrow* shall you sue for it as for life." Nettie is infuriated but not cowed: she says "I know you. . . . You think to frighten *me*, Garnet Seabright, into the promise to become your wife, and endow you with the broad lands of Mount Calm, upon condition of your sparing me" (336–337). Unlike Alice, Nettie recognizes that men use intimidation to force women to yield rights legally theirs. Fortunately Lionel is killed in a struggle with a woman— Hugh's long-lost mother— who suddenly appears.

However, when Hugh returns to his mother's deathbed, Nettie finds in the man of her dreams a worthier opponent to her possession of her lands. Hugh informs her, for the first time, how she comes to own the Mount Calm estate and urges her, in the cause of justice, to return it to Alice Chester. "He who gave you the Mount Calm estate had no just right to do so. The whole of the estate came by his *wife*, and should descend to *her* daughter." Nettie's immediate reactions make her sound like Mary Monson. She comprehends her legal position, pointing out that Garnet "must have had a legal right to the property, else he could not have conveyed it to me" (363). She defends her grandfather's alienation of the property, arguing in a way that would greatly upset Cooper: "I think two centuries quite long enough for any one family to hold any one landed estate. I think it quite time the property had passed into other hands" (363). Nettie is intensely conscious of the power that great wealth gives her, and asks Hugh, "is there a man, woman, or child, now living . . . who would voluntarily yield up an estate . . . of two millions of dollars—for—what?—a point of conscience!" (368). The climax of the battle, and of the diabolic imagery that has been associated with Nettie and her grandfather, comes when Nettie leads Hugh up on the roof to see the estate. The young man sums up Southworth's moral point in an analogy: "Nettie, when Satan wished to tempt Christ, he took Him up into a very high mountain, and showed Him the kingdoms of the earth and the glory thereof, and said, 'All these will I give Thee, if Thou wilt fall down and worship me'" (370).

In the end Nettie cannot resist her own "true nobility of soul" (369). Though it might appear she is swayed by the choice Hugh offers her between the estate and himself—between money and marriage—Hugh asserts that it is Nettie's own morality that conquers: "Nor was it through *my* persuasion that she made this glorious sacrifice to right. . . . No; I simply set the truth before her, and let it work its way. . . . I might have gone to Patagonia or Bhering's Straits, and the result would have been the same. She would never have known an hour's peace until she had restored the property" (387). With a little prodding from Hugh, Nettie even refuses Alice's grateful attempt to give her a percentage of the estate as a marriage portion. Returning the estate becomes almost a religious act proving Nettie's worth. Alice, seeing the girl for the first time, is struck by the resemblance to her dead husband, but "the only difference was, that in place of the latent diabolism under General Garnet's countenance, all Heaven shone from Miss Seabright's" (392).

The difference between Garnet Seabright and Mary Monson—both bright, proud, educated, and accustomed to command—is thus the difference between a heroine whose madness seems to consist more in claiming her legal rights than anything else, and one who, in the best tradition of the domestic novel, is strengthened by adversity and renounces even the rights to which she is legally entitled. Cooper is sure that control of money will lead women to licentiousness: Southworth shows the scorn with which Nettie treats Lionel's threats to slander her and her horror at the insinuation that she may be illegitimate. Similarly, though both novels have heroines who leave their husbands, in *The Discarded Daughter* this is the man's, rather than the woman's, fault. Alice only agrees to go west after Magnus asks the General what he would do if "the doors of that vault where you laid her fly open and yield up its beautiful dead," and the General replies that "*could* she be restored to me, . . . and *should* the first boon she craved . . . be the reconciliation you desire, that boon would be refused, though that refusal should send her back into the grave!" (286–287).

Through *The Discarded Daughter* Southworth, like Cooper, participates in the national debate over women's power, here particularized as the power to control property. In this novel it is a man, not a woman, who uses the property laws to disrupt the orderly progression of society. Southworth believes that protecting inheritance through the female will maintain family estates and social stability, and through Nettie's actions she argues that woman's legal power over property will be tempered by her superior morality. Regardless of the legal changes, however, Southworth contends that no law can sufficiently protect women from threat or coercion by the men in their lives. Cooper was persuaded that under the new laws, men could not control their wives; Southworth demonstrates instead that wives cannot control their husbands, even if they do hold property. Every woman in *The Discarded Daughter* who is not otherwise compelled chooses love over money. Marriage in the midcentury feminine view is not about property and alliance but about personal relationships.

The extent to which the propaganda for the various Married Women's Property Acts had altered public opinion is clear from a comparison of *The Discarded Daughter* to *Redwood*. The earlier novel acknowledged that Redwood would receive societal approval for dividing the estate he had received from Caroline's mother between his daughters from both marriages. Reader sympathy lies with Ellen rather than with spoiled Caroline, and we share Squire Lenox's dismay that Redwood has, apparently, only one child to leave his money to, for "such a fortune as you have to give makes a girl a sort of a prey to all the hungry hunters after money" (1:241). It is proof of Ellen's moral disinterestedness that she tells Caroline, "your mother's fortune is as entirely yours as if I had never had an existence. I have not the right, and, certainly, I have not the wish to interfere with your inheritance. . . . All that I covet, is an equal share of our father's affections" (2:268). Rather to the reader's frustration, she convinces Redwood that he has "no right to make any disposition of a property which descends to [Caroline] from her mother" (2:279). What Ellen wants from her father has little to do with property.

Thirty years later, in *The Discarded Daughter*, the reader's sympathy has been switched from the child by a secret marriage (Ellen or Nettie) to the rightful female inheritor, in this case Alice Chester. In *Redwood* Ellen implied that property should descend within the family, but neither the story line nor the characters were constructed to support this belief. Furthermore, Sedgwick teases the reader's sympathies with a final uncertainty about the disposition of the property. Caroline dies shortly after her marriage, leaving her child to Ellen. As his deceased wife's fortune is entirely within Redwood's disposition, will it go exclusively to Caroline's daughter, or will Redwood now give or leave some of it to Ellen? In *The Discarded Daughter* there are no similar ambiguities of law and attitude. The Chester estate must rightfully go to the Chester girl, and the only way that can be ensured is to remove a husband's control over his wife's property. Interesting as Nettie is, the reader never fully approves of her until assured that Alice will regain her property. In this case, law and virtue are on the same, rather than opposing, sides.

Southworth was not the only woman writer to emphasize that law alone was not enough to protect a woman's property or earnings from rapacious men. Fanny Fern, actually Sara Payson Willis Parton, made the same point in her two novels. In *Ruth Hall* (1854) the autobiographical heroine discovers that she is at the mercy of men as soon as she is widowed. Her husband's father claims his clothing, certain that Ruth is too ignorant to protest. "The law allows the widow the husband's wearing apparel. . . . The law is on her side, undoubtedly, but luckily she knows no more about law than a baby." He is wrong: Ruth questions his legal right to the clothes, but her protest is cut off when she is told, "in the present state of your affairs, you cannot afford to refuse." [48] Even more striking, in *Rose Clark* (1855) the artist Gertrude is bitterly reminded by her second husband, when she protests his going through her first husband's letters, that "the law says you can have nothing that is not mine." The author comments, "O, how many crushed and bleeding hearts all over our land can endorse the truth of this brutal answer." [49] Even after the husband forces a divorce on Gertrude, he persists in claiming what is not his. Chatting with a friend at Niagara, where Gertrude has gone with her family, he says that it would gall him to see her so flush of money "had I not the way of helping myself to some of it." The friend inquires, "How's that? The law does not allow you to touch her earnings, now you are divorced." But the ex-husband believes "all women are fools about law matters. . . . I will frighten her into it" (345). And indeed, Gertrude is saved by the conventional protection of male family members, rather than by the law. We never learn if she would have been a fool about law matters, as her brother, overhearing, beats the ex-husband and drives him away.

Property and Biography

Fanny Fern's heroines in *Ruth Hall* and *Rose Clark* echoed elements of her own life. She had learned through hard experience the ways in which fathers, fathers-in-law, and husbands can claim a woman's property.[50] But nothing in Cooper's history suggests that he should have been personally terrified at the prospect of married women's independence. He himself had married young. Susan De Lancy had some property, and while there was, in 1822, a quarrel between Cooper and Susan's brothers over this, Susan herself seems never to have attempted to interfere with her husband's control of all money matters.[51] James Grossman's description of the Coopers' marriage as "one of those thoroughly happy old-fashioned marriages in which the husband's formal rights of mastery were rigidly respected and the wife, through her delicate sensibilities and the other arts of love, had her way"[52] is entirely borne out by Cooper's long, chatty, and affectionate letters to his wife throughout his life.

Cooper's letters and journals furnish a clue to Mary Monson's inception and to Cooper's anger.[53] For many years they are full of details of the notorious troubles between Henry Cruger and his wife, Harriet Douglas Cruger. Harriet Douglas was a wealthy heiress from New York, famous in Europe as a "lion-huntress," to borrow Sir Walter Scott's description of her. Born in 1790, in 1823 she met Henry Cruger of South Carolina, a lawyer ten years younger than she. Cruger proposed; she hesitated, declaring "her unalterable determination never to marry except upon the condition of retaining sole and absolute control of her fortune."[54] Cooper met Harriet Douglas and Cruger, who was in pursuit of her, in Europe in 1830. The couple was married in 1833; Cruger, in a final effort to retain some self-respect, refused to take the name Douglas as demanded but renounced all interest in and rights to his wife's property. Unfortunately for him, he then gave up his law practice to manage the property, in exchange for a promise of the income or some part of it. Harriet was never satisfied with the arrangements and constantly changed them, sometimes without notifying her husband, who could and did find his checks refused and dishonored. After eight stormy years the couple separated for good, and there then ensued a protracted legal battle that lasted until 1850, as Cruger, unable to reestablish his career, tried to obtain some compensation.

At first Cooper seems to have been impartial, but gradually his friendship with Henry Cruger deepened and he became convinced that Harriet was responsible for the difficulties. Beard comments that Cooper was "endlessly fascinated by Harriet's unpredictable antics."[55] The final period of litigation coincided with the writing and revision of *The Ways of the Hour* (May–November 1849, with revisions until February 1850). The novel was originally titled *The Ways of Manhattan*, and Cooper frequently visited at the Douglas Manhattan mansion while writing it.

Mary Monson seems to be partly drawn from Harriet Cruger. The most important resemblance, of course, is that both women are very rich and wish to keep control of their own property. Both reject the argument that if a wife has entrusted herself to her husband she ought to entrust her property also. Second, Harriet Douglas really was not quite sane. Cooper calls her "the queerest woman I have ever met with." In February 1849 Cooper sent his wife an example of Mrs. Cruger's strange behavior:

> Finding nothing to do in Albany, Mrs C[ruger] went on to Henderson [her estate, on which Cruger was living]. There she *took* lodgings in the porter's lodge, making a great stir about the hardship of her case. At night she prayed for him in a voice so loud as to be heard by all in the lodge. The community is much exercised with all this.

In June 1850 he writes further: "Cruger has resigned Henderson. His wife behaved like a crazy woman—broke into the house—cut all sorts of capers." Apparently it was difficult to pinpoint Harriet's madness in her early years—wealth excuses eccentricity—and this may partially explain Cooper's uncertain description of Mary's mental condition. But Beard comments that Mrs. Cruger "died, as Cooper might have predicted, an utterly demented old woman." [56]

The Crugers perfectly exemplified a family where money had created two sets of interests. Harriet was Dunscomb's tyrannical capricious woman, at one time giving, at another clutching back. Dunscomb's complaint that women give petty reasons for leaving their husbands, including minor points of religious practice, reflects Harriet's behavior once she came under the influence of her brother George. She "introduced religion as an extra justification of her own conduct; any divergence of Cruger's point of view from her own was now represented as a moral offense." [57]

Toward the end of *The Ways of the Hour* Cooper writes, "There is no mode by which an errant wife can be made to perform her duties in boldly experimenting New York. . . . The 'cup and saucer' law comes in aid of this power, and the men who cannot keep their wives in the chains of Hymen . . . may just as well submit . . . to be the victims of an ill-judging and most treacherous regard for the rights of what are called the weaker sex" (479). Even this was temporarily borne out in the Cruger case. In January 1850 Cruger finally obtained a settlement from the court, but the Douglas brothers refused to pay. Cruger had to get a bench warrant to compel payment, and the financial wrangling went on until May. While writing *The Ways* Cooper may well have believed that Cruger's rights would never be vindicated.

The Cruger case gave Cooper his closest view of the social evil that could grow from the independence of women. *The Ways of the Hour* exemplifies the interaction between biography and the author's imagination. Even though Cooper had never suffered personally from woman's independence, he projects, onto the most exceptional of cases, his anger at all forms of the growing egalitarianism of the United States. Cooper writes with real people in mind, but ultimately the political construction he imposes on the case transcends the personal example.

The reflection of Southworth's experiences in *The Discarded Daughter* is more indirect. She was not heir to a great estate, but she knew what it meant to have a husband take from rather than give to a wife. By the time she was pregnant with her second child her husband seems to have been satisfied living off what she could bring to the marriage. The young family was residing in the home of Southworth's grandmother when Southworth's mother's second husband forced them to leave, "apparently because Southworth's husband was unemployed and expected the grandmother to provide support." At this point her husband deserted her. Southworth later told her daughter that he "had no mind for supporting wife or children." [58]

Southworth's books are "full of abandoned and otherwise mistreated wives," [59] who would be better protected if they had clear rights to their own property. It is possible that life followed art for Southworth. She never divorced her husband, although a bill was submitted to Congress that would have "made a legal dissolution possible." [60] She may even have continued to contribute to her husband's support. [61] However, when she went to England in 1859 and remained there for several years, [62] Frederick Hamilton Southworth apparently attempted a swindle of some kind in her absence. In January 1860 he filed "as owner of the story *Kathleen Vernon*, the title caption for copyright in New York, and . . . in Rio de Janeiro." When in February 1860 he "tried to sidetrack T. B. Peterson, publisher, in filing for copyright of *The Haunted Homestead* [h]e was unsuccessful . . . Peterson became owner of the copyright March 5, 1860." [63] A woman's earnings, unlike her property, were not generally protected from her husband by 1860; it is hard to know whether, like Alice Chester, Southworth could have been kissed or kicked out of them. As her husband died shortly after the Civil War began, Southworth was not forced to prove herself different from her heroine.

By the time Cooper and Southworth wrote their novels, the debate over whether to give married women legal control over the lands they brought to a marriage was settled in principle. [64] In some states local judges attempted to reverse the action of the legislature through judgments in individual cases, but on the whole the claim of a married woman to retain her property was given credence in society. The argument into which Cooper and Southworth enter through *The Ways of the Hour* and *The Discarded Daughter* is, therefore, over the results of giving women such legal power. Both authors understand that the new property laws change the legal status of husbands and wives, but they differ in their predictions of the consequences this change will have for the character of American women, for the institution of the family, and for the community.

Cooper sees the Married Women's Property Act as linked to a chain of social and political events, all of which lead to the destruction of the ideal American community. Granting women the right to control their real property will pervert the natural female character; Mary Monson represents the kind of woman—selfish, shrewd, and individualistic—who can be expected to emerge. Such powerful women, like Harriet Cruger, make a mockery of marriage and family by undermining the husband's authority and destroying the common interest of spouses. The breakdown of the appropriate relationship between husbands and wives contributes to the weakening of the social order, the displacement of the natural aristocracy, and the end of a republic built on virtue and the patriarchal family. The greed and self-centeredness of propertied women parallels the relentless self-interest of the masses.

Given Southworth's history—common enough for a midcentury woman—it is not surprising that she creates a contrary scenario. In *The Discarded Daughter*, Southworth shows that it is through the right of women to control estates that family properties such as Mount Calm can be passed down to succeeding generations, thus ensuring the continuity of a gentry class. Southworth fears not the wife's exercise of power but the husband's abuse of it. Where Cooper predicts that economic power will destroy the virtues of the female character, Southworth asserts that the natural morality of women will overcome greed and that their concern for personal relations will preserve marriage.

The passage of the married women's property laws worked to the advantage of the women of the wealthier classes and helped provide an economic base for widows. However, such laws had little effect on women from the lower or middle classes, where landholding meant, at most, the family farm. Many of these women were forced, either by the consequences of the Civil War or by family exigencies, to enter into wage work. The second part of the challenge to male economic hegemony therefore concerned control of wages.

4

Capitalism,
Sex, and Sisterhood

In 1873 Louisa May Alcott published a novel called, simply, *Work*. In the last third of the nineteenth century, no issue was more important to women than how they were to participate in an industrial and commercial society, a society where work increasingly meant leaving the domestic hearth, rural or urban, and going out among strangers. The repercussions, for domestic relations, for social policy, and for the economic well-being of the nation, were enormous.

The novel takes a strong stand on the place of wage work in a woman's life. *Work* begins with its heroine issuing a "new Declaration of Independence." Christie explicitly contrasts the situation of men and women: "being of age, I'm going to take care of myself. . . . If I'd been a boy, I should have been told to do it long ago."[1] Throughout her life she maintains that work is a woman's source of freedom. Rejecting an outwardly acceptable suitor a few years later, she asks, "What can you give me but money and position in return for the youth and freedom I should sacrifice in marrying you?" (87).

Alcott does not scant her depiction of the restricted opportunities open to a young white woman of the middle strata. Christie is not exceptional but "one of that large class of women who, moderately endowed with talents, earnest and true-hearted, are driven by necessity, temperament, or principle out into the world to find support, happiness, and homes for themselves" (11). True to this description, Alcott avoids the autobiographical temptation so frequent to female authors and does not turn Christie, like the heroines of *Ruth Hall*, *St. Elmo*, *Isa*, and even *Little Women*, into a successful writer. Instead Christie tries a number of common occupations, detailed in chapters titled "Servant," "Actress," "Governess," "Companion," and "Seamstress."[2] Though Catharine Beecher had praised teaching school as a way to "elevate and dignify" her sex,[3] Christie thinks it would violate her independence and avoids it; she is happy to have "no humdrum district school to imprison her day after day" (16).

Alcott also evades the most common solution for New England farm girls like Christie. Since the 1830s they had turned to the mills for work, yet Alcott never has her heroine consider the possibility of industrial work. The closest Christie comes to a factory is a "mantua-making establishment" (128), which Sarah Elbert calls a "factory-like workroom" (xxx). Christie's experiences parallel Alcott's own work history, but Alcott is constrained by more than autobiography. One major goal of this novel is to reject the division between domesticity and work that became a critical issue for working women in the late nineteenth century.[4] Alcott selects the kinds of work Christie undertakes to demonstrate the possibility of uniting independence and domesticity for women. In her vision, even marriage can become a form of work: as Elaine Showalter, who calls *Work* Alcott's "most feminist" novel, argues, the novel becomes coherent "once we substitute feminist definitions of 'work' for conventional definitions of waged labor. If work is reproduction as well as production, and domestic as well as commercial, then marriage is . . . a stage in Christie's working life."[5]

Although Alcott is determined to prove that a woman can be as independent as a man, she is unable to imagine a work situation where woman's sexuality is not an issue. In all of Christie's positions she is persistently a sexual object. As a servant she gets on better with the master than the mistress; as an actress she comes close to losing her dearest friend because Lucy is not only jealous of her as an actress, but as a woman; as a governess she attracts the attentions of her employer's brother; and even her idealized relation to David Sterling begins when she is employed in his nursery.

The most fully developed element of the plot turns on female sexuality. Christie loses her job in a sewing establishment for defending a fellow worker who, it is discovered, has "fallen." The climate of suspicion surrounding working women emerges when the owner says she cannot afford to keep Rachel even though it is years since the girl "went astray." No, to keep Rachel "would be the ruin of my establishment; not a girl would remain, and the character of my rooms would be lost for ever" (137). Cloaks must not only be neatly sewn; they must be the product of women above suspicion. Sarah Elbert writes: "In a dramatic confrontation between the necessities of production and the maintenance of social order, Rachel is fired as an undesirable influence on the workers, and the contradictions between true womanhood and waged work are made explicit" (xxxi). The problem of accommodating economic production with social attitudes toward women remained unresolved throughout the remainder of the nineteenth century.

Through Rachel's history, Alcott admits that not every woman who seeks independence through work is as steadfast as Christie. Christie herself will suffer the well-documented hardships of the independent seamstress—little work, late payment, loneliness, and illness—and attempt suicide. But a woman worker's pitfall was more likely to be sexual. Rachel's history is later explained by her brother David Sterling, "We were poor then . . . and she grew restless; tired of hard work. . . . She wanted to go away and support herself. *You* know the feeling; and I need not tell you how the proud high-hearted creature hated dependence. . . . For a time she did bravely; but life was too hard for her; pleasure too alluring, and, when temptation came in the guise of love, she could not resist" (343). Alcott's prudish reserve surfaces when Christie refuses to hear Rachel's story in detail, but she does acknowledge the sexual dangers that surround women working outside of the family.

Alcott was unusual in articulating the meaning of work for women of different races and classes. Whether women depended on wage work for survival at the most rudimentary level or to supplement their family's income, she saw them all as gaining independence and self-respect through employment. One of Christie's first companions at work is Hepsey, a former slave, who teaches Christie that as long as she can be self-supporting, she has not lost her freedom. When Christie rebels against polishing her employer's boots, protesting, "*Do* you think it's right to ask it of me," (22) Hepsey reminds her that there is far worse degradation than being a servant. Although Hepsey is the only black worker in *Work* and one of the very few appearing in any novel focusing on white workers, Alcott clearly understood the position of such women. As Jacqueline Jones notes, "the Afro-American woman found herself confined to [domestic service] . . . by virtue of her sex and race. A traditional form of 'women's work'—dirty, tedious, low-paying—service lacked the rewards of self-satisfaction and pride that supposedly accompanied such tasks when performed for one's own family." [6] Christie can leave service; Hepsey must accept it. Christie's other friends who must work run the gamut from a poor "clear-starcher" to wealthy young Bella Carrol, whose sister Christie serves as a companion until the depressed girl succeeds in killing herself.

The inherited insanity of the Carrols sounds as if it belongs in Alcott's pseudonymous thrillers rather than in pedestrian *Work*, but Alcott introduces the apparently irrelevant tale of the Carrols to make two points. First, Mrs. Carrol's trouble originates from choosing marriage to a rich man tainted with madness, rather than struggling independently to conquer her poverty. The symbolic consequences of this failure of self-support are her mad and miserable children. Second, once Helen Carrol is dead, her sister resolves not to pass on the curse. Bella, who has money, therefore confronts in its purest form the problem of what a woman is to do if she cannot marry.

Bella asks Christie to help her. Her brother has become a physician, but Bella does not contemplate a profession for herself. Charles Strickland complains that the solution *Work* proposes is "vague": "The best that Christie can offer is an appeal to . . . [Bella] to reform the upper classes by making her fashionable home into a center for the discussion of serious issues." [7] Yet the conversation between Christie and Bella emphasizes two of Alcott's strongest beliefs—that all women are sisters despite their class differences, and that, while their work may be different, women of all classes can and should find work.

Despite recognizing the difficulties that face the independent woman, *Work* has a utopian conclusion. *Little Women* had departed from the reality of Alcott's life most strikingly at the end, when Jo was rewarded for her efforts by a flood of men— husband, sons, and a whole boys' school. *Work* instead takes Christie through a brief marriage and widowhood to an all-female society on David's nursery, a female Brook Farm deeply tied to nature. Christie lives with her mother-in-law, sister-in-law, and daughter and receives visits from other women of differing ages, classes, and colors. On her fortieth birthday she has found a "new field of labor" (425) as a "mediator," an "interpreter between the two classes" of ladies and the working women "they wished to serve" (430). In this context the proposal to Bella, while inadequate, points forward to an idealized community of working women.

In the end Alcott hedges on the extent of the change she envisions. The nursery garden, like the world of women, exists in apparent isolation from the rest of the economy, with its problems of industrialization and competitive capitalism. Christie works in a domestic setting and shares her wealth with her family in a model of cooperation. Yet, in her relations with the outside world, Christie has become an independent small businesswoman. Thus Alcott depicts her heroine as having resolved the potential conflict between two of society's most deeply held values, capitalist freedom and female domesticity.

Alcott's novel adumbrates most of the major issues generated by that conflict: the integration of social expectations for women with their need or desire for economic independence; the threat presented by bringing their sexuality into the workplace; and the possibility that sisterhood could exist between working women and middle class women who stayed within the home. By keeping Christie out of the factory, Alcott avoids the additional question of whether working women could achieve solidarity with men in the industrial workplace. All of these issues were repeatedly addressed in other fiction of the post–Civil War era. And despite Alcott's optimism, the increasing presence of women in wage work, which flew directly against prevailing cultural norms, caused deep stress in American society.

Women and Wage Work in the Gilded Age

The increasing number of white women employed in wage work after the Civil War made visible the contradiction between the prevailing philosophy of political economy and the society's ideals of home and family. The culture placed its faith in unfettered capitalism as the means to economic progress and, at the same time, idealized the home as a refuge from the evils of the industrial system.

The rapid industrialization of the United States during this period was guided by the philosophy of laissez-faire economics. One of its best-known advocates, William Sumner, professor of sociology at Yale, clearly enunciated the obligations of citizens in this community: "We each owe it to the other to guarantee rights. Rights do not pertain to *results*, but only to *chances*. They pertain to the *conditions* of the struggle for existence, not to any of the results of it; to the *pursuit* of happiness, not to the possession of happiness." Each citizen's primary duty was "to take care of his or her own self." [8] In this amalgam of economics and Social Darwinism, those who did not succeed simply had not taken advantage of the chances offered.

The cornerstone of laissez-faire economics was the protection of business and industry from government regulation and interference. The late nineteenth century saw a great shift from the protection of individual political rights to the protection of corporate rights.[9] This shift was made possible by important changes in the interpretation of the Constitution. First, corporations were given the legal identity of persons. Using this legal fiction, corporations could claim protection under the Constitution from attempts by states or the national government to restrict their "life, liberty, or property without due process of law." The words of the Fourteenth Amendment, passed to protect the rights of ex-slaves, became the armor of corporations against state regulation. Such protection kept states from outlawing the unhealthful conditions so graphically portrayed in the "Reports of the Massachusetts Bureau of Statistics of Labor," which Elizabeth Stuart Phelps cited as her source for *The Silent Partner* (1871).[10]

Another important change in the legal system was the elevated importance of contracts. Sumner explained the benefits of the system: "A society based on contract is a society of free and independent men, who form ties without favor or obligation, and cooperate without cringing or intrigue. A society based on contract, therefore, gives the utmost room and chance for individual development, and for all the self-reliance and dignity of a free man." [11] This philosophy regarded the corporation and the lowest worker as equal partners to a contract. It assumed that each entered the contract as a free party and each could freely choose to end the relationship.[12] The rise of laissez-faire capitalism offered both economic opportunities and real economic risks to American women. During the Civil War, a labor shortage combined with increased wartime production to open factory employment beyond textile mills to women. The expanding activity of government and business during and after the war brought women workers into public and private offices as well. Although the economic conditions of the nation multiplied the number and range of jobs available to women, employers exploited the large number of job seekers through low wages and seasonal jobs. In addition, the emphasis on freedom of contracts and the Supreme Court's refusal to legitimate protective legislation for women meant that women who had claimed special rights within the home received no special protections in the workplace.[13] Not until the Progressive Era did the need for protective legislation for women workers become a national issue, when concerted efforts by the National Women's Trade Union League and the National Consumer's Union persuaded a number of states to pass maximum-hours legislation for women as public health and safety measures. Only in 1908 were these laws judged constitutional by the Supreme Court in *Mueller v. Oregon*[14] on the basis of the Brandeis brief, which argued that women have a special biological function in society and that their health needs to be protected for the good of the nation's future.[15]

Although the 1880s and 1890s saw increasing numbers of women in wage work, societal understanding of their motivation was quite narrow. The pattern girl—in the social consciousness as in novels—was single, living at home with her parents, and working out for wages to help her family and to fill her time until she married an acceptable man and retired to domestic life. Critics of such young workers emphasized the frivolous aims of working girls—their desire to buy fancy gowns and their constant husband hunting.[16] However, for many single women, work was essential for their own support or that of their families. The lives of young women who were "bound out" to the factory as children and others who, abandoned by their husbands, had to return to the mills for survival were reported by Lillie Chace Wyman in a series of articles in *Atlantic Monthly* in 1888, 1889, and 1896.[17]

Given the strong cultural proscription against married women entering the public sphere in almost any capacity, few accounts of married women in wage work appeared either in fiction or nonfiction. The fact that many of the married women in the work force were either foreign-born or black added to their invisibility. The ideology of the domestic sphere worked to deemphasize the economic contribution that married women made to the support of the family since it was widely believed that such economic power as women gained through wage earning might be detrimental to marital relations. The harmful impact on the family was seized on by the labor unions as yet another argument against the entry of women into the craft unions. As Edward O'Donnell, secretary of the Boston Central Labor Union put it, "The growing demand for female labor . . . is the knife of the assassin, aimed at the family circle—the divine injunction. It debars the man, through financial embarrassment from family responsibility, and physically, mentally and socially excludes the woman equally from nature's dearest impulse." [18]

Despite the cultural anxiety, women were welcomed by capitalist employers as cheaper and more docile labor than males. In the Social Darwinist economic scheme, women were for once the legal equals of men. They were free to contract for employment, and, if a factory owner could make greater profits using women workers, then it was his right, perhaps his duty, to hire them, in order for his firm and the whole economy to prosper.

Alongside the economic arguments for employing women as cheap labor, social and psychological defenses of women working arose. Though these arguments today appear as unwittingly supporting a hegemonic economic system, overtly they reverse the economic argument, stressing the value of work for women rather than for their employers. In her introduction to Annie Nathan Meyer's *Women's Work in America* (1891), Julia Ward Howe summarizes the main lines of argument. Work for women has positive value: "The new activities sap the foundation of vicious and degraded life. From the factory to the palace the quickening impulse is felt, and the social level rises. To the larger intellectual outlook is added the growing sympathy of women with each other." [19]

Meyer's was the minority view; most Americans considered woman's importance as the linchpin of domestic life undiminished. The ideal family life called for the wife to remain at home managing the household and nurturing the children. Industrialization had altered the wife's duties through the introduction of mass-produced goods, including prepared foods and labor-saving devices, but the middle-class homemaker of the late nineteenth century had new responsibilities as the leading consumer of the family. Middle-class families were tempted to "mimic, at least as much as they could afford, the elegant life-style formerly reserved for a small minority of wealthy families." [20] This meant that the wife and mother was as needed in the home as ever. An establishment in the city usually required household help that the wife was expected to supervise, and even if children were educated outside the home, the mother remained responsible for their moral guidance and discipline. Most important, given the dog-eat-dog world of business and industry, the home retained its function as a sanctuary from the outside world where the woman's role was to preserve for her husband "the single spot of rest which a man has upon this earth for the cultivation of his noblest sensibilities." [21]

The divergent points of view about women's work are epitomized in a series of contrasting articles by Gail Hamilton and Elizabeth Stuart Phelps that appeared in the *Independent* of 1871. Hamilton asserts simply: "the necessity of earning her own living is always a woman's misfortune," [22] while Phelps is certain that young women will inevitably be miserable if they do not work. Women are "human critters" with rights, and she tells parents to "urge them into the world. . . . Train them from infancy to 'be' something." [23] Where Phelps has a long article about the many ways in which women can gain self-support—everything from blacksmithing to dentistry—Hamilton invokes woman's heavy burden of maternity and claims that God is not so unjust as to expect her to take on the earning of bread as well.[24] Since Hamilton herself, in an earlier book called *Women's Wrongs*, had argued for women's work, she was attacked for inconsistency. Frances Willard's "A Specimen 'Girl of the Period,'" which holds up as a model a wealthy girl who has decided to study medicine in order to be useful, concludes with Willard asking a bookkeeper how she likes her work, and receiving the reply, "O, it used to go pretty well . . . but since reading Gail Hamilton's articles in THE INDEPENDENT I've concluded we women ought not to work at all. . . . I have about concluded the Oriental women are nearer right than we restless creatures of the West, and I verily believe Gail thinks so too!'" [25]

Hamilton's inconsistency was deeply rooted in fundamental contradictions of the Victorian United States. Women were more exposed to public life than at any time in the nation's history. Yet, their behavior was carefully restricted through elaborate sets of customs, such as the use of calling cards and the rituals of courtship.[26] Similarly, economic freedom in the marketplace was accompanied by ever stricter social and legal controls on daily life. In fields other than economics, individualism was less than dominant: "in the field of morality, the widest interpretation was given to the function of the state." [27] Even though the Supreme Court steadily overturned regulations on industry, states were free to regulate alcohol, immigration, prostitution, and birth control. Such regulation of social behavior reflected the belief that scientific "laws" governing social behavior could be discovered and reinforced by legislation in the same way that the laws of economic life were. These scientific laws were invoked to buttress arguments for limitations on women's activities.

The situation of working women crystallized the contradictions between the domestic ideal of the middle class and the needs of the economic system. The difficulty that Americans had in reconciling these two social imperatives is illustrated in an 1885 essay from the *Woman's Magazine,* titled "Two Types of Women." The first half of the article describes the "Woman Who Can Take Care of Herself," a self-sufficient woman who "goes where she likes and employs her talents at whatsoever she likes; who takes an honest pride in earning and handling her own money." This woman is rewarded by the respect of all. Neither she nor society has time to discuss "preconceived ideas of the proprieties of life, woman's sphere and all that have to stand aside; the question is bread, bread." But in the second half of the essay, entitled "The Woman Who Ought to Be Cared For," the author notes that all mothers believe that, if their daughters become wives and mothers, "their normal condition and that which would be the most favorable to their own happiness, would be that of being cared for." A woman in her maternal years needs a stronger hand to help her. "This is the period when woman's most sacred right is that of being cared for and protected." [28] The author, like many of her day, wants respect for both kinds of women, and yet cannot acknowledge that for thousands of women, neither being cared for nor caring adequately for themselves was an obtainable goal.

Fictional Critiques of Capitalism

While the consequences of industrialization and unrestrained capitalism for American society were frequently the subject of controversy in the last quarter of the nineteenth century, all parties to this debate—politicians, scholarly economists, reformers, journalists, or novelists—approached the question from within the dominant American ideology. Whether they endorsed laissez-faire capitalism or proposed drastic reforms, they agreed on the fundamental values of equality, liberty, and democracy. Most also agreed on the need to maintain the traditional family structure. The primary political question of the times was whether capitalism should be restrained or regulated and to what degree.

Novels contributing to this debate can be grouped into three broad classes: those that support the capitalist system, those that suggest amelioration and minor reforms, and those that propose the redirection of the political economy toward a different set of goals. Most fictional treatments of the problems of capitalism do not separate the concerns of working women from those of other workers. However, in portraying working conditions, the effects of poverty, and the consequences of strikes for family life, novelists discuss the effect of the economic system on the status of women.

The earlier novels tend to give a simplified view of factory life, emphasizing its benefits for women. *Effie and I; or, Seven Years in a Cotton Mill*, published in 1863, is dedicated jointly to "the owners and operatives of cotton mills." Written by Charlotte S. Hilbourne, the novel is set in the Lowell mills, which are praised as "an asylum for the oppressed, a home for the homeless, and a broad highway leading to wealth and honor." [29] The capitalist system is benevolent to the weak, including women, yet provides opportunities for the ambitious. The narrator emphasizes the altruism of the factory owners: when panics and famines come, they do not crush widows but "through the long cold winters . . . [let them live] securely in their factory homes, rent free" (9).

Even though the character of the Lowell mills had changed substantially by the mid-1840s, with the female operatives organizing to protest low wages and an increase in the employment of immigrant women, twenty years later this novel continues to idealize the mills as a morally pure and beneficial environment for women.[30] Not only do young women learn skills and good habits from working in the mills, but they enhance their chances to marry well, because "the great wheel of a cotton mill turns out some rare specimens of perfection" (238). Mills are also valuable social institutions when marriage fails. Deserted by her husband, the heroine returns to work and again finds dignity and self-support. The factory system is here defended as supporting democratic values and encouraging individual achievement while not modifying the place of women in society.[31] There is no hint that industrial life might, instead, threaten fundamental social values.

By the 1880s, the debate over the regulation of capitalism raged furiously. Advocates of laissez-faire economics and the Social Darwinism of William Sumner and Herbert Spencer defended the social effects of the capitalist system as the working out of natural laws: "the social order is fixed by laws of nature precisely analogous to those of the physical order."[32] A novel by Lillian E. Sommers, *For Her Daily Bread* (1887), illustrates how individuals work out their destinies within capitalism. This novel is particularly interesting because while it focuses on the individual's struggle to achieve, the hero is female.

In a familiar plot, Norma and her sister, who are orphaned, go to Chicago to find jobs. Like their real world counterparts, they discover that jobs for women that pay enough to survive are difficult to obtain. Yet not all working girls are in the same economic situation: "A number of the girls worked merely to obtain a little pocket money, others to assist in the support of the family, and the remaining few, silent, grave, and with tired faces and lagging steps, supported a mother, younger sisters and brothers on their scant earnings."[33] After working in factories and as a maid and servant girl, Norma learns stenography and typewriting in a business school. She is then able to secure a much better paying position, although she must deal with sexual harassment from the boss and the jealousy of fellow workers. Norma is frustrated that in her most pleasant working situation she is still only receiving $10 per week when her male counterpart earns $18, but the author seems to accept the inequity of women's pay as one more obstacle in her heroine's climb through adversity.

In his preface to the novel, Col. Robert Ingersoll asserts that there is no viewpoint here: "You will find no theories of government, no hazy outlines of reform, nothing but facts and folks" (3). Ingersoll, who was deeply interested in Darwinism as a support for his agnosticism, disingenuously ignores the ideological bias of the novel.[34] Toward the end, Norma and the boss's son discuss the unfortunate. With characteristic noblesse oblige, the rich young man suggests that the poor have been defeated by forces beyond their control. Norma, a true Social Darwinist, responds that "all should be held responsible for their lives even to its minutest details"(168). The successful owe their situations to "long and persevering labor, to untiring energy, to economy, long, sleepless nights and weary, anxious days," while the poor and thriftless weakly attribute their problems to "Ill Luck, or Fate" (169). She rejects the suggestion that such beliefs show her as cold and without pity.

For Her Daily Bread moralizes capitalist individualism, illustrating how a woman, through personal effort, good character, and determination, can succeed in the world of business despite the burden of her sex. Norma faces sexual harassment, job and wage discrimination, and social ostracism because she is a working girl, yet she perseveres and, in the end, marries the owner's son. Sommers recognizes that some women fail, but she and her heroine agree with William Sumner's view of the human struggle: "Certain ills belong to the hardships of human life. They are natural. They are part of the struggle with Nature for existence. We cannot blame our fellow-men for our share of these." [35] The author's ambivalent treatment of sex discrimination reveals that the society was only beginning to understand that a pure Social Darwinism would logically give women, like men, an equal share of Sumner's "chances."

By the turn of the century, acceptance of the capitalist system in its broadest outlines would provide the context for the writing of the "romance of business struggle." [36] A far greater number of novels, however, continued to criticize the failures of the Gilded Age: terrible working conditions, economic panics and depressions, squalid living quarters for families in the cities, materialism, and the loss of community. Since these conditions were rooted in the political culture of individualism and personal liberty, no revolutionary change in the industrial structure was proposed. [37] Instead, the novels suggested ways in which conditions could be ameliorated, particularly through the charitable efforts of the upper classes.

The most powerful example of these "reform" novels is Phelps's *The Silent Partner.* Perley Kelso, a wealthy young woman, inherits her father's interest in a mill when her father dies. Trying to assume "whatever responsibilities rest upon me, as sole heir to my father's property," she is informed by the other partners that she may be only "a silent partner." When she asks if a silent partner has a vote, her fiancé, another partner, answers, "No, none at all. . . . If you have your husband's, that's another matter. A woman's influence, you know; you've heard of it." [38] Perley justifies her desire to participate in the management because "it is not my property . . . which I am reluctant to intrust to you" but instead it is "my people,—the people" (63–64). Forced to accept her role as the silent partner, Perley undertakes social work among the mill workers.

The Silent Partner is an impassioned outcry against conditions in the New England mills. Drawing on reports to the legislature and other factual documents, Phelps creates a stark portrait of factory life. The other heroine of the book, Sip, a factory girl, has "cotton-cough" from "sucking filling through the shuttle." Her deaf sister, Catty, is going blind from a "wool-picking" disease (81–82, 186). Through Sip, Perley meets Bub Mell, a ten-year-old boy who works in the mill despite laws setting age minimums. Later, Bub is killed by falling into the machinery of the factory, and Catty, unable to hear or see those trying to warn her away, falls from a bridge during a flood. When Perley tries to discuss the situation of the mill workers with her fiancé, Maverick, he simply ignores her.

The economic position of the book is clarified when the mill workers threaten to strike after a wage cut. Perley wants Garrick, a sympathetic manager, to explain the reduction to the people, but the workers cry out to hear the "young leddy." She justifies the wage reduction as a result of larger market forces and thus averts the strike. Judith Fetterley attacks Perley as betraying the workers because she "reinforces the mythologies through which the masters obfuscate reality and thus maintain power," but there is no reason to expect her to do otherwise. At no time in the book does Phelps suggest that the basic capitalist system should be altered.[39] She stresses the common humanity of laborers and the owners rather than class conflict, and seeks only humanitarian reforms. Her primary concern is building the reader's sympathy toward the workers as fellow creatures of God. As in Phelps's other novels, such as *The Gates Ajar* series, the underlying meaning of *The Silent Partner* is religious. The final solution, for Sip, and for Perley as she rejects Garrick, is to find love for one another through faith in Christ.

William Dean Howells's minor novel, *A Woman's Reason* (1882), also argues for amelioration and reform. On the surface, this is a version of the classic plot of women's fiction: Helen Harkness's father dies, leaving her alone and impoverished; her fiancé is shipwrecked and apparently lost at sea; Helen has to learn to manage for herself as these supports are withdrawn; in a dramatic finale the fiancé is rescued and returns, they marry, and all is well. The strength of the novel comes from the precision with which Howells traces Helen's social descent and realistically strips away the familiar assurance of domestic novels that a willing woman can support herself by her "accomplishments." The lesson is that a well-educated, middle-class young woman of the day is, "as the sum of it, merely and entirely a lady, the most charming thing in the world, and as regards anything but a lady's destiny the most helpless."[40]

Helen's attempts to be independent are continually shadowed by offers of hospitality from old friends and by her own low opinion of her abilities, an estimate confirmed when she tries such expedients as writing reviews or painting boxes to be sold on commission. Her new friend, Miss Root, an art student, tells her candidly that such "gimcracks" are only bought charitably by those who "know *you* did 'em." Even she has "never sold a thing yet" (311).

In Miss Root, Howells provides a careful contrast to Helen. Coming from a lower-class background, the art student is surviving as a single woman on money previously earned through teaching and taking boarders. She recognizes that women of the upper classes are not trained to face the economic struggle, and points out to Helen that most work for women requires preparation. Quite unsentimentally she summarizes her views on the weakness of women workers: "If a man takes a thing up, he takes it up for life, but if a woman takes it up, she takes it up till some fellow comes along and tells her to drop it. . . . I don't know whether I want to join in any cry that'll take women's minds off of gettin' married. . . . But if women are to be helped along independent of men . . . —why, it's a drawback" (316–317).[41]

After Helen is reunited with her lover, she is invited to lecture at a newly established Institute of Industrial Arts for Young Ladies, Howells's reformist solution for the problems of women like Helen. Yet his heroine, lecturing to "girls brought up as ladies" (461), gives ambiguous advice. She has previously admitted that "it would have been better for me if I had been . . . trying to help myself because I respected work. . . . But I wasn't. . . . I was merely doing it because I couldn't bear to be a burden to any one" (388). Therefore, she first echoes Miss Root's sentiments on work: "Do learn to do something that people have *need of*, and learn to do it well and humbly, and just as if you had been working for your living all your life"(461). But later she regrets not telling each girl one more thing—"Not to omit the first decent opportunity of marrying any one she happened to be in love with" (462).

A Woman's Reason is fairly early Howells. It expresses only mild and, through Captain Butler, rather bewildered criticism of an economic system in which bright and wellborn young men cannot find work. Nevertheless, the novel is unsparing in its sobering picture of women's economic liabilities. Howells saw no real possibility of a woman surviving in the world without marriage, though he was uncomfortable with his conclusion. His last comment is about Helen: "She has acquired no ideals of woman's work or woman's destiny; she is glad to have solved in the old way the problems that once beset her; and in all that has happened she feels as if she had escaped, rather than achieved" (466). Years later, after the Haymarket riot and his immersion in Tolstoy, Howells became an outspoken socialist critic of the economic system. *A Woman's Reason*, however, accepts capitalism while conceding that few women can survive in its competitive environment.

Work is a very early example of the third group of novels, those which outline a different economic and social structure for society. Agrarian and cooperative, Alcott's model is identified with the domestic economy of the family. The financial arrangements of her communal utopia are characterized as inherently female. When Christie visits the elderly uncle on whose farm she grew up, he inquires about her monetary situation. Learning that she gives two-thirds of what she makes to Rachel and Mrs. Sterling, Uncle Enos objects: this is not a "fair bargain." She replies, "Ah, but we don't make bargains, sir: we work for one another and share everything together" (419). His response suggests Alcott's view: "So like women!"[42]

During the 1880s, a number of solutions to the problems of capitalism were proposed, including Henry George's single tax and the cooperative societies popularized by Laurence Gronlund.[43] One such reform of industrial organization is propounded in *Troubled Waters* (1885), a novel written by Beverley Ellison Warner. The story is set in a New England mill town dominated by several woolen factories. The workers in one factory, owned by a particularly cold and cruel man, express numerous dissatisfactions with the system. As one skilled workman puts it, "Why, we fools of workingmen first create wealth, then we hand it over to people we call capitalists, who deal out to us just enough to keep us from starving, while we keep adding to their pile."[44] Wilton, the employer, uses the language of laissez-faire when he defends firing senior employees: "I go on supply and demand, y'know, I do; an' when one o' my men's workin' for a dollar 'n a half, while half a dozen other fellers are hungry for the job at a dollar, why I'm losin' money an' p'litical 'conomy's sufferin'" (46). He is so despised by his workers that when three of them set his house on fire, the crowd that gathers cheers at the blaze.

Warner's portrait of the mill town underscores the threat of violence and disharmony that results from a confrontational relationship between owners and workers. The conflict destroys the character of good men, the morality of young women, and the harmony of families. The consequences of the economic system are demonstrated by the misfortunes of the Crofts. The father, a skilled foreman, is laid off because the owner can hire cheaper labor. Mrs. Croft upbraids her husband: "who'd have thought you'd 'a been only a machine-shop foreman after twenty years . . . ?" But the question she continues with, "And whose fault is it, I'd like to know?" (23) suggests an indictment of the economic system that allows Croft to be abused and underpaid. This system destroys working and nonworking women: the Crofts' daughter, Nellie, is corrupted by work in the factory, and Mrs. Croft is embittered by her husband's failure.

Warner believes the impetus for change is likely to come from outside the system. His preferred scheme, cooperation or profit sharing, is proposed by a wealthy young woman, Sydney Worthington, who offers to fund a new mill to be run on the cooperative principle in which all workers are part owners of the company. Sydney's idealism is symbolized by her romantic attraction to Rev. Winchester, a sensitive and intellectual cleric who devotes his time to the poor; Winchester challenges her to engage in philanthropy much as Rev. Powers does for Christie in *Work*. These two sets of parallel characters, Sydney and Rev. Winchester in *Troubled Waters*, and Christie and Rev. Powers in *Work*, are classic illustrations of the alliance between women and ministers that Ann Douglas described in her study of American culture.[45] In both novels, the pairs symbolize a "feminine" view of the social order, one that, in Douglas's view, was subordinate to the dominant male culture of the day. In fact, implementation of Sydney's plan is carried out by two virile male characters, Sydney's brother and a crusty newspaper editor who describes the workings of cooperative ventures and cites empirical evidence from England that they are successful.

By the end of the novel, two mills are operating on the new principle with economic and social success. Through the cooperative principle, "the element of hope . . . transferred the Tradelawn help into men and women, from having been dulled, embittered, and helpless slaves" (318). Although Warner admits to "a trinity of problems. . . . The problem of labor, the problem of poverty, the problem of wealth" (323), he eschews revolutionary change; he ends the book by calling for a return to the old spirit of the American gentry, for capitalists to acknowledge the "stewardship" of their wealth, to understand noblesse oblige, and to see that "the profit of the earth is for all" (325).

In the most famous of American utopian novels, *Looking Backward* (1888), Edward Bellamy lays out a plan for a democratic state socialism. All production would be controlled by the state. All men would be part of the great "industrial army" for twenty-four years, retiring at age forty-four. All individuals within the society would have an annual "credit" with the state for goods and services, and the American need for personal liberty would be satisfied by allowing persons to spend their credits as they desire. Bellamy attacks the idea that men need to have competition for material goods and substitutes honors and status. He is at his most radical when his spokesman, Dr. Leete, explains the rationale for equal credit for every man: "His title, . . . is his humanity. The basis of his claim is the fact that he is a man." [46] This statement, which does not depend on Marxist assumptions about materialism, found favor in American eyes because of its ethical basis.

A rare exception among the authors of economic novels, Bellamy directly addresses the dependency of women. He sees the marriages of the nineteenth century as, at best, humiliating to women and, at worst, as subjecting them to a form of serfdom. In the world of 2000, women are freed from the need to marry by their equal share of credit with the state, but Bellamy justifies giving them a life that is "separate but equal" because of their biological role. They are employed, but at different jobs, do lighter work, are assured more frequent rest, and take longer vacations than men. They work because Bellamy believes that "a regular requirement of labor, of a sort adapted to their powers, is well for body and mind" (263). Ultimately, his interest in women is instrumental. By choosing mates who have attained honors and status, women will improve the species, and competition for women will add "zest" to men's lives. Thus Bellamy frees women from economic dependence, but the primacy of their sexual and reproductive functions keeps them circumscribed.

One final novel arguing against the capitalist system, Mary Wilkins Freeman's *The Portion of Labor* (1901), in modern criticism is usually attacked as ultraconservative. Typical comments are Edward Foster's summary— "Calvinistic determinism is linked with economic conservatism and decorated with a touch of self-righteousness"—and Perry D. Westbrook's "Miss Wilkins had not one suggestion in regard to the betterment of the system. . . . Her book is . . . infused with a Calvinistic fatalism that would be enraging to a reformer."[47] The entire novel has been read backward through its conclusion, with the failure of the strike and the heroine's marriage taken as the author's ideals rather than as her concessions. Yet examined sympathetically, this novel is one of the most politically engaged of the period, despite its failure to provide solutions to the economic problems it describes. An anonymous contemporary reviewer praises the tale as "a drama of the people" and finds "Mrs. Wilkins Freeman's imaginative power . . . strikingly demonstrated . . . in the noble play of sympathy and creative insight which takes this portion of the working-man's life, and lifts it from out the commonplace view on to a plane of understanding and nobility."[48] Yet it is even more striking that Freeman takes as her central figure a working woman and integrates her completely into an economic vision.

The chief radical voice in *The Portion of Labor* is that of the heroine, Ellen Brewster. Daughter of a factory worker, Ellen is chosen valedictorian of her high school class. The beautiful and charming young woman rises and addresses her parents and classmates on "Equality." She does not talk about the American founding but about the distribution of wealth between capital and labor. Her essay "flung all castes into a common heap of equality. . . . She forced the employer and his employé to one bench of service in the grand system of things; she gave the laborer, and the laborer only, the reward of labor." Risley, a wealthy lawyer, recognizes the import of Ellen's speech: "She may have a bomb somewhere concealed among those ribbons and frills."[49] And indeed, later Ellen leads out an entire factory full of workers, men and women, whom she has persuaded not to accept a wage cut just because times are hard. She reminds them that "it is the great capitalists who have made them hard by shifting the wealth too much to one side. They are the ones who should suffer, not you" (477).

Ellen is courted by Robert Lloyd, nephew of the factory owner, and much of the tension of the novel occurs when he and Ellen argue about the fairness of the system. Incredulously Robert asks whether she really believes that "all the property in the world ought to be divided, that kings and peasants ought to share and share alike?" Equally amazed that anyone could doubt, Ellen replies, "Why, of course I do! . . . Don't you?" She is persuaded that "the men earn the money," and when Robert reminds her that "there is the capital," she flashes back that "the profit comes from the labor, not from the capital" (211–212). Through Ellen's rhetoric, through the speeches of a local radical, and through the plot of the novel, Freeman emphasizes the injustice of the system. Men are turned out when they get older; young girls fall ill due to hard work; factory girls lose class status; workers who protest, like Ellen, are blacklisted. Even though this is a small community where the owner knows all of the workers personally, he lives in remote luxury.

Freeman also examines the way in which women's entrance into the marketplace can backfire on the workers. When there is "a demand for girls and not for men," Ellen's aunt must work in the factory after her husband is fired. She tries to protect his ego, refusing to let him do housework because "it ain't a man's work," but nevertheless Jim "took his wife's earnings and despised himself" (171–172). It is not long before he takes off with another woman, and Eva understands the castrating effect of the role reversal: "He lost his good opinion of himself. . . . He began to think maybe he wa'n't a man. . . . And he was ashamed of his life because he couldn't support me and Amabel, ashamed of his life because he had to live on my little earnin's" (285). By 1901 Freeman thus suggests that it is the free play of capitalism rather than feminism which has changed woman's economic position in the family, even though the resulting anxieties are played out on the psychological and social levels.

Freeman recognizes that the movement for reform may be contaminated by extremism. Ellen's views on the relationship between capital and labor are affected by the radical thinkers among the workmen who gather at her home. The wildest among them, Nahum Beal, who speaks "with a strange abandon of self-consciousness and a fiery impetus for one of his New England blood," foresees a time when his colleagues will "all thank God that you belong to the poor and down-trodden of this earth, and not to the rich and great. . . . The hand that marks the time of day on the clock of men's patience with wrong and oppression has near gone round to the same hour and minute" (100). Beal is not quite sane and later assassinates the mill owner. Yet Freeman is careful not to picture this radical as a foreigner or as an outside provocateur; Beal is an American, a native of the town, who symbolizes the explosive anger of the laboring people.

It is true that Freeman finally backs away from any revolutionary proposition. She lays out the debate in Marxist terms, attacks capitalism for its worst failings, and shows the effects of the industrial system on the family, but ultimately she bows to the status quo. Critics who believe the novel to be a conservative manifesto always point to the religious resignation of Ellen's father. Andrew Brewster, a man of "judicial mind," represents the native American laborer who is unpersuaded by revolutionary schemes. And Ellen, though a powerful figure deeply aware of the injustice of the capitalist system, does marry her employer. Writing after the panic of 1893, the Pullman strike of 1894, and the jailing of Eugene V. Debs, Freeman's conclusion mirrors the political climate of the day. The 1896 election saw the realignment of the political parties in the United States, with the working classes of the Northeast rejecting Populist and Democratic platforms to vote with the Republican industrialists. The cleavages in the country after this event were between the poorer agricultural sections of the West and South and the industrial Northeast, where owners and workers saw a common interest.[50] Ellen's marriage to the mill owner symbolizes this union of worker and employer. Freeman's acquiescence should not, however, obscure the power of her attack on the system in *The Portion of Labor*.

Howells and Phelps on Work and Sisterhood

Into the many-faceted debate regarding the impact of capitalism on American society was injected the debate over women as wage workers. Late nineteenth-century American novels repeatedly address one fundamental question: Do women lose their essential feminine character when they engage in wage labor? Three forms of the question recur. Do working women lose their sisterhood and common ideals with women who are exempt from waged work? Will the exposure of a woman's body at work have sexual consequences? And finally, can a working woman identify with other workers when they are male?

The Silent Partner and *A Woman's Reason*, both told from the point of view of an upper-class heroine, take differing positions on what Christie, in Alcott's *Work*, called interpreting "between the two classes" (430). Though one is essentially a story of uplift and the other the reverse, each examines the relations possible between "working" women in a class-based society. Phelps, like Grace Dodge, founder of working girls' clubs, believes that working girls include those who "have received their wages in advance, that is, money, responsibility have come to them through birth, inheritance and surroundings" and that when such women "work out their wages in loving, hearty, faithful services . . . Mutual admiration and love bring about cooperation, which naturally leads to a sisterhood among women, made up from all branches of work and responsibility."[51] Howells is not so sanguine about the natural sisterhood of women.

In *The Silent Partner*, the potential similarity between women of disparate classes is immediately suggested on the rainy night when Perley first talks to Sip. Although she is herself on the way to the opera, she criticizes the unknown working girl for going to the theater rather than home. When *Don Giovanni* is over, Sip, who has followed Perley, stops her to ask, "I want to know why you tell *me* the Plum is no place for *me*? What kind of place is this for you? . . . I tell you it's the plating over that's the difference;

the plating over"(29–30). The pointed parallel between the two women here extends an earlier hint that they share a bond in limited freedom of choice. Perley notes how many working girls are out alone in the rain and innocently comments on "how little difference the weather appeared to make with that class of people." But when Sip tells her, "*You*'re not cold and wet, at any rate," Perley can think of no answer except "I cannot help that" (22). Most of the book explores the limits on what either Perley or Sip "can help."

Neither Sip nor Perley is able to change her situation much. Perley cannot get into the mill because of her male partners, so she holds evening socials for the workers, sends children to the seaside, joins the workers' church, and visits with Sip. Sip cannot get out of the mill, though Perley attempts to rescue her. As Sip says after she fails at several other jobs, "I told you it was no use. . . . It's too late. . . . I knew I should come back. My father and mother came back before me. It's in the blood" (199–200). Nevertheless, both women gain power: they learn to talk. Perley uses her voice when she speaks to the potential strikers. Once Perley has "blazed out" (251), the threat dissipates. Despite the opposition of the active partners to Perley's "work," it is the silent partner who can be heard. As so often for women, power is expressed as public discourse.

Sip also learns to talk: she becomes a preacher. Symbolically, she takes no credit for her new voice, explaining that she began to talk because her retarded, deaf-mute sister, who has drowned, "had such things to say! . . . *God had things to say.* I'd been talking Catty's words. *God had words.* I cannot tell you how it was; but I stood right up and said them; and ever since there's been more than I could say" (292). As Perley becomes a voice reaching out from the owners, Sip becomes the voice of the silenced masses.[52]

No bond in *The Silent Partner* is stronger than the bond of sisterhood, and the relationship of Perley and Sip is measured against Sip's feelings for Catty. Everything that Sip does for Catty, whose unpleasantness and bad habits Phelps does not sentimentalize, is done "for love's sake." Indeed, Sip first yields to Perley when she uses the same expression. Later, Sip's worst moment comes when an oculist tells her that Catty will go blind. When Perley asks if she can do anything Sip replies, " 'Do you suppose . . . that you could—kiss me?' Perley sat down . . . and held out her beautiful arms. Sip crept in like a baby, and there she began to cry" (190).

Phelps believes that the shared experience of work and love, rather than class origin, is the ground of sisterhood.[53] At her evening *réunion* for workers Perley shocks Mrs. Silver and Miss Van Doozle by playing Beethoven, which they are sure "the people can*not* appreciate" but which "could not have asked a stiller hearing" (229). These evenings are Perley's versions of the working girls' clubs, based like Dodge's on "democratic principles."[54] Perley's relationship to the workers is measured against the growing distance with which other women of her own social circle regard her. Mrs. Silver proclaims that Perley is "dead and buried . . . as far as Society is concerned" (236), and her daughter Fly shows how far she is from her old friend by choosing the life Perley has rejected and marrying the man Perley has refused.

The contrast at the end of *The Silent Partner* is between idleness and dependence on males, and work and bonding with women. It is not surprising that in an essentially positive review, which calls *The Silent Partner* "the best, though perhaps it will not be the most popular, of Miss Phelps's novels," *Harper's New Monthly Magazine* complains that "the book is defective . . . for not coming to any natural end. It ravels out, and leaves a ragged and unfinished edge." [55] That is, in open defiance of the conventional conclusion of romantic fiction, having acquired sisterhood, Sip and Perley choose independence over dependence, work over marriage. *The Silent Partner* admits that married women do work—Sip's mother gave birth on a Tuesday, returned to the mill on Thursday, and died on Saturday—but the novel's plot adheres to the division between marriage and work in order to argue for the empowerment of work. Though it pains Sip to tell her admirer that "I'll never marry anybody, Dirk. . . . I'll never bring children into this world to be factory children . . . and to grow up as I've grown up," once she has rejected marriage she finds "her work" in preaching and becomes "a very happy woman" (287, 291–293). [56]

Similarly, Perley, who has broken with Maverick because he cannot understand her attitude toward the mill, also refuses Garrick, a suitor who shares her values. "I have no time to think of love and marriage. . . . That is a business, a trade, by itself to women. I have too much else to do" (260). Phelps reemphasizes the connections between marriage and silence, work and voice, when she has Perley continue, "I believe I have been a silent partner long enough. If I married you, sir, I should invest in life, and you would conduct it. I suspect that I have a preference for a business of my own" (262). [57] This business requires her to bond with women rather than men, and her most important bond is with her sisters in the working class.

A decade later William Dean Howells, in *A Woman's Reason*, disputes Phelps's idealistic picture of relations between women. For Howells, sisterhood is not strong enough to bridge class divisions and economic disparity. When his heroine is at her lowest point, she has lost the sympathy of her wealthy friends and is unable to gain true acceptance by any other group of women. Just as Howells cannot imagine economic self-sufficiency for women, he seems resigned that the class differences among them are almost impenetrable.

Howells traces the limitations of sisterhood and the incomprehension between classes first through the relationship of Helen Harkness and her friend Marian Butler. Marian is oblivious of the depth of Helen's financial exigencies: for instance, she sends Helen a gift on which she can hardly pay the duties. And when Marian does think about assisting Helen, she is moved more by her own embarrassment than by sympathy: learning that Helen has been reduced to making servants' bonnets, Marian says indignantly, "I think that you might have had some little consideration for us—for all your friends, if you had none for yourself" (390). Unimpressed by Helen's efforts at self-support, Marian can imagine only one way out of Helen's situation: she introduces her to an eligible Englishman and cannot see why Helen refuses his proposal. Yet accepting aid from the Butlers and "marrying for a home" are both forms of the dependency that Helen wants to avoid.

Howells sees class distinctions as deep and permanent. Helen's most practical help comes from Cornelia Root. But Miss Root does not treat Helen as a sister, because she cannot forget—or forgive—Helen's origins. She disciplines herself "into accepting Helen as worthy her esteem and regard, in spite of her beauty, her style, and her air of a finer world," but clever Mr. Evans points out that she does "hate her just a little . . . for her superiority to us all—which she can't conceal" (312–314). Miss Root harbors her own sense of class superiority. When Helen offers to drape a dress and mentions having done so for her cook, Miss Root has "to discipline with uncommon severity the proud spirit that revolted at having the same hands drape its corporeal covering which had draped the person of an Irish cook" (321).

Thus class categories extend all the way down the social ladder. The narrative voice refers to the servants who buy hats from Helen as "simple, stupid things" with "mistaken tastes" (373), an appraisal quite unlike Perley's view that working girls are sensitive to high culture. Helen herself tells Marian that her clients are "as full of prejudice and exclusiveness as any one. I've never seen distinctions in society so awful as the distinction between shop-girls and parlour-girls" (389). She develops no sisterhood with her customers, though she has no more money than they.

To survive as a milliner Helen moves in with her former servant, Margaret. It is in the relationship of Helen and proud Margaret—the Irish cook whom Miss Root despises—that Howells is most original. After Helen's father's death, Margaret cares for the Harkness house and grandly announces, when the time comes to pay her, that "I should wish to consider Miss Helen my guest for the past two weeks" (89). Now Helen comes to Margaret's house and insists on being a boarder, not a guest. Helen has no theories about equality, but she struggles to make Margaret understand that there is no difference between them any longer.

Yet this is not quite true. Unlike the relationship of Sip and Perley, the relationship between Margaret and Helen is governed by their dependence on men. Margaret is now married, and it is her new husband who rules. When he tells Margaret that he wants to be "master in his own house . . . he was going to turn that girl and her bonnets into the street," Helen and Margaret "could not look at each other" (447), for their friendship is powerless before him. Even when the husband is fortuitously killed in an accident, the women do not become more independent or set up a *Work*-like commune. As Margaret "could not live upon the little sum that Helen paid her for board" she is forced "to break up her little establishment and find a servant's place" (448). Just at this point Helen regains masculine support when her presumably drowned lover, Fenton, reappears.

Howells can envision loyalty and devotion between the classes, but not sisterhood. Though Helen lives with Margaret, Margaret continues to pour her tea. And in the arrangements of Margaret's home, "There were no evidences of the better taste to which she had been accustomed half her days." Instead of Beethoven, "she had an infant Jesus in wax under a glass bell" (369). Yet Helen and Margaret, starting from such different points, are women with similar work histories. Margaret works until she meets her husband aboard ship returning from Ireland; then she stays home until she loses his support through death. Helen, having apparently lost male support through death, works until she, too, marries a man returning from a voyage. Where Sip and Perley, despite their different class backgrounds, both choose work over marriage, when they can Helen and Margaret both choose marriage over work.

The class boundaries are maintained: it is part of the happy ending that once Helen and Fenton are married, "Margaret came to live with them. . . . It was something that Miss Helen kept no other girl; and it was everything that she could be with her when Lieutenant Fenton should be ordered away to sea again" (457). Any hint of equality between the women is swept away as Helen gives up work for marriage, and Margaret, widowed, returns to work.

At the end of *Work*, Christie's actions as a "mediator" between the classes of ladies and working women are left vague. Sisterhood was a splendid ideal, but as the lives of working women diverged from those of middleclass women in the home, it took someone like Phelps to suggest that work might be more important than marriage, that relations between women might be as important as relations between women and men. Howells, a more conventional male expositor of American values, gives his heroine a lover rescued from a desert island and never imagines that she loses anything in the exchange.

Work and the Body

The story of a young girl seduced and abandoned by a rakish young man, often of a higher social class, formed the plot of the first American bestseller, *Charlotte Temple* (1791), and countless other volumes. There are variations, but usually the young girl becomes pregnant, she—and often the baby—dies, and the young man is left alive but remorseful. Although there are rhetorical nods to the wickedness of seducers, most novels assume that a woman bears the responsibility for resisting temptation.[58] If she does, like Pamela, she may ultimately receive the greatest of all rewards—an offer of formal marriage.

Late nineteenth-century novels about work, like *Work* itself, use variations on the seduced-and-abandoned plot to buttress their larger positions about women in the work force. Two factors, one practical, one ideological, account for the connection. First, where Charlotte Temple had to sneak out of her boarding school to meet her lover, by the end of the Civil War women worked alongside men. Therefore, the work situation might itself be held responsible for a young girl's fall, especially if the author wished to condemn industrial conditions. In contrast, Social Darwinism, with its talk of the survival of the fittest, implied that strong individuals would overcome even the most oppressive conditions. On this theory, a young girl who did not resist temptation demonstrated her own, rather than the workplace's, corruption. Such belief offered support to laissez-faire capitalism, which could then ignore sexual danger along with the other difficulties contractual workers faced.

M. L. Rayne, author of *What Can a Woman Do, or Her Position in the Business and Literary World*,[59] wrote a novel revealing American uncertainty about who to blame for seduction in the workplace. In *Against Fate* (1877), three young girls come to Chicago to earn money; their histories, as workers and sexual beings, inscribe three different theories of responsibility.

Jennie leaves her Bible at home; she becomes a servant in a wealthy home where she is easily seduced, and later abandoned, by a rich young gentleman. Jennie's fall is largely due to her own weakness, abetted by man's evil. On the other hand, the temptations that come to Eva, working in a store, result from her work situation. For one thing, because she models clothes all day, her work reduces her to pure body. For another, it is the boss who attempts to seduce her. Only the sisterly intervention of Margaret Holmes, one of his previous conquests, saves her. In a predictable conclusion, both the fallen women, Margaret and Jennie, repent and die.

Meanwhile, Lucia, the third young girl, easily resists the city's temptations. The contrast Rayne draws between Lucia and Jennie seems influenced by the distinction between the fit and the unfit, and Lucia herself delivers a Social Darwinist speech urging Eva to have no pity for fallen women but to follow her own method in school, where she will expel a "depraved" child "and so prevent its hurting twenty good children."[60] Later Lucia and Eva debate the sources of Jennie's fall. Lucia is sure that "a girl with a high purpose in life and a mind above pleasures and amusements, will never come to any harm." Eva instead thinks that Jennie needed "friends to protect her" and blames "that man!" (152–153). Rayne's novel thus never settles on man's wickedness, unfit female character, or exposed work situations as the cause of woman's sin.

Though stores and offices could be dangerous, it was the easy camaraderie of the mills and factories that most alarmed society.[61] Phelps summarizes the combined dangers of a man's overtures, a woman's weakness, and the opportunities offered by work when she has Sip send Nynee Mell home from an assignation with her fellow worker Jim. Jim is "a miserable Irishman" who has been in town "long enough to show his colors, and a devilish black mustache." Sip explains to Perley: "You see, they put him to work next to Nynee; he must go somewhere; they put him where the work was; they didn't bother their heads about the girl; they're never bothered with such things. And there ain't much room in the alley. So she spends the day with him, pushing in and out. So she gets used to him and all that. She's a good girl, Nynee Mell; wildish . . . but a good girl. She'll go to the devil, sure as death, at this rate" (123). The language is openly suggestive of the sexual interplay between workers. Though Jim is wicked and Nynee weak, Phelps plainly blames the conditions of work for the downfall of girls like Nynee.

Such an analysis ran counter to the prevailing cultural view that held women responsible for their own purity. *Troubled Waters* demonstrates how much difficulty Americans had in maintaining any other position. Warner uses the seduced-and-abandoned plot in an explicitly industrial context. Ellen Croft is easily led astray by bad companions, partly because the workers themselves internalize the division between domesticity and work. "Mill life, even for mill-girls, has its ideal and romantic side. A certain class, of which 'Nellie' and her friends are the type, never look upon the humdrum daily work as a profession which they are to learn thoroughly, and by which they are to earn their livelihood. . . . Mill-work is only an occupation by the way. . . . Matrimony they are taught, and not work, is the true heritage of women" (26–27).[62]

Responsibility for Ellen's fall lies not simply in her exposure to men on the job, but in the broader ramifications of the factory system. Ellen is driven to spend nights walking "the street with a pair like herself, flirting boldly and brazenly with men" (28), because of the "bitter or spiteful" words her mother gives her at home. These, too, are caused by the inequities of competitive capitalism. Mrs. Croft's bitter temper is created by industrial injustice and represents the simmering resentment of the working class. Thus Ellen's fall symbolizes the damaging effects of factory life on family and purity.

Yet Warner soon retreats to a more conventional, mother-blaming position. The lack of a warm and loving home, rather than conditions impinging on that home, becomes the causal factor in Ellen's destruction. The narrative voice asks:

Was this Nellie altogether to blame? Answer me, wife of Robert Croft.
. . . Has your daughter no excuse for meeting men on the street. . . .
Did you not cause it? . . . You, with your . . . sinking down under the
very circumstances that should have spurred you rather to hold up the
hands of a husband and throw protecting arms about the form of a
daughter. You, with your sullenness and bitter tongue. Your daughter
walks the street to get beyond your reach. . . . Whose fault is it . . . that
your daughter has no companion in her own home? (148–149)

In this passage Warner invokes the middle-class model of the home as a
haven. He calls for women to protect daughters and husbands against the
"circumstances" of industrial life, rather than calling for change in those
"circumstances." Presumably, if mothers provide that "single spot of rest"
in an industrial world, girls like Ellen will stay pure. The model girl of the
novel, Margaret Lane, who does stay at home with her mother despite poverty, easily rejects tempting offers of riches and marriage from Richard
Wilton. She is eventually rewarded with a proper lover and ownership of the
mill.

Ellen elopes; the results are inevitable. Found abandoned by the minister,
she returns to her repentent mother. And of course she must die: "It seemed
to them like a dream, for the little baby died in the first week of its life. . . .
Ellen Croft died the other day in a yellow fever hospital . . . with the blood-
red emblem of the Geneva Cross upon her simple dress,—over a heart that
had beaten in sympathy with many sorrows, the more tenderly perhaps for
the buried sorrow of her own young life" (249). By the end Warner has
separated economic causes from women's failings: he appears to approve
Robert Croft's angry charge that Mrs. Croft, for lack of a "single mother's
instinct . . . gave [Ellen] over to this shame" (189). Mrs. Croft repents, but
her change comes entirely from realizing her earlier faults, not from the
good effects of the cooperative system.

Ellen Croft's story recalls Rachel's, in *Work*. Both girls find work weary-
ing and yield to love and gaity. Both girls repent and do good works. Both
are welcomed back, eventually, to their families. Each novel ends with a
vision of a cooperative workplace, though without clarifying whether the
resolution of larger economic issues will cause the sexual dangers to women
to disappear. But only Alcott, of all of these authors, lets her fallen woman
live. Throughout the other novels it is clear that no matter what the cause of
a woman's fall, it is irrevocable. A woman's purity remains her prime responsibility; wage work does not change that.

Freeman and Worker Solidarity

The Portion of Labor is a powerful portrait of woman as worker. Much
of the novel's strength comes from Freeman's ability to intertwine her her-

oine's emotional and sexual awakening with her political solidarity with her fellow workers. The greatest conflict Ellen Brewster faces is between her allegiance to abstract principles of equality and justice for her class, and her personal feelings as a woman. The book appears to end like *For Her Daily Bread*, with marriage between the beautiful worker and the boss, but Freeman modifies the romantic convention. Robert Lloyd is not simply a Prince Charming rescuing Ellen from the need to work, but a man who will, even in marriage, continue to challenge her attachment to her class.

Ellen goes to work in the factory when her family's circumstances overwhelm them. A wealthy woman, Lloyd's aunt Cynthia Lennox, had offered to send the young valedictorian to Vassar, but when Ellen's father loses his job and her Aunt Eva suffers a breakdown, Ellen feels she must sacrifice her education. As she enters the factory she identifies herself entirely as a worker:

> Suddenly it seemed to her that the greatest thing in the whole world was work. . . . She realized all at once and forever the dignity of labor, this girl of the people, with a brain which enabled her to overlook the heads of the rank and file of which she herself formed a part. . . . She never again felt that she was too good for her labor, for labor had revealed itself to her like a goddess behind a sordid veil.(350)

In the factory Ellen becomes, as Cynthia's friend Risley had predicted, "a good female soldier in the ranks of labor." Risley is opposed to sending Ellen to Vassar because, he half-teasingly says, she should remain "in her sphere of life, the daughter of a factory operative, in all probability in after-years to be the wife of one and the mother of others" (165). Ellen, too, accepts that by going to work in the Lloyd factory she has determined her social class permanently. When Robert ignores her in the factory she assumes that she has put herself out of his life. "Still . . . she realized no degradation of herself as a cause of it. She realized that from his point of view she had gone into a valley, but from hers she was rather on an opposite height . . . . the height of labor" (357).

Ellen, however, is a woman as well as a worker, a woman whose sexual awakening Freeman has delicately traced from early childhood on. Her first kiss, from her childhood sweetheart Granville Joy, is described as part of midsummer "growth and bloom . . . the revolutions of those unseen wheels of nature" (161–162). Ellen also has deep attachments to women, which Freeman depicts as a natural part of the girl's sexual development. It is easy for Ellen to squelch a rumor that she will marry Granville by telling her friend Abby, "I think more of you than any man I know" (229). Similarly, when Cynthia Lennox appears, Ellen falls under the "old fascination," going back to the time when she ran away from home and Cynthia, deeply lonely for a child, detained her. Josephine Donovan considers Ellen's

infatuation with Cynthia of a "lesbian nature," but Risley, Cynthia's admirer, understands Ellen's feelings better: Ellen, he tells Cynthia, worships
her, "as a nymph might a goddess. . . . It is one of the spring madnesses of
life, but don't be alarmed, it will be temporary. . . . She will easily be led into
her natural track of love. . . . She is one of the most normal, typical young
girls I ever saw" (270–271).[63]

In fact, on the very night when Ellen, visiting, is disappointed not to find
Cynthia alone after she had "dreamed, as a lover might have done, of a tête-
à-tête with her. . . . She had thought . . . that possibly Cynthia might kiss her"
(268)—the passage that persuades Donovan of Ellen's lesbian feelings—
Cynthia's nephew Robert walks Ellen home, and she realizes "that he had
not left her, that he would never in her whole life. . . . She fought against the
feeling of utter rapture. . . . But the girl could no more escape than a nymph
of old the pursuit of the god" (281).

Ellen's love for Robert, who inherits his uncle's factory after Nahum Beal
kills the older man, forces her to confront her conflicting loyalties to class
and lover. Since their first meetings, when Robert was surprised at her militant rhetoric, they have recognized their differences, but Robert originally
has "no mind to enter into an argument with this beautiful girl" (211).
When she goes into the mill Robert wants to "lift [her] out of this forever,"
but she insists that "there is nothing for me to be lifted out of. . . . You speak
as if I were in a pit. I am on a height" (390).

Ellen's choices become harder when conditions worsen and Robert
lowers wages. Her first allegiance is to the laboring class. Like the other
women in the factory, she begins by asking, "What do you think the men
will do?" (473). But when the men seem resigned to the wage cut, Ellen
urges them to strike in a speech at an impromptu mass meeting: "If you men
will do nothing, and say nothing, it is time for a girl to say and act." And she
concludes, "If I were a man . . . I would go out in the street and dig—I
would beg, I would steal—before I would yield—I, a free man in a free
country—to tyranny like this!" As she speaks, "she was freedom and youth
incarnate, and rebellious against all which she conceived as wrong and tyrannical. . . . All the griefs of her short life . . . were directly traceable to the
wrongs of the system of labor and capital" (477–479). Though the men are
intimidated by Robert's adamancy, she exhorts them to think only about
"whether we are doing right or not, whether we are furthering the cause of
justice and humanity. . . . There have always been martyrs" (485).[64]

Critics who condemn *The Portion of Labor* usually base their attitudes
on dislike of Ellen Brewster. Foster, who calls the novel "Miss Wilkins' most
ambitious and least successful," finds the heroine "tedious"; Westbrook,
who praises the "verisimilitude . . . [of] the drab, gray manufacturing town,"
calls Ellen a "virago" and a "grotesque."[65] Similarly, in the 1880s, at the
time of the carpet weavers' strike, "unsympathetic local newspapers . . .

commonly referred to trade union women as 'amazons.'"[66] Clearly both critics and contemporaries are offended by such strength—and speech—from young women. Yet Ellen Brewster is neither a virago nor an amazon: she is a Marianne, a natural leader of the masses, and feminine values are the ones she ultimately elects.

Ellen's final choices are made emotionally, as a woman. After a terrible winter—in which Ellen, blacklisted as an agitator, is reduced to sewing by the piece with her mother—Abby comes and tells her they must give in. She lists domestic disasters: her family has no food, her sister is threatened with tuberculosis, one woman has taken laudanum, and another "has gone to the bad." Abby, like Phelps, believes that moral failure may come from industrial conditions: "She didn't have enough to pay for her board, and got desperate. . . . It's all on account of the strike" (515–516).

Again Ellen speaks, this time to a group composed only of men, and she expresses a specifically female concern for personal suffering: "I think I did wrong. . . . I did not count the cost. All I thought of was the principle, but the cost is a part of the principle. . . . [The strike] has brought about too much suffering upon those who were not responsible for it, who did not choose it of their free will" (516). The next morning, as the group of workers approaching the factory is threatened by union men, "She was in the very front of the little returning army. She saw the threatening faces of the pickets; she half turned, and waved an arm of encouragement, like a general in a battle. 'Strike if you want to,' she cried out. . . .'If you want to kill a girl for going back to save herself and her friends from starvation, do it. I am not afraid!'" (526–527).

It is as a woman that Ellen also eventually yields to Robert. Freeman describes their love as a natural force greater than either of them: early in the relationship Robert speaks to her with that "masculine insistence which is a true note of nature, and means the subjugation of the feminine into harmony," and "every line in her body betrayed helpless yielding" (388). But Robert is unable to comprehend the depth of Ellen's dedication to her work and her fellows. Freeman emphasizes the conflict between woman as worker and as sexual object by switching from Ellen's to Robert's point of view. Looking into the factory, he can see her only as his future wife. "It seemed to him he could not bear it one instant longer to have her working in this fashion. . . . That the cut in wages affected her relation to him never occurred to him" (474). He is incredulous when he learns that it is she who has led the workers out.

He goes at once to find her, and Ellen receives him in a symbolically frigid parlor where she assures him that she prefers "no one before my own, before all these poor people who are part of my life" (494). Though "it was all he could do to keep himself from seizing her in his arms," she insists that "the matter at hand . . . is too close to my heart for any personal consideration to come between" (496). This is the choice of her intellectual conviction, but she suffers for it. When the strike ends and Robert remains away, she looks in the mirror and sees in her eyes "the eternal, unanswerable question of humanity, 'where is my happiness?'" (549).

The last scene takes place in springtime, in a public park. The atmosphere is one of rebirth; even "the birches stood together in leaning, white-limbed groups like maidens" (555), and Roman candles and fireworks go off. Every eligible woman named in the novel, from Cynthia to Abby, is rapidly paired off. Ellen, "with the sight of the happiness of these others before her eyes," feels crushed. "She was only a young girl, who would fall to the ground and be slain by the awful law of gravitation of the spirit without love" (560). At this point Robert appears, explaining that he knew she would not yield until he had put the wages back on the old basis. Yet Ellen's Cinderella romance has its limitations: she will marry her prince, but "never as long as he lived would he be able to look at such matters from quite the same standpoint as that of the girl beside him. She knew that, and yet she loved him. She never would get his point of view, and yet he loved her" (561). Edward Taylor praises this "reunion of Robert and Ellen, following their bitter struggle . . . [as] one of the most finely imagined passages in the economic novel."[67]

In *The Portion of Labor*, Freeman develops all dimensions of a woman worker in the context of capitalism. There is extensive sisterhood in this novel: between Ellen's mother Fanny and her sister Eva; between Ellen, an only child, and her friends Maria and Abby, sisters themselves; and in an intuitive way that cuts across classes, between Fanny and Cynthia Lennox, who understands what Fanny must have suffered when her child was missing. Ellen herself is the clearest representative of the potential class flexibility of a woman worker. At the same time, she is a physical being, set against a backdrop of realistic sexual interplay in the mill. Finally, she, more than any other woman in these novels, experiences and articulates her solidarity with all other workers, male as well as female. In the end, however, the biological imperative wins out, and Freeman backs away from her depiction of oppression in the capitalist system. By 1901 no other choice seemed possible to most Americans.

Collectively these novels, written over a period of thirty years, express the cultural conviction that a woman did not lose her gender through work. Indeed, she could not lose it. Conservative or progressive, the novelists all emphasize the ways in which a woman worker can, at almost any moment, be reduced to her body. Some writers construct this as romance, others as sexual harassment in the workplace or, at worst, as seduction. But Americans found no way to think of women workers as members of a sexually undifferentiated labor force.

Insistence on the sexuality of the woman worker affected the answers to all other questions raised about her. Most notably, Americans concluded that women workers keep their sisterhood with other women because sexual identity is a primary bond. Only the idealists—Phelps and Alcott—argue that sorority might be stronger than class divisions, but conservative authors express a version of this belief when they assume that all women, whether wage earning or middle class, will put the "female" values of love and family first.

If a woman was always tied to the exigencies and dangers of a female body, if she would inevitably put sisterly and domestic values first, how could she be expected to adhere to the call of a labor movement confronting the power of capitalism? Novelists use strikes—moments when the women had to be counted in or out— to express their positions on the solidarity of women to male workers.[68] In *The Breadwinners* (1883), an antilabor novel published anonymously by the journalist and diplomat John Hay, nonworking women are concerned only with domestic necessities and indifferent to ideological justifications for a strike. Telling their men that "their lazy picnic had lasted long enough, that there was no meat in the house, and that they had got to come home and go to work," a crowd of wives breaks a railroad strike.[69] In Warner's *Troubled Waters* women workers are denied any opportunity to declare their solidarity with their fellows. Though the women are "operatives as well as the men," they are excluded from the strike meeting "by command of that mysterious organization, 'The Central Committee'" (104). It is thus scarcely surprising that the strike is once again broken by women—now undifferentiated between workers and nonworkers—who "grew stronger in their rebellion from day to day" (151).

Freeman—writing last—makes her heroine personally confront the choice between domestic values and solidarity, a choice that is constructed as female or male. In her speech urging the strike Ellen repeatedly tells her fellows she would strike "if I were a man"—and then she does. On the other hand, when she returns to work it is as a "girl" leading in her fellows, and her concern is for "those poor women . . . the little starving children" (520). Ellen's capitulation returns her to the safer world of love and care; it also makes her powerless.

Ellen Brewster is, temporarily, the strongest woman in these novels, the only one really able to identify as a worker. She is crushed more by the unregulated power of the industrial machine, the factory system of which the owner himself is only a tool, than by her femininity. Freeman leaves us with the final paradox in the debate about giving women power through work. Once a woman claimed her independence to work, she gained power within her domestic relations. But as long as the working class in the United States was overwhelmed by the power of capital, working women risked merely exchanging one kind of powerlessness for another.

5

The Power of Professionalism

In 1871 Harriet Beecher Stowe prefaced her new novel, *My Wife and I*, with remarks about the function of literature. Her narrator, Harry Henderson, says, "It is now understood that whoever wishes to gain the public ear, and to propound a new theory, must do it in a serial story. . . . We have prison discipline, free-trade, labor and capital, woman's rights, the temperance question, in serial stories. . . . In our modern days . . . it is not so much the story, as the things it gives the author a chance to say." [1] One of the "things" Stowe's own story, serialized in the *Christian Union*, gave her a chance to comment on was women professionals, especially doctors. Two years later, in *The Gilded Age*, the eponymous novel of the period, Mark Twain and Charles Dudley Warner again focused on a woman doctor, and by the 1880s William Dean Howells, Sarah Orne Jewett, Elizabeth Stuart Phelps, and Henry James had all had their say about female physicians. Their common interest in this new form of women's activity was not coincidental. The national debate about appropriate forms of public power for Gilded Age women found an outlet in a twenty-year discussion, partly conducted through fiction, of women's entry into the professional classes, most particularly into the medical profession.

In their portrayal of women who become doctors, Stowe, Twain, and Warner raise most of the important questions female physicians faced themselves and presented to their society. The authors first examine why any properly brought up young woman would want to enter the professions. Stowe, who sends two women into medicine, gives two answers. Ida Van Arsdal has no inclination for the life of a society belle; unlike her sister Eva, the "wife" of the novel's title, Ida is uninterested in men. This "young lady philosopher" is described as having short hair, as well as "promise of vitality and power of endurance—without pretensions to beauty" (200). A "strong-minded sister" who has "made my declaration of independence" (168, 184), Ida works for her father and saves enough money to study as she pleases. We hear nothing suggesting her particular attraction to science or the practice of medicine.

Caroline, the hero's cousin, on the other hand, "has a fine philosophic mind, great powers of acquisition, a curiosity for scientific research; and her desire is to fit herself for a physician" (121). But natural inclination is not sufficient: in a plot twist that will be often repeated, Caroline is revealed as the victim of a disappointment in love. Professional activity is a displacement for her grief and lost domestic life. Caroline argues the economic necessity of work—"the customs and laws of society might be modified so as to give to women who do not choose to marry, independent position and means of securing home and fortune" (112)—and her alcoholic lover argues its value as sublimation: "the pain she feels now in leaving me will soon die out in the enthusiasm of a career" (437).

Where for Ida the study of medicine represents independence and power, and for Caroline it provides intellectual stimulation, support, and a substitute for marriage and family, Twain and Warner's heroine merely wishes to escape the repression of a young girl's life.[2] Ruth Bolton is bored. She asks her father, "Why should I rust, and be stupid, and sit in inaction because I am a girl?" (1:141). Feeling "what a box women are put into" (1:140), Ruth thinks of "the medical scheme" as "the only method of escape" (1:255). Warner demonstrates through Ruth's weakness and eventual failure that restlessness is not a good enough reason for undertaking a medical career.

Both Warner and Stowe spell out the difficulties of obtaining a medical education. Elizabeth Blackwell had received her medical degree from Geneva Medical College in New York state in 1849, but the medical schools even of most coeducational institutions remained closed to women. Caroline and Ida, like many women of the 1860s and 1870s, go abroad for their medical training. Ruth, daughter of Philadelphia Quakers, takes the other possible route, entering the "woman's medical college" in that city. The college, founded in 1850 by Quakers, was still struggling in 1873: only in 1871 did the state medical society recognize its graduates.[3] Warner gives a fair picture of its early days: "The college was a small one, and it sustained itself not without difficulty in this city . . . the original of so many radical movements. There were not more than a dozen attendants on the lectures . . . so that the enterprise had the air of an experiment, and the fascination of pioneering for those engaged in it" (1:149). Warner emphasizes the physical and emotional strain of Ruth's studies, especially the terrors of a night Ruth spends in the dissecting room with a male Negro corpse.

In these novels marriage and medicine are posed as incompatible opposites. Caroline and Ida will not marry—one from necessity and the other from inclination. For Ruth the choice is difficult. Though she resembles Caroline in her desire for intellectual activity, and proudly tells her mother she "shall not marry young, and perhaps not at all," she is fond of Philip Sterling. The key conversation, which echoes for twenty years in novels about women who choose to be doctors, takes place between Philip and Ruth in Ruth's last year of study. Philip asks:

> Ruth, do you think you would be happier or do more good in following your profession than in having a home of your own?
> What is to hinder having a home of my own?
> Nothing, perhaps, only you never would be in it—you would be away day and night, if you had any practice; and what sort of a home would that make for your husband?
> What sort of a home is it for the wife whose husband is always away riding about in his doctor's gig?
> Ah, you know that is not fair. The woman makes the home. (2:172–173)

Finally Ruth, overstrained by working to support her suddenly impoverished family, falls ill. Recovering, she admits to Philip, "I would not have cared to come back [from death] but for thy love," and he questions, "Not for thy profession?" Her response is to tease him, "Oh, thee may be glad enough of that some day, when thy coal-bed is dug out and thee and father are in the air again" (2:323). As the coal bed will be "a fortune to them all" (2:323), Twain and Warner are assuring the reader that Ruth will give up medicine and "make the home." They thus conclude with a negative appraisal of women's physical ability to withstand the rigors of medical practice. Their book appeared in the same year as Dr. E. H. Clarke's *Sex in Education*, which argued that women were biologically unable to support the strain of higher education.[4] In such an atmosphere, for many readers Ruth's physical limitations would settle the question.

Implicit within these analyses of apparently private and individual life choices were two of the most difficult issues raised by the appearance of women professionals. Both address the question of the kind of power that such activity confers; one issue is political, the other psychological. In both *The Gilded Age* and *My Wife and I* the female physician is contrasted to a woman who overtly asserts her power in the political system. Twain depicts that terror of Washington, the female lobbyist, and Stowe parodies Victoria Woodhull, a notorious women's rights reformer. Both novels suggest that becoming a woman physician is a more moderate, attractive, and reasonable way for a woman to secure "influence, and position, and fame, just as man can" (*My Wife and I*, 119). But Ruth leaves medicine, and at the end of Stowe's novel Ida and Caroline have all their training before them. Within the confines of both narratives the woman who exercises open political power, even through questionable means, is more effective than the polite professional.

The second issue is the relationship between women's ability to claim professional power and the absence or emasculation of sustaining men around them. Both Ruth's and Ida's fathers lose their money; failure in the central male role, that of breadwinning, weakens their authority and facilitates their daughters' entrance into medicine. Ida only sails for France when her father is in no position to stop her; Ruth leaves medicine when her father and lover are reestablished financially. Neither Warner nor Stowe imagines a world in which women can exercise power while leaving men equally empowered. This challenge remained, in fiction and reality, for the rest of the century.

The Window of Opportunity

The same laissez-faire public philosophy that encouraged the unrestricted growth of American capitalism and the exploitation of women as wage workers permitted several thousand women to attain the status of professionals in the male-dominated field of medicine during the latter third of the nineteenth century. The entrance of women into medicine caused consternation among regular medical practitioners, because women physicians not only competed for patients but also challenged exclusive male social control over the community. Yet despite opposition from most of the medical establishment, women were impelled by two historical forces to enter the profession: the window of opportunity that opened in the Jacksonian era, and the women's rights movement with its demand for giving women a public role.

The relatively weak state of medicine during most of the century partly explains how women were able to gain access to a medical education and consequent medical authority within their communities. By 1846, when the American Medical Association was founded, the medical profession was in a state of crisis. Most of the states had repealed all licensing laws for doctors, thus allowing almost anyone to practice medicine or to open a medical school and certify its graduates. The earlier laws, while giving physicians the right to organize in societies and to sue in the courts for the recovery of their fees, had not been very effective but had given physicians some legitimacy.[5] This legitimacy was badly undermined by loss of public confidence in the practice of medicine and by the prevailing Jacksonian philosophy. The 1830s and 1840s were the era of the common man and common sense; the idea of licensing doctors smacked of monopoly, and the science of medicine was perceived as both unnecessarily mystical and highly ineffective. Jackson, as Joseph Kett puts it, embodied "native ability over artifice, simplicity over ostentation, independence over servility,"[6] and public opinion of his time similarly rejected the claims of science and the elitism of physicians in favor of simpler therapies and open competition among practitioners.

Not only was the doctors' political authority stripped away by the Jacksonian movement, but their claim to be the legitimate deliverers of health care was challenged by several competing schools of medicine. Samuel Thomson originated a method of herbal medicine which, after obtaining patents for his concoctions, he franchised to home practitioners. Since herbalists were exempt from licensing laws, he was able to proselytize very successfully for his system. Joseph Kett credits part of the success of the Thomsonian method to its ability to capitalize on the antimonopoly political movement and its congruence with the "popular romantic culture of nature."[7] Since the Thomsonian franchise permitted home practice on family members, it enabled women to practice some forms of medicine without challenging the established cultural boundaries.[8] The Thomsonian premise that any individual could learn this medical system paralleled the political belief that any individual could be competent in political office. Thus, Paul Starr concludes, the Thomsonian protest was directed "not at science, but at a particular way in which knowledge was controlled."[9]

Another, more serious challenge to regular medicine was the rise of homeopathy, a theory of medicine that rejected most of the "heroic" methods—bleeding, cupping, and purging—for a more "natural" treatment of symptoms through very small doses of medication, known as attenuations. Originated by a German physician, Samuel Hahnemann, who experimented with the effects of pharmaceuticals on healthy patients, homeopathy appealed to many orthodox doctors because it seemed to have a scientific foundation.[10] By the 1840s, the Hahnemannian system had converted many American doctors. Homeopathy increased in popularity as its practitioners formed their own national society and established medical colleges and hospitals. Along with the desire to improve medical standards, one of the main purposes of the founding of the AMA in 1846 was to deal with competition from sectarian medicine. The code of ethics adopted in 1847 included a "consultation clause," under which no physician who adopted "an exclusive dogma," meaning homeopathy or Thomsonianism, could be a member, nor could a regular physician consult with such a believer.[11]

The end of the licensing laws and the rise of competing philosophies of medicine opened the field to extraordinary competition between practitioners. Most medical colleges were proprietary, with the faculty enhancing their income through teaching.[12] Schools were established to teach regular or allopathic medicine, homeopathic medicine, natural and herbal medicine, or a mixture of therapies, known as eclectic medicine. The growing number of schools meant competition for students, leading some of the homeopathic or irregular schools to admit women and blacks. Since the best regular schools of medicine refused to consider admitting women, women physicians like Elizabeth Blackwell took advantage of the lack of public regulation to open medical colleges for women and to establish hospitals where female physicians could train and practice. Given this window of opportunity, the number of women who attained the status of physician doubled (from 200 to 544) in the decade of the Civil War and quadrupled in the 1870s.[13] Regina Morantz-Sanchez concludes that the "temporary fluidity [of the medical profession] allowed women who wished to achieve professional status to do so before definitions of professionalism crystallized once more."[14]

The opportunity to become a doctor that the chaotic situation in American medicine offered was not alone sufficient to explain the increase in and acceptance of female doctors. As in the campaign for married women's property rights, conservatives and feminist forces joined to support the right of women to obtain medical education. Led by such advocates as Sarah Josepha Hale, male and female conservatives worked for the establishment of medical schools and hospitals for women because they felt that women's delicacy could only be preserved by having women physicians. Furthermore, they believed that medical education would strengthen woman's position as the guardian of her family's health and welfare. At the same time, supporters of the women's rights movement saw the entrance of women into medicine as an opportunity for individuals to achieve independence and self-fulfillment and as a way to bring women's special talents into the public sphere. As Morantz-Sanchez rightly notes, not all female physicians were feminists; some opposed suffrage for women while others were disinterested. Yet "however much they differed over specific issues or strategies, women physicians expressed feminism in their behavior."[15] Feminists, traditionalists, and some of the women doctors agreed that medicine would be improved by the entrance of female physicians because women had special qualities of nurturing to bring to patient care.

Where antifeminists and women's rights advocates differed most was in their vision of the power that would be exercised by women physicians. Conservatives imagined the woman doctor attending female patients and children within the home, adding her expertise to the natural talents of women in the household. They did not anticipate women doctors playing a public role. Supporters of women's rights, as well as those who opposed female doctors, instead recognized the inherent power that the physician exercises over the patient through the physician's knowledge of science and the dependence of illness. As scientific knowledge grew, the power of female doctors would grow within the community and could extend to authority over men. As a profession, medicine was a meritocracy. Potentially the success of an individual physician rested on competence rather than gender.

The opposition to women physicians drew on many of the familiar arguments used to oppose other public roles for women. A woman who left the domestic sphere to enter medical school would never be able to fulfill her responsibility as a wife and mother. Male physicians, who worked to keep women out of the regular medical schools, asserted that women had limited intellectual capacity, were much too passive to become physicians, and were likely to be nervous, excitable, and hysterical. The natural delicacy of women made them unsuited for the "ghastly" rituals and "blood and agony" of the dissecting room.[16] Any woman who did endure the horrors and hardships of a medical education would be so hardened that she would no longer be a woman, and thus would have no special sympathy to give to her patients. Surgery, in particular, required unfeminine strength. As Edmund Andrews put it, "The primary requisite of a good surgeon, is *to be a man*—a man of courage."[17] The belief that women were not strong enough to be physicians, coupled with the notion that those who might be fit enough would be defeminized, kept women out of men's medical colleges and medical societies for more than forty years.

By the 1870s, well aware that the medical profession had not secured the public trust, the medical community in the United States was torn by dissension over upgrading the standards for physicians through education and licensing. There was general agreement that standards for medical colleges should be higher and that there should be some way to distinguish qualified physicians from other types of practitioners, but confronting either issue meant dealing with two troublesome groups: homeopaths and women physicians. Homeopaths, while comprising less than 15 percent of the physicians in the United States, had been very successful in gaining patients and, in particular, the respect and patronage of upper-class families. Given the prestige of their clientele, all attempts to pass legislation to restrict their practices met with political failure.[18] Some state medical societies either ignored the AMA's consultation clause or accepted the presence of homeopaths in the regular hospitals. In Massachusetts, where a public trial was held in 1871 to expel several homeopaths from the state medical society, public sympathy for the homeopaths was so great that contributions poured in to endow the homeopathic hospital at Boston University.[19]

Soon after the Massachusetts furor over homeopathy, the regular female physicians of Boston, having been rebuffed for more than two decades, began another campaign for acceptance as members of the state medical society. They argued that if the purpose of the society was to designate publicly those doctors who had received the best training and who were most qualified, then patients had a right to know which female physicians also met those standards. In earlier days, the opponents of admitting women had charged that they received inferior training; in the battles of the late 1870s, faced with women with excellent educational qualifications, opponents reverted to the notion that women just weren't "fit" for medicine. After several polls of the membership and annual convention fights, the first woman was finally admitted to the Massachusetts Medical Society in 1884. By that date, seventeen state societies admitted women as regular members, and there were more than twenty-four hundred female physicians working in the United States. In fact, almost 15 percent of Boston's doctors were female.[20]

The argument about female physicians, which continued well into the twentieth century, was part of the larger division of public opinion over women's political power. For a brief period when women physicians were associated with homeopathy, both could be dismissed as "irregular," transient, and inferior phenomena. But once women were a prominent part of the regular medical force, it became apparent that debate over women doctors was really a debate over women's rights. Writing about female physicians gave novelists another entry into the ongoing discussion of woman's place in the political culture.

Three out of Four for Homeopathy

Ten years after *My Wife and I*, William Dean Howells published the first of four important portraits of a female doctor which capitalize on public fascination with the tumultuous medical profession. These novels, Howells's *Dr. Breen's Practice* (1881), Elizabeth Stuart Phelps's *Dr. Zay* (1882), Sarah Orne Jewett's *A Country Doctor* (1884), and Henry James's *The Bostonians* (1886), appearing in rapid succession, constitute an active debate about the capacities, power, and professional standing of female physicians.[21] Furthermore, unlike the novelists of the 1870s, these authors are aware that attitudes toward women doctors had become intimately connected to attitudes toward that other disruptive group in American medicine, homeopaths.

The fictional discussion of women doctors was conducted among friends and acquaintances. Mark Twain had moved to Hartford in 1871, the year of *My Wife and I*, because it was an "enclave of the Beechers"; Stowe, Warner, and he were neighbors as they wrote their novels.[22] Twain and Warner were also close friends of Howells, who as editor of the *Atlantic* was at the center of the most important literary network in the United States. James was his good friend; Phelps a contributor; Jewett a "familiar dinner guest" at Howells's home.[23] The women also knew each other: Phelps was a young girl in Andover when Stowe lived there, and Jewett admired both Phelps and Stowe.[24]

Howells's project was soon known to his friends On September 11, 1880, he heard from James that a mutual friend "speaks of your writing a story about a 'lady-doctor'! I applaud you that subject—it is rich in actuality—though I cannot, I think, on the whole, say I envy you it."[25] When Phelps wrote to propose her own novel about a woman doctor, Howells asked that she hold back publication until his story should finish running.[26] As a result *Dr. Breen's Practice* appeared in the *Atlantic Monthly* from August to December 1881, and *Dr. Zay* from April to September of 1882, with a prefatory note by Howells.

Dr. Breen's Practice is the single most negative portrait of a female physician from the entire period. Grace Breen is not fitted by personality, inherited abilities, or even desire to be a physician. Unlike many of the other women doctors, she does not come from a medical family. Like Caroline in *My Wife and I*, she has taken up medicine after suffering a "disappointment" in love, but she is moved by neither scientific nor feminist conviction. The very title of the book is ironic, as Grace treats—or more accurately, does not treat—only one patient.

Grace Breen has neither influence nor power within her community, in this case an old-fashioned, inexpensive summer resort full of women, where Grace is regarded with considerable diffidence. Grace recognizes that "talk about men being obstacles! It's other women! There is n't a woman in the house that would n't sooner trust herself in the hands of the stupidest boy that got his diploma with me than she would in mine." [27] Yet she refuses to take a feminist stance in response. One boarder, Miss Gleason, expects Grace to do great things for women, but Grace herself "would not entertain the vanity that she was serving what is called the cause of woman, and she would not assume any duties or responsibilities toward it" (15). Nevertheless, Miss Gleason astutely observes that if Grace fails, "you make it harder for other women to help themselves hereafter, and you confirm such people as these in their distrust of female physicians" (79).

Grace's female incapacity is symbolized by her apparent inability to drive a carriage. The successful female physician always drives: as early as *The Gilded Age* Twain and Warner satirize the "one woman physician driving about town in her carriage, attacking the most violent diseases in all quarters with persistent courage, like a modern Bellona in her war-chariot" (1:150). Phelps, whose novel was constructed to answer Howells point by point, has a heroine first seen driving through the forest in a phaeton pulled by the fastest horse in town, and the hero's sense of her importance and status increases when he realizes she keeps *two* horses.[28] In *A Country Doctor* Nan Prince grows up driving her doctor-guardian out at night and in storms. But Grace is dependent on men for transportation. The reader is thus not surprised when she gives up medicine to marry the young man who chauffeurs her.

Grace is not merely a woman doctor; she is also a homeopath. Her patient, Mrs. Maynard, is dubious about homeopathy, and as her condition worsens she fears that Grace's medicine "is n't active enough" (65). Even Grace's mother thinks that Mrs. Maynard would get better with a more active treatment (128–129). Eventually Mrs. Maynard requests "a *doctor* . . . a *man* doctor!" (64), thus apparently identifying Grace's personal weakness, the weakness of her medical system, and her sex. Indeed, the only "man doctor" in the neighborhood proves to be an allopath. Though at first Grace will not consult "with a physician whose ideas and principles I kn[o]w nothing about" (66), she is eventually persuaded to call in Dr. Mulbridge.

Mulbridge regards Grace, his first female physician, as "an extraordinary specimen," but agrees to consult until he learns that she is a homeopath. Then he turns pale and refuses, insisting that "it has nothing to do with your—your—being a—a—a—woman." The reasons are "purely professional—that is, technical—I should say disciplinary" (94–99). He reminds Grace of the case in which "one of our school in Connecticut was expelled from the State Medical Association for consulting with . . . his own wife, who was a physician of your school" (101). Grace responds with uncharacteristic force. She labels the ban on consultations ridiculous, and when she realizes that Mulbridge will not waive it in a case of immediate danger she cries, "I withdraw the word! It is *not* ridiculous. It is monstrous, atrocious, inhuman!" (100). Feeling she has no choice, she yields the case to him.

The unusual strength of Grace's protest against the consultation ban betrays Howells's own anger at the physicians' code of ethics and at the notorious Connecticut case, which occurred in 1878.[29] Howells himself was a follower of homeopathy as early as 1874; his physician was Dr. Walter Wesselhoeft, a general practitioner of homeopathic medicine, who taught at the Boston University School of Medicine. In September 1881, just as *Dr. Breen's Practice* was appearing, Howells wrote to his father about the treatment of his daughter Winny, saying that "I should like to put the case in the hands of Dr. Wesselhoeft again as soon as he gets home from Europe. After being used to homeopathy, it is hard to have patience with allopathotic [*sic*] methods." By December he himself was being treated by Wesselhoeft.[30] In 1882 reaction similar to Howells's prompted the Medical Society of New York to propose a new code permitting fellows to consult "with any legally qualified practitioners of medicine." Their justification recalls Grace's outburst: "Emergencies may occur in which all restrictions should . . . yield to the demands of humanity."[31]

But if it is not homeopathy that makes Grace weak, then it must be her sex. Indeed, "even those among [the ladies at Jocelyn's] who were homœopathists insinuated a fine distrust of a physician of their own sex" (22). The personal contrast between Grace and Mulbridge symbolizes the opposing qualities that Howells believed male and female physicians bring to their art. Grace is sympathetic, nervous, physically delicate, and naturally submissive, while the female guests remark that Mulbridge is "a perfect conception of a man: so abrupt, so rough, so savage." For Howells, the ideal combination is the male doctor assisted by a subordinated female physician. Even Miss Gleason accepts this: "the perfect mastery of the man-physician constitutes the highest usefulness of the woman-physician. The advancement of women must be as women" (171).[32] Mulbridge's idea of what to do with Grace is to reduce her to nursing and then offer her marriage; she has the sense to accept her other suitor.

The end of *Dr. Breen's Practice* foreshadows the end of *A Woman's Reason*, which appeared the following year. Helen patronizes a school of industrial arts for young women while still urging the students to seek marriage; Grace treats the sick children among the operatives at her husband's factory, but only at her husband's behest. This situation, Howells admits, "amount[s] to begging the whole question of woman's fitness for the career she had chosen" (271).

One can only imagine Phelps snorting as she read the successive installments of *Dr. Breen's Practice*. In her 1896 autobiography, *Chapters from a Life*, Phelps criticizes Howells's objection to novels that address the "ethical sense, not the aesthetical sense." She responds with the literary creed of *The Silent Partner* and *Dr. Zay*: "even moral reforms, even civic renovations . . . have their proper position in the artistic representation of a given age or stage of life."[33] The difference between *Dr. Breen's Practice* and *Dr. Zay* is neatly summarized in a review in *Lippincott's* for September 1884: "The subject of female doctors has been treated by Mr. Howells, who allows a young and pretty woman to practice medicine just as he allows her the indulgence of any pretty whim or caprice, and by Miss Phelps, who shows the coming of the Golden Age together with the days and works of female doctors."[34]

Phelps is careful to take up each characteristic of the female physician that Howells had treated; the two books can be charted under such headings as "success in practice," "devotion to science," "ease in consultation." Unlike Grace, but like the women physicians in Jewett's *A Country Doctor* and Garland's *Rose of Dutcher's Coolly*, Dr. Zay (Zaidee Atalanta Lloyd) is "naturally" inclined to medicine as the daughter of a doctor. A Vassar graduate, she attended a homeopathic medical school in New York (presumably the same one as Grace), but then studied in Zurich and Vienna, and consults frequently with a famous surgeon. Reflecting current reforms, she assures the young male accident victim who becomes her patient that "three years are necessary to a diploma from any reputable school" (79). She has been in practice several years, and earns three thousand dollars annually, exactly the average that Rachel Bodley, dean of the Woman's Medical College of Pennsylvania, found in her survey of graduates in 1880.[35] Unlike Grace, she is strong physically and undaunted by the demands of medical practice: she "enthusiastically" sews up the leg of a man who has cut a muscle on a mowing machine (133); she saves half of the town from diphtheria and scarlet fever; and she coolly assures the injured hero, Waldo Yorke, that her hand will inflict all the pain "that it ought" (43).

Phelps uses sets of metaphors to describe her heroine The first, flowers and wild animals, are metaphors of nature conveying a complex mixture of feminine beauty and threatening strength. Dr. Zay is first seen in the forest, as blooming as the apple blossoms that she drops in the path of Waldo Yorke to show him the road. Roses, carnations, and honeysuckle decorate her rooms, and she only barely loses her "bloom" as she fights an epidemic.

But the other side of her nature is shown by repeated mentions of her furs: she wears "leopard fur" or "furs," "long seal-skin gloves" or "fox-skins"; she is "a beautiful wild creature, a leopardess" (222–234) whom Yorke will find it a challenge to tame.

The second set of metaphors are mythological. Michael Sartisky has pointed out that the myth of Atalanta structures Zay's love affair with Waldo Yorke: he finally catches this woman who always runs—or drives— faster than he, when she emerges weak and shaken from dealing with a man in delirium tremens who has been shooting a revolver inside his house. Yorke himself says, "I have overtaken Atalanta this time. She stopped for a leaden apple,—for a revolver ball,—and I got the start" (254).[36] Less noticed but equally important is the persistent comparison of Dr. Zay to a caryatid (22, 24, 25, 26, 28, 31). A caryatid, originally a priestess of Diana, is a female figure made into a supporting column, for example on the front of a temple. Although Zay's romantic history repeats the myth of Atalanta, the references to caryatids symbolize her role as a source of strength to her community.

Dr. Zay practices medicine out of feminist conviction. She tells Yorke that "I had learned how terrible is the need of a woman by women, in country towns. . . . There is refinement and suffering and waste of delicate life enough in these desolate places to fill a circle of the Inferno." She became a doctor after watching her suffering mother be "comforted, during a part of her illness, by the services of a woman doctor in Boston. . . . I said, When she is gone, I will do as much for some one else's mother" (75–76). But she is more than a medical support to women. Phelps emphasizes her social and political power. The most revealing incident occurs when she is visiting Molly, who is pregnant out of wedlock. When Molly's lover, Jim, falls into the mill pond, Dr. Zay forces Yorke to drive for help ("Do as I bid you!" she says imperiously). She directs the men in giving artificial respiration for longer than they think worthwhile ("'Give him up? *No!*' came down the ringing cry") and then sends for the minister and compels Jim into an instantaneous marriage to Molly, threatening him with her "rights in your life." Zay even defies legal authority; when the minister worries that there may be a large fine for a marriage performed without notice of intention, Zay answers, "I will be responsible for it" (139–148).

The role of Dr. Zay in bringing about the marriage of Jim and Molly demonstrates the female physician's authority and specifically her power over men. This belief was widely shared by supporters of female physicians. A short story included in *Daughters of Aesculapius*, stories written by the alumnae and students of the Woman's Medical College of Pennsylvania and published in 1897, has an almost identical plot to the Jim and Molly tale, only in this case set among the upper classes. Dr. Anna Fullerton, class of 1882, recounts how she met a young unmarried mother on the maternity wards, and how she, the doctor, confronted the child's father and his society matron mother and brought about the marriage. Once again the female doctor is a caryatid upholding true morality and improving the community.

Phelps must have been particularly annoyed at Howells's ambiguous treatment of homeopathy. For Phelps there was no uncertainty. In *Chapters from a Life* she includes a creed that begins, "I believe in the Life Everlasting" and continues, "I am uncertain whether I ought to add that I believe in the homeopathic system of therapeutics. I am often told by skeptical friends that I hold this belief on a par with the Christian religion."[37] Yorke, a typical son of the Boston upper class, is reassured to find his doctor a homeopath, although he emphasizes the special relationship between women and homeopathy—his mother "would never have been able to bear it, if I had died under the other treatment. Women feel so strongly about these things" (39). In an exact reversal of the events in *Dr. Breen's Practice*, when Dr. Zay is angry at her patient, she threatens to give him over to the incompetent, male allopath of the town.

It is in *Dr. Zay* that we first begin to hear about the need for a new kind of marriage, a "new type of man" (244), if the female physician is to marry. Historically the opposition between medicine and marriage was not as absolute as novelists—or perhaps their readers—liked to think it was: in her 1881 address to the graduating class, Dean Rachel Bodley of the Woman's Medical College of Pennsylvania reported that of the 276 graduates of the school since its founding, 75 were married when they began study and 54 married after graduation.[38] More than a decade later, a writer in the *Woman's Medical Journal* for October 1894 notes, "Our experience is that the majority of women in the profession are married and being married, still maintain their profession."[39] But such marriages required shifts in the family hierarchy, as Phelps recognizes. Waldo Yorke may capture his Atalanta when she is worn out by epidemic and danger,[40] but she has already warned him what marriage to her will mean, in terms that echo the discussion between Ruth and Philip in *The Gilded Age*:

> You would come home, some evening, when I should not be there. . . .
> You would need me when I was called somewhere urgently. You
> would reflect, and react, and waver, and then it would seem to you
> that you were neglected, that you were wronged. You would think of
> the other men, whose wives were always punctual at dinner in long
> dresses . . . I should not blame you. . . . I should like somebody myself
> to come home to, to be always there to purr about me. . . . Generations
> of your fathers have bred it in you. You would not know how to
> cultivate happiness with a woman who had diverged from her heredi-
> tary type. (244)

It is this marriage that Yorke accepts; at the end of the novel, Dr. Zay has both professional and personal control over the men around her.

By the time Jewett's *A Country Doctor* appeared, reviewers openly regarded the spate of novels about women doctors as entries into a debate and began to examine them in the context of the medical profession's struggle to upgrade standards and to limit competition. Thus *Lippincott's* reviewer regrets that "Miss Jewett should have encumbered her first novel . . . with such a controversy. The fault we have to find with the endless debate is the infusion of an intense seriousness into the argument for female doctors, as if a void existed which must be filled. There are already many more male doctors . . . than the world needs." The reviewer expresses doubt about the scientific foundations of medicine, complaining that the male doctors work "with their highest abilities and intense beliefs in their dogmas without successfully grappling with the problems which disease presents." The solution to this problem is not an influx of women, because they are "not usually considered scientific and endowed with keen, accurate intellectual vision." [41] The arguments made by this reviewer are exactly those made by the faculty at Harvard Medical School in their decisions not to admit women students.

In *The Nation* another reviewer objects that neither *Dr. Breen's Practice*, *Dr. Zay*, nor *A Country Doctor* gives a realistic view of the obstacles facing most young physicians beginning practice in an overcrowded field:

> No one of the heroines works for her living. . . . They are all beautiful.
> . . . Each has had the best special training for her career that the times
> afforded. That they count two out of three for homœopathy may go
> for what it is worth. . . . The great fact remains, no one yet ventures to
> represent a woman struggling as most men struggle to gain a footing in
> the professions. No one ventures to present her without the attractions
> that are distinctly feminine. [42]

But the parallels exist because Jewett was responding as much to her literary predecessors as to the medical realities. [43] Nan Prince must have the same beauty and fortune as Grace Breen and Dr. Zay so that her choice of medicine over marriage will not seem forced upon her. Nevertheless, there are two novelties about *A Country Doctor*. First, Jewett undermines her argument in support of women's freedom to choose a profession instead of marriage by her strong emphasis on genetic inheritance, and second, at a moment of great national ferment about homeopathy and allopathy, she goes out of her way to ignore all irregular medicine.

Nan Prince is the daughter of the brief marriage between a doctor and a farm girl with an inherited tendency to alcoholism. Neighbors comment shortly before her mother dies, "There's an awful bad streak in them Thachers. . . . I expect there'll be bad and good Thachers to the end o' time." [44] After her grandmother also dies, Nan is raised by her guardian, Dr. Leslie. Leslie justifies his unusual treatment of his ward with a deterministic argument: he believes that children up to the age of eight "are simply bundles of inheritances" and that a little later they assert their own "individuality" (102). Nan early shows "a real talent for medical matters," and Leslie finds that "the law of her nature is that she must live alone and work alone" (105, 137). Therefore he intends to "help one good child to work with nature and not against it. . . . I don't care whether it's a man's work or a woman's work" (106).

The result is that Nan's career, which she thinks is freely chosen, is perceived as inevitable in the context of contemporary arguments for natural selection. Her "medical" genes assert themselves precociously when as a child she sets a turkey's broken leg, and the road to marriage is blocked by her other inheritance: she believes she should not have children for fear of passing on the alcoholism that has skipped her. "I have no right to the one way of life [marriage], and a perfect one . . . to the other." Medical training only increases her understanding of "the wretched inheritance I might have had from my poor mother's people" (317).

The clue to Jewett's attitude toward homeopathy lies in her novel's peculiar geography. *A Country Doctor* takes place in New England, and several times Nan and her guardian go to Boston, where he has medical friends.[45] The reader assumes that Nan's boarding school is also located near Boston. However, when the time comes for Nan to receive formal medical training, Jewett becomes vague about its location. Even though Dr. Leslie has medical acquaintances and Nan finds former school friends in the city where her training takes place, it is never named.

The reason is simple: unlike Dr. Zay and Grace Breen, Nan is a "regular." She could not, however, receive her medical training at Harvard, where Jewett's own grandfather had trained, since women were not admitted there. Medical training for women in Boston took place at the New England Female Medical College. Founded in 1848 by Samuel Gregory, the school had already acquired a poor reputation by 1862.[46] An informed reader might well believe that Nan is attending the New England, because she is dissatisfied with her education: she receives "little encouragement . . . from the quality" of her school, which offers "inferior instruction" (192–193). Modern scholarship also describes the New England as "the only major regular woman's medical college that in any way deserved the accusations of inferior teaching." [47] Yet Jewett cannot place Nan at the New England because that medical school adopted the homeopathic method when it merged with Boston University in 1873.

Homeopathy, as a method or even a controversy, is a conspicuous absence from this novel. Presumably, Jewett's desire to avoid the taint of such an irregular practice leads her to describe Nan's medical education anachronistically, suggesting that the preparation of women doctors was much worse than it was. Because of the drive to improve standards of medical education, generally, "by the 1880s students at the regular women's medical colleges were receiving an education comparable to men at the best schools."[48] Yet Jewett, fearful of homeopathy and more conflicted than she can admit, cannot imagine such a high-quality medical school for women.

Jewett's discomfort about women's medical education is further suggested by a significant misprint in the first edition. As Dr. Leslie "somewhat contemptuously overlooked the building and its capabilities . . . he told himself that like all new growths it was feeble yet, and needed girls like his Nan . . . who would make the college strong and to be respected. Not such doctors as several of whom he reminded himself, who were disgracing their sex, but those whose lives were ruled by a pettiness of detail, a lack of power, and an absence of high aim [*sic*]" (194). In the missing "not" is revealed a surprising ambivalence about female physicians.

The effect of denigrating Nan's formal medical education is to highlight her dominance by Dr. Leslie. Jewett's first description of Dr. Leslie emphasizes his power: "one felt that he was the wielder of great powers over the enemies, disease and pain. . . . Wherever one might place him, he instinctively took command" (33). Though Nan demonstrates her medical competence when she sets a farmer's dislocated shoulder, at no time do we see her exercise authority similar to Leslie's. The novel depicts her as locked in an Oedipal relationship with the doctor, who serves both as her father and her medical preceptor. She is the only one of the successful female doctors who does not reduce the power of the men around her. Her indifference to public opinion and her refusal to marry seem to be her declarations of independence, but the reader doubts her freedom. The book ends with her refusing opportunities to go work in the "city hospitals" or, like Dr. Zay, to continue her studies in Zurich. Instead, she returns to the farm on which she grew up, embracing her future as a country doctor and as assistant to aging Dr. Leslie.

Two years later James finally had his say about this subject "rich in actuality." The "lady-doctor" is one element in the "very *American* tale" he set out to write, "a tale very characteristic of our social conditions."[49] As in *My Wife and I*, the female physician in *The Bostonians* appears alongside women more directly demanding rights for women. But James differs with his predecessors. His woman doctor is scarcely a woman; she is apparently opposed to demands for women's rights; and her homeopathy indicates a commitment to foolish and outdated reform.

Basil Ransom meets Dr. Prance at Miss Birdseye's on his first evening in

Boston. He is struck by her boyish appearance: like Ida van Arsdal, she is "a plain, spare young woman, with short hair and an eyeglass. . . . It was true that if she had been a boy she would have borne some relation to a girl, whereas Doctor Prance appeared to bear none whatever" (31, 41). Dr. Prance is not at all impressed by the evening's women's rights speaker: as she says, "I guess I know more about women than she does" (42). Ransom quickly gathers that she was "bored with being reminded, even for the sake of her rights, that she was a woman—a detail that she was in the habit of forgetting, having as many rights as she had time for. It was certain that whatever might become of the movement at large, Doctor Prance's own little revolution was a success" (48–49).

Dr. Prance has the independent control that the other heroines fight for. This is nicely symbolized in the Cape Cod section, when Basil goes fishing with her every morning. In *Dr. Breen's Practice* Grace was taken out in her suitor's boat, and only he rowed when the wind died down. Unlike Grace, Nan Prince can row, though the night she goes out on the river with her suitor she too leaves the oars to him. But Dr. Prance is "devoted to boating and an ardent fisherwoman" (399), as self-sufficient on the water as she is professionally.

Less ambiguously than Howells, James uses homeopathy to mark his female physician as different and of dubious medical worth. James's brother William had trained as a regular physician at the Harvard Medical School, and although "lifting, hot irons, ice packs, blistering, galvanism, the water cure" all figure among the treatments used by some member of the James family, homeopathy never appears.[50] For the first time in these novels, homeopathy is stigmatized as an outworn reform. When Basil Ransom learns from the dying Miss Birdseye that the medicine Dr. Prance gives her is homeopathic, he says, "I have no doubt of that; I presume you wouldn't take anything else." Miss Birdseye comments, "It's generally admitted now to be the true system," and Ransom replies, "It's a great thing to have the true system." The intruding authorial voice adds that Ransom "was not often hypocritical; but when he was he went all lengths" (372).

The attack on Miss Birdseye's medical beliefs is part of the satire on Miss Birdseye's "systems" throughout the novel; she is a "confused, entangled, inconsequent, discursive old woman, whose charity began at home and ended nowhere" and who has spent fifty years of "humanitary zeal" on assorted causes (27). Rather than associating homeopathy with Beacon Street, as Phelps does, James tars it with the brush of quackery. The scene has an amusing historical resonance. Mary Putnam Jacobi, the outstanding female physician of the period, was the niece of Elizabeth Peabody, the model for Miss Birdseye, who "kept her in touch with every new social ism." As early as 1869 Putnam Jacobi wrote to her mother, in a letter prescient of the reform milieu of *The Bostonians*, "I detest vulgarity, pretention.

. . . No homeopaths, no spiritualists, few 'female' orators."[51] In 1891 she was still complaining that "the greatest . . . resistance has been offered to woman's entrance at the best schools, while inferior and 'irregular' colleges have shown an odd readiness to admit them. It would seem that co-educational anatomy is more easily swallowed when administered in homœopathic doses!"[52]

James sends a double message. On the one hand, he accepts Dr. Prance's entrance into the professions. Unlike Verena Tarrant, she is not "made for love," and her shrewd observations, her desire to get back to her studies because "I don't want the gentlemen-doctors to get ahead of me," her passage across a room "as if she had been traversing a hospital ward" (48), all give her a professional aura. On the other hand, she is described as a sport of nature. She is so comfortably masculine that at one point Basil wishes he could offer her a cigar (362). She bypasses any hierarchical relation to men by essentially becoming one, thus embodying the fears of defeminization that recur in objections to giving women professional stature.

Unlike her predecessors, Dr. Prance seems to have neither father nor mother. In the treatment of family in these novels we can trace shifting public attitudes toward women doctors. In the novels of the 1870s, fathers had to be weakened or dead before women could study medicine. Men were the obstacles to women's professional advancement. In the novels of the 1880s, it is mothers who must disappear before women can be strong enough to become physicians. Characteristically, Grace Breen still lives with her mother, who, although she "had never actively opposed her studying medicine," treats her like a child and reminds her that "a man would n't" feel timid about going into practice alone (13–14, 42). The mothers of Nan Prince, Dr. Zay, and perhaps Dr. Prance are dead. These newly powerful women are, by training, occupation, and attitude, profoundly different from the women who had preceded them. One way to symbolize this difference was to cut them off from their mothers.

The novels about women doctors from the 1880s all tend to become absorbed in the heroine's personal life or qualities. Dr. Breen is unsuited for the profession by her sex; Dr. Prance is unsexed by her profession. The most difficult dilemma facing both Nan Prince and Atalanta Lloyd is how—or whether—to integrate marriage with their profession. The obsession with the marriage question is not merely novelistic convention; marriage serves as a metaphor for all the newly fluid power relations between men and professional women. On the other hand, the novels of the 1880s skirt the issue of professionalism as a form of public political power, even though James, whose entire novel is about women's rights, clearly prefers Dr. Prance to Olive Chancellor, and Jewett and Phelps both demonstrate a physician's natural authority over a community of patients. By the 1890s, novelists would directly address the woman physician's public position.

The New Doctors

In contrast to the fictional lady doctors of the 1880s, the women professionals who appear in the novels of the 1890s are successful "regular" physicians exercising power within the medical community as well as over patients and associates. The achievement of professional status by the women physicians who appear in Annie Nathan Meyer's *Helen Brent, M.D.* (1892) and in Hamlin Garland's *Rose of Dutcher's Coolly* (1895) accurately represents the change that had come to medicine in the United States. In retrospect, women achieved a higher status in medicine and had brighter prospects in the profession during the decade of the 1890s than at any time during the next sixty years.

The conflicts and uncertainties that had characterized the American medical community were beginning to be resolved by the 1890s. Women were taking their place within the profession, and after the New York Medical Society accepted homeopaths as members, a number of other states followed suit, regardless of their official codes. Gradually, as the views and practices of the homeopaths converged with those of the regular physicians, homeopaths joined the staffs of municipal hospitals and medical colleges. The integration of the two groups was hastened in most states by the advent of licensing legislation that either forced homeopaths and regulars to sit on the same examining board or allowed each group to form its own board, thus giving equal legitimacy to the homeopaths. The result was a more homogeneous screening process that raised the standards for all legitimate physicians.

It is thus not surprising that no mention of homeopathy or other irregular practices appears in these two novels of the 1890s. Instead, both focus intensely on the dual nature of a woman doctor's power, public and private. Public power is immediately obvious in *Helen Brent, M.D.*, which opens as Dr. Brent gives the address at the dedication of the Root Memorial Hospital and Medical College for Women. Mrs. Root has endowed the institution after receiving extraordinary care from Dr. Brent, a renowned surgeon and gynecologist. As an intern Helen Brent had achieved fame by confronting a leading male physician who excluded women physicians from his hospital, even though the hospital had been specifically endowed "for their clinical instruction." [53] At this triumphal moment Helen Brent sees that physician, Dr. Manning, in the audience, as well as her former fiancé, Harold Skidmore.

By the end of the first few pages of the novel, Annie Nathan Meyer has demonstrated that Helen Brent is well educated, influential in the city, a fighter for women's rights, and a practitioner of the specialty requiring the most physical strength, surgery. Inevitably, Meyer also endows her heroine with beauty and grace; the newspaper account of the address describes Dr. Brent as "the figure of a very Juno" (18).

Dr. Brent's behavior as a professional woman of science is beyond re-proach. She lives by the norms that the medical community was trying to establish for all of its members. After trying to raise the standards of medical education for more than fifty years, in 1889 the Association of American Medical Colleges finally required member schools to have three-year graded programs and entrance standards. In 1893 the Johns Hopkins medical school opened with the latest in equipment and a commitment to research.[54] The Root Memorial College follows the same principles: it is equipped with superb laboratories, students follow a three-year course, and there are re-search facilities to encourage advanced work (43–44). Helen Brent, a pro-fessional more than a feminist, is interested in making the hospital "advance the condition of medical preparation all over the country." She cares more that the college encourage "original research," and inculcate "the love of science, for science's sake" than that it is "another college open to women without restrictions" (50). Brent justifies including male faculty members and hiring a male architect as necessary for building the best institution.

The parallel between Helen Brent and Annie Nathan Meyer as founders of institutions for women's education cannot be ignored. Annie Nathan, daughter of a prominent Jewish family in New York, enrolled in the Collegi-ate Course for Women at Columbia without her father's knowledge. She was chagrined to find out that the women's course was essentially a readings course and that women were barred from the lectures attended by the male students. After marrying a doctor in 1885, Meyer embarked on a campaign to create a woman's college as an annex to Columbia University. Almost single-handedly, she lobbied the Columbia trustees, raised funds, and gath-ered support from leading citizens. In 1889, the board of trustees of Colum-bia approved the opening of Barnard College.[55] Like Helen Brent, Meyer insisted on the highest standards for Barnard's students. On the first day of entrance examinations, she personally convinced the Columbia math-ematics professor to administer the same exams that the male applicants had to take, so that there would be no hint that the Barnard exams were easier.[56]

While Meyer creates a very impressive portrait of the physician as public figure, she is less sanguine than Phelps about whether a professional woman can achieve private happiness. After Helen returns from her studies in Eu-rope, her ex-fiancé tries one more time to persuade her to give up medicine and marry him. The personal strength that Helen has acquired through her profession repels her lover. Hopeful that she has been exhausted by study, Harold is "irritated at seeing her so beautiful and so strong," and he senses a change in the balance of their relationship, wondering, "Where had fled all his masculine sense of superior power?" (24–25). Accusing Helen of being unfeeling, Harold paints a conventional picture of female self-sacrifice: "If you really loved me, you would have given up all this, your ambition, your profession—everything. That is love" (25–26).

Meyer's plot is constructed to show that some sacrifice of professional ambition is necessary for both men and women who marry. She lays the groundwork in this interview. Helen proposes that she could work only on consultation and therefore supervise a household, but she will not give up medicine altogether and points out that no man is ever asked to give up his profession for his wife. In reply Harold ridicules "the idea of comparing the ambition of a man, his very career, his breadwinning, with the day dreams of a woman" (27). Disparaging her proposal as "fairyland," he announces that "it is generally conceded that a man's career is more important than his wife's. It is so in the nature of things." Helen responds that she will never marry "until I can find the man that together with me will be courageous enough to try to change the world" (30–33).

Helen's authority is strong enough to create a hospital, but her limits as a woman are revealed when she talks to Harold, and her limits as a doctor are revealed when she attempts to interfere with social codes and male sexual behavior. Having learned from a poor patient that her "utterly ruined . . . physical condition" (73) was caused by Mortimer Verplanck, a wealthy man who is about to marry young Rose Bayley, she visits Rose's mother "with a tale of approaching disease . . . that was going to attack her daughter" (75). Mrs. Bayley thinks it preposterous to "break off the match at this late day," and calmly says she never expected "a handsome young fellow" with an enormous fortune to have "lived the life of a saint." Even when Helen speaks "so low that Mrs. Bayley could scarcely catch her words," presumably with explicit information, she only mutters, "Doctors sometimes mistaken—think they know everything—change of habits—marriage." Helen leaves the house having found "how far a mother's ambition will permit her to go" (77–79), and how far a woman doctor cannot go.

The consequences of the Verplanck marriage allow Meyer to continue her exploration of inequitable social expectations for professional men and women. Mortimer Verplanck marries Rose, who as Helen predicted soon dies of syphilis, and Harold Skidmore marries Louise Cushing, the beautiful social butterfly Helen refused to be. Extremely successful in his career, Harold lives just as he feared Helen would—with continuous work, frequent travel, and neglect of his spouse. In his absence Louise has an affair with Verplanck and falls ill. Skidmore, who has been away too much to have any idea that all New York is talking about his wife, asks Helen to take the case from Dr. Manning. Ever the professional, she refuses until Manning requests the consultation, and then, having cured Louise, and well aware of the true situation, she prescribes a trip to Europe for both of the Skidmores. Harold will not consider the sacrifice to his career. Louise elopes with Verplanck, and Harold's reputation and health are destroyed.

In the final passages, Meyer hints that Harold has learned the need for mutual respect and sacrifice, and that Helen and he may eventually marry.

Helen receives a letter from Harold who hopes, someday, to return "as a suppliant . . . kneeling in the dust" (196). But Meyer retreats from making that role reversal a reality. Throughout the novel she insists on the right of women to pursue careers, but hesitates to endorse marriage for professional women. Harold Skidmore intuits that Helen Brent's life is not complete without a husband and children, yet Helen herself "knew it would have been far less complete, less satisfying, had she subdued the intellectual rather than the emotional side of her nature" (53). This is true even though as a social eugenicist she worries about the loss of her genes, wondering aloud, "Is the highest type of woman destined never to be handed down to the succeeding generation?" (128). The message of *Helen Brent, M.D.* is ambivalent: the current state of marriage is unjust to women, but Meyer will not promise that it is possible for the professional woman to marry and fulfill woman's natural role as a mother.[57]

The female physician who appears in Garland's *Rose of Dutcher's Coolly* (1895) provides a direct contrast. Garland's novel, which traces the life of a young girl from a farm in Wisconsin, is best known for its description of the innocence of childhood in rural America. His heroine, Rose, however, is too extraordinary to believe: tall, statuesque in figure, beautiful, intelligent, self-disciplined, sexually aware, and driven to find the perfect mate.[58] After completing college at the University of Wisconsin, she leaves her father's farm, arriving in Chicago with a strong desire to become a writer but no clear notion of what an independent life would be like. Isabel Herrick, a doctor in the city, becomes Rose's mentor, the model of a professional woman who has resolved both the career and marriage questions.

Like Helen Brent, Isabel Herrick proved her strength and determination when she confronted sex discrimination in the course of medical education. As a medical student she was one of the first women in her school. When refused admittance to the dissecting room, she announced, "Men—I won't say gentlemen—I'm here for business, and I'm here to stay. If you're afraid of competition from a woman you'd better get out of the profession."[59] Garland is clear about Dr. Herrick's personal power: known as "the little Corporal," she "ordered [the male students] about so naturally and led them so inevitably in everything she undertook" (288). As Dr. Brent is a surgeon, a specialty demanding physical strength, Dr. Herrick is an alienist or psychiatrist, a specialty requiring emotional strength.

Herrick and Brent share other characteristics that mark them as full members of the profession. Both have urban practices and, rather than driving around in carriages, see patients largely in their own offices. This change of scene reflects a modification that took place in the lives of many American doctors; an urban practice could serve more patients than a rural one that depended on house calls to distant farms.[60] Both women doctors have circles of influential friends: Helen has to evade society functions, and

Herrick is associated with progressive politics in Chicago, hosting a dinner party where her guests include a famous professor and a leading newspaper editor.

Again like Helen Brent, who tells a young protégé that her "chief aim in working is to make all women find themselves" (104), Isabel Herrick feels responsible for setting out the life choices of young women. She introduces Rose to two potential suitors: an attractive young man of good family who could give Rose comfort and appreciation, and Mason, the newspaper editor, who challenges her intellect and independence. On a single day Rose faces her choice: she watches a terrible storm on the lake with Mason, after which he leaves her, alone and soaked, to report on the storm. She is rescued by his rival, Elbert Harvey, who takes her to his home where she is coddled by his family and servants. Rose knows that Harvey would give her "a life of ease, of power, of grace and charm," but she would "need to give up her own striving toward independence" (358). Her model for this independence has become Isabel Herrick.

Dr. Herrick uses her position as a doctor and a friend to give Rose a vision of the new marriage. Another eugenicist physician, she recognizes Rose's natural endowment for motherhood. When Rose objects, "I hate to think of marrying as a profession," she tells Rose that she herself would give up her profession rather than her "hope of being a mother," but expects to have both. Amazed, Rose asks, "Will it take away your power as a physician?" Echoing Mary Putnam Jacobi, Herrick gives the feminist response: "If a woman has brains and a good man for a husband, it broadens her powers" (327, 330).[61] More directly than any of the novelists of the 1880s, Garland claims that professional training will empower women in both the community and the domestic sphere.

At the end of the novel, Garland gives us two modern couples. Herrick finally marries her medical school classmate. According to Dr. Sanborn, "he had the judge come in to give him legal power to compel Isabel to do his cooking for him, and Isabel replied that her main reason was to secure a legal claim on Sanborn's practice" (361). Mason proposes a similar marriage to Rose: "I want you as comrade and lover, not as subject or servant or unwilling wife. . . . You are a human soul like myself, and I shall expect you to be as free and as sovereign as I, to follow any profession or to do any work which pleases you" (380).[62] The novel ends before we can see either Rose as the companion/wife or Herrick as the mother/physician, but Garland's position is clear: Women can pursue professional goals while remaining essentially feminine. Marriage will enhance the power of a professional woman, not end it.

A Utopian View

In 1911 Charlotte Perkins Gilman published *The Crux*, which directly emphasizes a woman doctor's public power. Using this power, Dr. Jane

Bellair accomplishes what even Helen Brent failed at: she saves a lovely young woman from venereal disease. But her true goal is larger: she is working for the improvement of the human race.

Dr. Bellair is a "breezy woman, strong, cheerful, full of new ideas, if not ideals, and radiating actual power, power used and enjoyed."[63] These new ideas are identified with the West, where, she says, "people have a chance to grow" (162). She persuades a number of her old friends from New England to join her in Colorado. Here young Vivian Lane renews a childhood romance with Morton Elder, a man whom her wise grandmother regards with great suspicion. Finally Mrs. Pettigrew goes to see Dr. Bellair. Speaking of Morton she says, " 'fine boy—eh? Nice complexion!' Dr. Bellair was reading a heavy-weight book by a heavier-weight specialist. . . . 'Better not kiss him,' she said." The two women understand each other immediately. Grandma says she will look out for "that girl of mine"; with a suggestion of her larger vision, the doctor adds, "Yes—or any girl" (134–135).

The central scene of the book is the one in which Jane Bellair breaks the truth to Vivian. The contrast between Dr. Bellair's power as a physician and her previous powerlessness as a woman is very pointed: she confesses to Vivian that years earlier she married a diseased man, became ill, and lost the ability to have children. "Never be able to have a child, because I married a man who had gonorrhea. In place of happy love, lonely pain." When Vivian protests that "I didn't know," the doctor bursts out impatiently, "No! You don't know. I didn't know. Girls aren't taught a word of what's before them till it's too late." But Bellair intends to change that. "I left him. When I found I could not be a mother I determined to be a doctor, and save other women, if I could" (221). She tells Vivian why she must not marry Morton Elder; her directness contrasts vividly with the euphemistic recounting of Helen Brent's fruitless conversation with Rose Bayley's mother—not Rose —twenty years earlier.

Vivian's grandmother, consoling her, points both morals of the book. "All this about gonorrhea is quite newly discovered—it has set the doctors all by the ears. Having women doctors has made a difference too—lots of difference" (244). *The Crux*, more than any of the earlier novels we have examined, spells out the nature of this difference. Women doctors will exercise their authority to stop men from harming women. Vivian's conservative parents dislike women doctors, and Morton concurs, but all three would keep Vivian ignorant and permit her destruction. The woman doctor saves her from physical and moral degeneration. Reversing the action of Dr. Zay, Dr. Bellair prevents a marriage rather than forcing one.

The difference between male and female medical practice is explicitly examined. Before she talks to Vivian, Dr. Bellair tries to get help from her best friend and medical school classmate, Dr. Richard Hale. She is unable to persuade him to stop his "dangerous patient" from marrying. She argues: "You are a member of society. Do you mean to let a man whom you know has no right to marry, poison the life of that splendid girl?" (210–211). Hale is hero enough so that he himself will eventually marry Vivian, but he still has limited vision. He is more concerned with professional confidentiality than with the social imperative to preserve the race. To him "it is a matter of honor—professional honor." Furious, Bellair says, "I won't leave you to the pangs of unavailing remorse. . . . That young syphilitic is no patient of mine" (212). Her last words evade the question of what Dr. Bellair would do with a patient's confidences, but clearly Gilman is arguing that female physicians will regard social welfare as more important than qualms about professional ethics.

Gilman wrote *The Crux*, as she avows in the preface, "first for young women to read; second, for young men to read," and she admits its goals by referring "anyone who doubts its facts and figures . . . to 'Social Diseases and Marriage,' by Dr. Prince Morrow" (5).[64] But her book is more than a social hygiene tract. It is a logical culmination to the nineteenth-century fictional discussion of the forms of social and political power that women attained by becoming physicians. Dr. Bellair—that breath of fresh air—is impelled by her own experience of woman's powerlessness to become a doctor, and then to exercise her newfound power to guide her community. It is not accidental that the novel includes one other vision of female power. Urging her aunt to go west with them, Vivian's friend Susie says, "I suppose you could teach school in Denver. . . . And you could Vote! Oh, Auntie—to think of your Voting!" (67).[65] Only the full exercise of political rights could give a woman more power than Dr. Bellair exercises in *The Crux*.

Political Power,
Direct and Indirect

Ten years after the Civil War ended, Mary Clemmer Ames, a well-known Washington journalist, articulated a major choice facing American society as women became politically visible:

> Thus some of the highest prizes in the Government are won. Unscrupulous men pay wily women to touch the subtlest and surest springs of influence, and thus open a secret way to their public success. No longer the question is: Shall women participate in politics? shall they form a controlling element in the Government? But, as there are women who will and do exert this power, shall it remain abject, covert, equivocal, demoralizing, base? Or shall it be brave and pure and open as the sun?[1]

Ames's conclusions, reached after a decade of reporting on the political scene in Washington, D.C., outline a new form of the controversy about the appropriate way for women to exercise political power. The issue of method, of *how* women were to participate in political life, was central to the debate over women's suffrage in the last four decades of the nineteenth century. Should women influence the political sphere through direct means, through public speaking, petitioning, and voting, or should women exercise their power indirectly, by influencing men who in turn would represent the women's interests? And what would be the consequences of women acting in the political arena: would they be corrupted by the system or would women improve the moral tone of American politics?

The belief that women should exercise only indirect influence on politics is a logical extension of the view that "the family and not the individual, has been the political unit and the head of the family . . . has been the political representative of the rest." Therefore, Francis Parkman concluded in 1879, "to give the suffrage to women would be to reject the principle that has thus far formed the basis of civilized government."[2] Arguing in 1866 against giving women the right to vote in Washington, D.C., Senator Davis explained, "I concede that woman, by her teachings and influence, is the source of the large mass of the morality and virtue of man and of the world. . . . but that woman should properly perform these great duties . . . it is necessary that she should be kept pure. . . . To keep her in that condition of purity, it is necessary that she should be separated from the exercise of the suffrage."[3] The antisuffragists believed that entering politics would not only remove women from their true duties, but would corrupt their natural purity and femininity. Thus, like the women who spoke against abolition, suffragists were ridiculed, defeminized, and silenced. The *Albany Evening Journal* opined that suffragists had "hookbilled noses, crow's feet under their sunken eyes, and a mellow tinting of the hair," while the *New York Tribune* prescribed as a cure for women who had signed petitions for suffrage "a wicker-work cradle and dimple-cheeked baby."[4]

Those who supported suffrage for women had a fundamentally different concept of the structure of society: the basic unit was the individual, and each individual was vested with certain natural rights. As George William Curtis, the editor of *Harper's Weekly*, declared at the New York Constitutional Convention of 1867, "a woman has the same right to her life, liberty, and property that a man has, and she has consequently the same right to an equality of protection that he has." The best protection for the individual, according to the Founders, was a government formed on the consent of the governed, and "right reason and experience alike demand that every person shall have a voice in the government upon perfectly equal and practicable terms."[5] Natural rights adherents argued that women, like men, had a moral right to express their views publicly, to petition the government, to try to influence Congress directly, to vote, to serve on juries, and to hold office. Speaking in favor of women's suffrage in 1866, Senator Benjamin F. Wade foresaw no unfortunate consequences: "I do not believe it will have any unfavorable effect upon female character if women are permitted to come up to the polls and vote. I believe it would exercise a most humane and civilizing influence."[6] Twenty years later, the Senate minority report reprised the same theme: "Woman's vote is needed for the good of others. . . . She is an enemy of foreign war and domestic turmoil; she is a friend of peace and home. Her influence for good in many directions would be multiplied if she possessed the ballot."[7]

Debate over the political power of American women was fueled by the debate over extending suffrage to the male Negro after the Civil War. Caught between its commitment to the rights of the ex-slaves and the need to push for women's suffrage, the women's rights movement split into rival camps, with one group continuing the campaign for a national suffrage amendment and the other working state by state. Supporters of suffrage were forced to choose between the two groups, which had philosophical as well as strategic differences.[8] Yet despite divisions within the movement, women rallied to fight for suffrage at local, state, and national levels. Not only did women speak for suffrage in campaigns across the country, but they testified before Congress, gathered and presented petitions, raised funds, and published their own newspapers for the cause. The territory of Wyoming, where women gained the vote in 1869, sat on juries, and held political office, served as an example of the positive benefits of suffrage for countless prosuffrage speeches.

During the era of Reconstruction, partisan battles between the Radical Republicans and the Democrats robbed the prosuffragists of the opportunity to gain the vote for women. As a strategy to defeat the Fourteenth and Fifteenth Amendments, which assured citizenship and the vote to (male) ex-slaves, many Democrats espoused the enfranchisement of women, knowing that an amendment to grant suffrage to both blacks and women would fail.[9] When the prosuffrage forces accepted Democratic support, the Republicans, who had previously favored their cause, deserted them as traitors. In the years that followed, corruption and political bargaining between the parties and business interests dominated the Washington scene, to the exclusion of the suffrage question.

While the women's movement was unable to find any leverage with which it might bargain for the vote, women lobbyists, who asked only for indirect paths of influence, exploited the opportunities for political power. Even as Senator George Vest led the opposition to suffrage by insisting that the vote "would take [woman] down from that pedestal where she is today, influencing as a mother the minds of her offspring, influencing by her gentle and kindly caress the action of her husband toward the good and pure,"[10] he and his fellow legislators were quite aware of a new model of female behavior, that of the woman who used the same techniques of persuasion in the public world of politics.

Washington abounded in women exercising indirect power for their own personal gain or for powerful interests. Edward Winslow Martin hints at the tactics of these paid lobbyists: "If the man fails, the female lobbyist is called in to exert her arts, which are more potent than those of the sterner sex. Congressmen and officials are famous as being the most susceptible men in the world, and the fair charmer is generally successful." In pursuit of special legislation, some interests were known to rent houses and employ women to entertain legislators, using "the lever of lust" to gain votes.[11] The abundance of female lobbyists in Washington during the Gilded Age gave credence to the dualistic view that any good woman would be corrupted by politics and no good man could resist a corrupt woman's powers. Such a view betrayed an extremely ambivalent judgment of women—were they inherently pure and moral or were they inherently corruptible?

The Temptation of Politics

After the Civil War, controversy about woman's political role in the Republic was widespread. Congressional debates over suffrage began with the 1866 resolution to grant suffrage to women in the District of Columbia; attempts to vote by Victoria Woodhull, Susan B. Anthony, and Virginia Minor generated extensive publicity; and there were books and speeches on all sides of the issue.[12] Discussion of the woman question in fiction took two forms. One group of novels directly addressed the demand for women's suffrage through favorable or satirical depiction of those involved in the campaign. At the same time another group of novels, each of which focused on a female lobbyist, revealed divided national opinion about the consequences of political action for women.

There are profound differences between the two sets of novels. Those that deal with women who use indirect influence to affect government decisions draw their conclusions primarily from the authors' views of woman's *moral* nature. In contrast, the novels directly concerned with the demand for suffrage are constructed around an argument from woman's *biological* nature. Another major distinction is that the antisuffrage novels are usually written as if contemporary women remained remote from the day-to-day work of politics. The lobbyist novels are well aware that, as Ames says, already "there are women who will and do exert this power."

Four major novels about female lobbyists—Mark Twain and Charles Warner's *The Gilded Age* (1873), John William De Forest's *Playing the Mischief* (1875), Henry Adams's *Democracy* (1880), and Frances Hodgson Burnett's *Through One Administration* (1883)—all appeared within a decade. From the earliest reviews these novels have been compared, usually as "political novels," sharing a joint preoccupation with late nineteenth-century government corruption.[13] Little attention has been paid to their implications for the debate over political rights for women. Yet these books address the major topics of that debate: why women might want to enter politics, whether they needed to, and what the effect would be, on women and on government. All four analyze the motivation of a woman involved in the political sphere. Each examines how such a woman is embedded in a family situation and whether she is provided with male representatives to the political world. Though usually it is the lack of male relatives that drives a woman to assert her own powers, Burnett, the only female author in the group, offers a radical dissent, suggesting that it may be these very male relatives who deflect a woman's indirect influence outward into the public sphere. The four authors divide, as American opinion did, about whether women are too pure or too impure for politics. In *The Gilded Age* and *Playing the Mischief*, sexual corruption is one of many causes of political corruption; in *Democracy* and *Through One Administration*, cause and effect are reversed, and the heroines are sullied by their contact with Gilded Age Washington politics.

Twain and Warner open the discussion with *The Gilded Age*, where a notorious murder case is linked to a satire of the Washington lobbyist to prove that women should remain outside the loci of male power.[14] There are two parts to the story of Laura (van Brunt) Hawkins: her romantic history, in which the beautiful orphan foundling, raised by the Hawkins family, is seduced into a mock marriage by Colonel Selby during the Civil War, and the amusing analysis of Laura the lobbyist, working as Senator Dilworthy's assistant for the passage of the Knobs University bill, which would make her adopted family wealthy from the proceeds of their Tennessee lands. The connection suggested between these two is that once seduced and abandoned, Laura loses any moral scruple and is therefore willing to manipulate men. For Laura the political remains secondary to the sexual: as she connives for passage of her bill, she takes a generalized revenge on men, frowning "upon no lover when he made his first advances, but by and by, when he was hopelessly enthralled, he learned from her own lips that she had formed a resolution never to marry. Then he would go away hating and cursing the whole sex, and she would calmly add his scalp to her string."[15]

As Bryant Morey French has demonstrated, Laura's eventual murder of her betrayer and her acquittal on grounds of temporary insanity are based on the life of Mrs. Laura Fair, a notorious Californian who "received the ardent support of a group of extremists in the women's rights movement . . . advocates of direct action against their male oppressors."[16] Mrs. Fair was not a government lobbyist, and in fact Laura shoots Colonel Selby in a scene basically irrelevant to her political activities. But for Twain, who was just coming to the purity argument for giving women the vote, the female lobbyist was a logical stumbling block, and it served his purpose to suggest that she was as exceptional and dangerous as Mrs. Fair.[17] In the same year as *The Gilded Age*, Twain wrote a sketch called "The Temperance Crusade and Woman's Rights" in which he defended female temperance crusaders as

> thoroughly justifiable. They find themselves voiceless in the making of laws and the election of officers to execute them. Born with brains, born in the country, educated, having large interests at stake, they find their tongues tied and their hands fettered, while every ignorant whisky-drinking foreign-born savage in the land may hold office, help to make the laws, degrade the dignity of the former and break the latter at his own sweet will.

He "dearly" wants women to be allowed to vote, for "the present crusade . . . will suggest to more than one man that if women could vote they would vote on the side of morality."[18] Women lobbyists, deeply immersed in the manipulation and thievery rampant in Washington, were an obvious contradiction to his opinion of women.

And Laura is indeed engaged in most of what lobbyists were accused of. Twain only hints at the details, but the outline follows Edward Martin's analysis of the "working of the lobby." Laura is one of the "corps of operators who act as bushwhackers between the line of conventionality and the verge of looseness."[19] We never hear that she sleeps with any of the Congressmen, but her flirtations have the desired effect. When Senator Dilworthy asks if another senator has been "free in his manner," Laura indignantly replies, "Free? . . . With *me!*" but afterward she is amused: "Wouldn't Dilworthy open his eyes if he knew some of the things Balloon *did* say to me" (2:41–42).

During her stay in Washington Laura addresses Senator Dilworthy, that grand religious hypocrite, as "Uncle." The title emphasizes Laura's anomalous situation. As an adopted child, she is without any real family. She is temporarily excited by the knowledge that a man, presumably her father, looked for her after the steamship explosion, but, as Twain and Warner say in an ironic appendix, despite the "ease with which lost persons are found in novels . . . the man was not found" (2:329). Squire Hawkins, her adoptive father, dies when she is an adolescent. The only competent male left in the family, Clay, another adopted child and thus doubly unrelated to Laura, goes to live in Australia. Her marriage turns out to be false, bringing her no husband to act on her behalf. The remaining man whom Laura might have depended on to represent her, both generally and in the attempt to convince the government to buy the Hawkins family's Tennessee lands, is Washington Hawkins, the most inept man in the novel. Laura thus has two choices: she can gracefully consent to being poor and powerless, or she can use her influence on males outside her family to gain indirect power.

In *The Gilded Age,* previous sexual corruption explains a woman's involvement in political corruption: Selby, Laura says, has killed "all that was good in me" (2:65). Though Twain satirizes the temporary insanity plea as an excuse for murder, he accepts sexual betrayal as the cause for Laura's political behavior, because it allows him to continue to think of most women as a moral force for good. Women are naturally pure; however, once corrupted, they are capable of distorting the political process as much as men.

In *Playing the Mischief,* De Forest does not give his female manipulator even as much excuse as Laura has. Josie Murray, the most successful of all these female lobbyists, is motivated only by greed. Josie is a young widow who goes to Washington to claim reparations for a barn destroyed during the War of 1812. The claim is unjust in many ways: the government is not obliged to pay for property damaged in battle; the claim has been settled once already; and Josie asks first $20,000 and obtains, finally, $100,000 for a barn worth less than $2,000. The barn belonged to her husband's family, with whom she lives in Washington. Reverend Murray and his brother, a colonel in government employment, are opposed in principle to personal claims on the government and actually offer Josie an income if she will abandon the claim. But Josie refuses; thus her plea for sympathy, "What do I know about earning a living? What *can* a lady do?" is unconvincing.[20]

The exploration of women's power in *Playing the Mischief* is structured by a triangular contrast between Josie; Belle Warden, a model of traditional female influence; and a woman lawyer, "Squire" Nancy Appleyard. Appleyard, a "woman's rights woman," is the great comic success of De Forest's novel. She wears man's attire and has a "small head . . . full of wild notions about the early coming and the great glory of the millennium of female suffrage. When ladies should vote, go to Congress, sit on the bench of the Supreme Court, conduct banking, sail ships, and command armies, then politics would be pure, law infallible, business honest, war humane, and the world holy and happy" (75). De Forest's satire consists not only in ridiculing Appleyard's ideas, but also in demonstrating her inadequacy. Though she claims to be a lawyer, she is "without clients, or position, or anything that is legal" (43). Furthermore, she is in love with Sykes Drummond, one of Josie's conquests, and repeatedly fails to win him through aggressive actions that she thinks befit her male stance. Instead Drummond notices Nancy's prettiness and soft outlines, "signatures of a sex which is clearly doomed to rely for power upon its sweetness, rather than upon its strength" (74).

De Forest has several targets in his satire of Appleyard. Her ineffectual aggression spoofs the defense of Laura Fair and perhaps mocks Twain's heroine as well. After Appleyard fails in her second attempt to shoot Drummond, De Forest writes,

> It was really dreadful. Here was a man who would not permit himself to be shot either by night or by day. There was no precedent in the history of American heroines for the treatment of such a willful, irrational, and brutal wretch. The Jael of California herself, that spotless and fearless *protégée* of the eloquent strong-minded, would have been perplexed to deal with a wretch who thus abused his superior strength. (184)

The similarity of Nancy Appleyard's masculine costume to that of Dr. Mary Edwards Walker, a familiar sight in Washington in this period, has often been noticed.[21] Starting out as a "Bloomer," eventually Walker wore "a masculine jacket, shirt, stiff wing collar, bow tie and top hat."[22] But Walker was only a partial model, important primarily for her manner and notorious appearance. Nancy Appleyard's professional aspirations are a parody of those of Belva Lockwood, who studied law at National University Law School from 1871 to 1873 and was admitted to the bar of the District of Columbia—a distinction Appleyard is "clamoring" for—in that year. Lockwood is famous as the first woman admitted to practice before the Supreme Court, an event that required an act of Congress in 1879. Mary Walker briefly lived with Belva Lockwood, and "for a time the two women jointly promoted various feminist causes, particularly woman suffrage," so it was easy for De Forest to combine them in Appleyard.[23]

Josie, who ridicules Appleyard's strategy for gaining power, has no moral scruples against applying her own methods of persuasion. Belle's claim-hunting mother, Mrs. Warden, instructs Josie in how to proceed: "You must pick out your man, and then you must enchant and bewilder him, and then you must put your case in his hands" (26). Josie tries her skill on a number of public men, going so far as to engage herself simultaneously to two different congressman, Sykes Drummond and G. W. Hollowbread. Her tactics are epitomized by her treatment of the professional lobbyist Jake Pike, whom she employs to get her bill through and then refuses to pay. Though Pike protests, she terrorizes him by threatening to work against him, and he yields because "he knew what handsome and clever women could do in Washington" (155). The *Atlantic Monthly* reviewer, though amused, protests that De Forest has undertaken an "unpleasant problem" and probably refers to Josie's unscrupulousness in complaining that "much in the book . . . is downright disagreeable," dealing with the "vulgar phases of society in this country." [24]

De Forest's novel suggests that men are rightly frightened of female power. Hollowbread tells Josie, "If ever we let you ladies vote, you will easily get control of the inside of politics, and put us on the outside" (68), but Josie needs no more weapons than she already has. The opening scene of the novel foreshadows everything that happens thereafter: meeting Josie on the train, Hollowbread intends to make "a conquest of her," but "it did not so much as cross his statesman-like mind that, from this young lady's point of view, he was the mouse, and she the cat" (10). Shortly she has "bewildered and bamboozled and completely deprived of his common sense this really able Congressman" (98), so that eventually he has no "thought now of statesman-like honor; not a compunction as to robbing the treasury. . . . He was . . . a bewitched old Lothario, sacrificing others and himself for a passion" (159). When Josie wins her claim and breaks her engagement, he goes mad.

Josie perfectly understands the difference, in style and results, between her methods and the direct political participation sought by Appleyard and the suffragists. Mrs. Warden, in a low moment, says, " 'I wish women could vote; then it wouldn't be so [that one has to go to men for everything]. If I *do* fail in this demand of mine . . . I solemnly mean to turn woman's rights woman, and go to agitating. If we had a Congress of ladies—' 'Then you and I wouldn't get any money,' interrupted Josie. 'Pretty young gentlemen would have it all. I think we had better trust our affairs to male legislators'" (26).

The proper use of woman's power is demonstrated through the character of Belle Warden. Josie and Belle compete for the attentions of Congressman Edgar Bradford, and in the end Belle conquers. Although Josie set her snares for Bradford, he has always "draw[n] my line of proprieties" at "the confines of my official business" (62) and is frightened of Josie's fraudulent claim. He agrees with Edward Martin that "if a legislator allows to himself the slightest access from the [lobbying] woman, from that time he either is won to her interest, or tied up from proceeding averse to it." [25] Bradford's speech about Belle to Colonel Murray, who had been his superior officer during the war, epitomizes De Forest's vision of woman's contribution to the community: "She is my superior. . . . She is fit to be my officer. She will uphold me. This is a place of horrible temptations, colonel. She will be just such a wife as a Congressman needs. She will not let me do an unworthy action" (160). Though Belle Warden is the most colorless woman in *Playing the Mischief*, she will always achieve what she wishes, through Bradford. Even her mother admits "there is no man who will work for one like one's own husband" (29–30).

Playing the Mischief expresses profound doubts about female morality. Colonel Murray concludes that "there was one code of honor for men, and another, far less exacting, for women" (135). Hollowbread, realizing that Josie's claim is an "audacious project . . . for swindling Government," wonders "whether women generally are not less moral, at least in matters of property, than man; whether . . . they might not be fundamentally incapable of radical, unimposed, self-sustaining honesty" (53–54). Even the weapons used by the most virtuous are sexual and thus of questionable morality. Belle, who envisions asking her husband for "nothing which he is not able to give and willing to give," does not deny that she will "coax" him (26). In the early 1870s, with Victoria Woodhull preaching free love along with women's suffrage, the Beecher-Tilton scandal emerging from women's rights circles, and women lobbyists operating successfully in Washington, it was easy to conclude that women are too immoral to be trusted with political power.

We last see Josie going into dinner at Banker Allchin's, where she is honored "as a power in politics, as a successful claimant, as a goose worth picking" (184). De Forest tells us that she cannot escape "without being stripped of the golden plumage which she has filched from Uncle Sam's eagle. . . . On the whole, our hopes for her are feeble—feebler even than our good will" (185). The book thus ends with a straightforward authorial condemnation. A feminist, resisting-reader approach to this novel, as well as to

The Gilded Age, might argue for responding positively both to Laura, who is seduced and abandoned, and to Josie, who is alone in the world with little support besides her clever coquetry. Josie is a petty thief compared to the men who will inevitably "strip" her. But the undeviating authorial voice in *Playing the Mischief*, less ambiguous than that which lends Laura some sympathy in *The Gilded Age*, the creation of such moral norms as Colonel Murray and Belle Warden, and the fact that Josie both refuses an income and destroys her uncle and aunt reveal how artificial such a reading would be. To gain sympathy for the woman manipulating power in Washington, a different approach was necessary. That is what we find in *Democracy* and *Through One Administration*.

Democracy analyzes the possibility of a woman actually doing what Bradford expects from Belle—using her personal power to keep a political figure from "wrong action." Adams, however, changes the terms of the debate by creating a heroine apparently attracted to power for its own sake, rather than for material reward. Madeleine Lee, a wealthy and charming New Yorker who has lost both husband and child in one tragic week, comes to Washington because she wants to see "the tremendous forces of government, and the machinery of society, at work. What she wanted, was POWER."[26] The question is how she is to gain it. Soon "there was a very general impression . . . that Mrs. Lee would like nothing better than to be in the White House. . . . Mrs. Lee was properly assumed to be a candidate for office" (47–48). To gain this office she will have to marry Senator Silas Ratcliffe, "the first public man of the day," but after all, to "all well-regulated Washington women . . . the President's wife is of more consequence than the President; and . . . they are not very far from the truth" (48).

Madeleine is, indeed, tempted; "to tie a prominent statesman to her train and to lead him about like a tame bear, is for a young and vivacious woman a more certain amusement than to tie herself to him and to be dragged about like an Indian squaw." Senator Ratcliffe encourages Madeleine's ambitious longings, telling her bluntly that "the pleasure of politics lay in the possession of power" (43). But Madeleine, like Belle, has moral scruples. Asked repeatedly by Senator Ratcliffe what he should do in dubious situations, she has always the same answer: "whatever is most for the public good" (42, 87). The senator, whose great strength is "the skill with which he evaded questions of principle" (81), attempts to entangle Madeleine in his dilemmas so that she cannot criticize his subordination of morality to ambition.

Ratcliffe is successful enough that soon Madeleine admits having "got so far as to lose the distinction between right and wrong. Isn't that the first step in politics?" (99). She reconciles herself "to accepting the Ratcliffian morals, for she could see no choice. She herself had approved every step she had seen him take. She could not deny that there must be something wrong in a double standard of morality, but where was it? Mr. Ratcliffe seemed to her to be doing good work with as pure means as he had at hand" (98). Rather than adding to government corruption, like Laura and Josie, Madeleine is in danger of being corrupted by contact with public life.

To complicate his critique of women who influence government, Adams adds Mrs. Samuel Baker, widow of a lobbyist and, as it turns out, source of the damning information about Ratcliffe that will finally break his spell over Mrs. Lee. Mrs. Baker candidly reveals to Madeleine the details of the work she did with her husband. Familiar with all the members of Congress, she claims she "could get round the greater part of them, sooner or later." When Madeleine, scandalized, asks, "Do you mean that you could get them all to vote as you pleased?" Mrs. Baker replies cryptically, "Well! we got our bills through," and spells out her persuasive methods, including dinner parties, elbow jogging, and bribes. Madeleine is horrified to realize that Mrs. Baker is "perfectly presentable [and] . . . knew more about the practical working of government than [she] could ever expect or hope to know" (104–105).

The parallel casts a deep shadow on Madeleine's desire for influence. Is she really any purer than Mrs. Baker in her attempt to "manage" Senator Ratcliffe? Mrs. Baker carried information about all the congressmen in her head; Mrs. Lee tells Ratcliffe that she has organized her own "secret service bureau" (36). Mrs. Baker offered "suppers and cards and theatres" and occasionally money (104–105). Madeleine offers Senator Ratcliffe much the same: he longs "for a civilized house like Mrs. Lee's, with a woman like Mrs. Lee at its head, and [her] twenty thousand a year for life" (76). Are her attempts to lobby for reform any different from Mrs. Baker's attempts to lobby for a bill? Madeleine's final self-judgment is firmly negative.

But this self-judgment raises the most complex issue in *Democracy*—that of Madeleine's motivation. Having received proof of Ratcliffe's corruption, Madeleine tells herself that the temptation to marry Ratcliffe had come from

ambition, thirst for power, restless eagerness to meddle in what did not concern her, blind longing to escape from the torture of watching other women with full lives and satisfied instincts, while her own life was hungry and sad. . . . She had actually . . . hugged a hope that a new field of usefulness was open to her; that great opportunities for doing good were to supply the aching emptiness of that good which had been taken away. (166)

This last is the argument from sublimation, from, ultimately, "woman's nature." According to its logic, a woman needs the fulfillment of husband

and "dimple-cheeked" baby; failure in this realm explains female attempts to play the power game.

While Adams toys with this idea, common in antisuffrage writing, he has two objections to it. First, he does not entirely dismiss the attraction of power for its own sake: he had known it too well in his own life and was willing to admit that women might feel it too.[27] Both he and his wife have been alleged as models for Madeleine.[28] Marian Adams suffered from childlessness, but childlessness alone cannot explain how Mrs. Adams, a "perfect Voltaire in petticoats" according to James, created a salon that, like Mrs. Lee's, became "a rendezvous for the political and intellectual elite."[29] Ratcliffe understands Madeleine's mixed motives: in his proposal he first tells her that she is "fitted better than any woman I ever saw, for public duties" (154), and only then does he appeal to her instinct for self-sacrifice by telling her that he needs her.[30]

Second, *Democracy*, like *The Gilded Age* and *Playing the Mischief*, is primarily concerned with morality in politics. Taking as his premise that both men and women have longings for power, Adams investigates the frequently proposed possibility of improving political morality through women.[31] Unlike Laura and Josie, Adams's heroine sets out as a reformer, yet soon corruption is "bespattering with mud even her own pure garments" (97–98). Adams concludes that politics will drag women down too, that they will become as complacent as Mrs. Samuel Baker or as confused about ends and means as Madeleine. More important than any personal emptiness that might lead Madeleine to politics is the inevitability of what happens to her. Madeleine is still without husband and child as the novel ends, and she is not thinking about filling the void. She is thinking about the way in which a pure woman can be harmed by participation in government. Once she dismisses Ratcliffe, she says, "I want to go to Egypt . . . democracy has shaken my nerves to pieces. Oh, what rest it would be to live in the Great Pyramid and look out for ever at the polar star!" (182).

In *Through One Administration* (serialized from 1881 on), Burnett replies to all three of the preceding novels; a recent writer chooses his verb well in suggesting that the book "may have been in part provoked by Adams' *Democracy*."[32] Bertha Amory is much like Madeleine Lee in her social position, her style, her wit, and her fundamental morality, but Burnett makes two critical alterations in the position of her heroine: first, Bertha is a married woman, surrounded by husband, children, and father, and second, she is compelled into the political world by her husband.

The political tale is not very different from that in *The Gilded Age*. Once again the owners of a large tract of territory need government intervention if they are to benefit from its natural resources. Bertha's husband Richard, a charming but unscrupulous man, invests Bertha's fortune, without her knowledge, in the project. Telling Bertha that "you would make the most successful little lobbyist in the world" (120), he gradually forces her to make herself agreeable to the men who control votes, especially Senator Plane-field, "a lady's man [who] . . . finds Mrs. Amory very charming" (128). Richard himself explains that women who become similarly involved

> rarely . . . even in the end, admit to themselves that they have done what they are accused of. Given a clever and pretty woman whose husband or other male relative needs her assistance; why should she be less clever and pretty in the society of one political dignitary than in that of another, whose admiration of her charms may not be of such importance? I suppose that is the beginning, and then come the sense of power and the fascination of excitement. (155)

It does not take long before Bertha is noticed as "a little married woman who flirts" (310) and finds that "it appears somehow that Richard belongs to Senator Planefield, and, as I belong to Richard . . . I am that glittering being, the female lobbyist" (424).

The costs to Bertha are great. She is cut socially. Forced to be more "glittering" than agrees with her, she becomes ill. She loses her self-respect and begins to quarrel with Richard, whom she has never loved but with whom she has always maintained amicable relations. Finally he contrives for her to give a bribing letter to another senator, Blundell, who sees that she is being manipulated and realizes that she is ignorant of the letter's contents. Blundell kills the bill, and Richard flees the country. Bertha is left to face her husband's perfidy and her loss of fortune.

Burnett creates a more complex connection between her heroine's motivation and her behavior than did Twain, De Forest, or even Adams. Bertha lobbies because her husband requires her to do so; frequently she mentions doing her duty. But her deeper reasons lie elsewhere: she obeys Richard because she feels guilt over her secret love for her cousin Philip Tredennis. She also hopes that if she seems "a dazzling and worldly creature," "false, and shallow, and selfish" (237, 280), she will destroy Philip's love for her and save him the pain of unfulfilled longings. Her erotic history and her lobbying thus have the direct relationship artificially imposed on Laura Hawkins's history.

This is the only novel of these four written by a woman, and the only one in which the heroine has men who could represent her. But Bertha's father, Professor Herrick, is so unworldly that he does not secure Bertha's fortune to her at the time of her marriage; her cousin Philip is paralyzed by his unspoken love and can only suffer as he hears Bertha's name connected with Planefield's "as—as no honest man is willing that the name of his wife should be connected with that of another man"; and her husband is so corrupt that, as Bertha replies, "Richard has not resented it" (325). In a stunning rejection of the antisuffragists' argument for confining women's political participation to indirect influence, Burnett demonstrates that rather than sparing a woman the need to represent herself, her male relations may be the very cause of her political involvement.

Burnett agrees with Adams that women are more likely to be corrupted by politics than politics corrupted by them, but she is much more dubious about the temptation of politics for women. Though Bertha makes a "pretence of being interested in politics . . . it was not a very serious pretence" (92), and her claim to be "fond of power" (209) is merely her attempt to discourage Philip Tredennis. In the end Bertha, tortured by her emotional conflicts, yields to her "nature." We last see her as she enters the nursery.[33]

The most striking parallel between these four books is that women are almost always successful in their indirect manipulation of government. Even in *Through One Administration*, where the bill for Richard's railroad does not pass, Planefield alleges that this is because Bertha has gone away just when she is needed. "One or two of her little dinners would be the very things . . . for the final smoothing down of one or two rough ones. . . . They'd only have one opinion when she'd done with them" (377). Indeed, one reviewer commented that the most unrealistic thing about the novel was that the bill did not pass: "We feel bound to say that it gives us a far higher notion of the purity of the capital . . . to know that the scheme failed. Any woman with the charms of Mrs. Amory who plays Mrs. Amory's part, however unconsciously, would in most cases, we fear, insure her friends' success."[34]

The lobbyist novels articulate American fears of giving women more direct political rights because of the conviction that the methods women already employed were quite successful. These novels contest the claim that the presence of women would improve political morality. Women who are corrupt themselves find government and politicians a ready field for their talents; pure women, rather than salvaging morality, are dragged into the morass. Rather than hastening the vote for women, the argument from morality seems to raise another barrier.

The Biology of Political Action

Americans who opposed giving women direct access to political power, especially through the ballot, preferred to shift discussion from the political morality of women to their biological "nature." Less concerned about the republic and more about the structure of the family, antisuffragists usually took the superior morality of woman as a premise but then used a set of assumptions about the physical differences between the sexes to argue against letting women into the political arena. Once again the argument about rights turned into an argument about bodies.

According to the antisuffragists, the very qualities of mind and temperament that made women the moral leaders of the home disqualified them from political participation. Their emotional nature was suited only to private life. As Senator Vest of Missouri asserted, "There are spheres in which feeling should be paramount. . . . That kingdom belongs to the woman, the realm of sentiment, the realm of love."[35] Yet, Francis Parkman stated that while "the impetuous property of feminine nature . . . may have its use at times," the danger of passing rash legislation would be "increased immeasurably if the most impulsive and excitable half of humanity had an equal voice in the making of laws."[36] In addition to their excitability, women were too subject to stress to be given the additional burden of politics.

The argument from nature led inevitably to the discussion of woman's role as wife and mother. Many antisuffragists implicitly admitted the attraction of power and politics for women when they expressed fears that a woman who became involved in political action would necessarily neglect her children and husband. Furthermore, she would be likely to bring the political world into the home, promoting "unhappiness and dissension in the family circle."[37] Rev. Horace Bushnell's imagination extended further: he predicted that if women were given the ballot, they would feel impelled to exercise their equality within the home, even to the point of taking different political positions from their husbands or running against their spouses for public office.[38] The ideal of the male antisuffragists was articulated by Senator Vest: "When I go to my home . . . I want to go back, not to be received in the masculine embrace of some female ward politician, but to the earnest, loving look and touch of a true woman."[39]

Many antisuffragists believed that giving women the "equality" of the vote would discourage marriage and encourage divorce. The Senate minority report in 1887 stated that "the largest number of divorces is now found in the communities where the advocates of female suffrage are most numerous and where the *individuality* of woman as related to her husband . . . is increased to the greatest extent." An increase in divorces, or in the number of women who chose to pursue a career and remained unmarried, signaled a serious problem for a society where population growth was valued. As the senator from Georgia declared, "It is the duty of society to encourage the increase of marriages rather than of celibacy. If the larger number of females select pursuits or professions which require them to decline marriage, society . . . is deprived of the advantage resulting from the increase of population by marriage."[40] This concern with the preservation of marriage and the hierarchical relationship between husband and wife should be read in the light of late nineteenth-century racism, which urged the northern European and Protestant elements of the population to reproduce themselves, both to preserve a "superior" gene pool and to outnumber blacks and more recent immigrants at the voting booth.

The concern for woman's emotional nature, for her physical weakness, and for preservation of motherhood as a primary duty all hint at a basic fear—that a woman who ventures into the political sphere will no longer be sexually controlled by her husband. After a long, rambling discussion of the physical differences between men and women, Francis Parkman arrives at his point: since women are weaker physically, they cannot protect their honor in public. He defends the need for sexual control over wives by reminding readers that "women, and not men, are of necessity the guardians of the integrity of the family and the truth of succession." These guardians cannot be trusted: Parkman anticipates that since "many women sell themselves; many more would sell their votes." [41]

Others who do not impugn a woman's fundamental morality distrust her resistance to tempting circumstances. They emphasize the conditions of politics, which would throw men and women (usually imagined as wives) together. Senators Brown and Cockrell raise the specter of the baser element rushing to the polls to "take pleasure in the crowded association which the situation would compel of the two sexes in political meetings and at the ballot box." [42] Writing some thirty years before, Bushnell was even more direct. In rural areas, he anticipates, men and women will have to travel together to the polls and may be forced to stay overnight in a tavern, "in some kind of general carouse that will comfort their defeat, or celebrate their victory. Finally, the next day the women voters are put down home— with some things to regret, which are only worse if not regretted." [43]

Three significant novels, Bayard Taylor's *Hannah Thurston* (1864), Henry James's *The Bostonians* (1886), and Hamlin Garland's *A Spoil of Office* (1892), deal directly with the demand for women's suffrage. Where the lobbyist novels argue about woman's moral nature and the effect on government of permitting women to participate, contemporary novels about suffrage join the debate about woman's biological nature and the effect on male-female relations within the home if women gain new "rights." The novels demonstrate the ways in which women's increased power in the public realm would have consequences played out in the domestic sphere. The first group of novels is openly political; the second group, especially when defensive against change, is psychological.

In 1859 the women's rights speaker Anna E. Dickinson appeared in Kennett Square, Pennsylvania, [44] and in that same year Bayard Taylor, a well-known travel writer, returned from Europe to the town and began to build a house there. [45] Whether he heard Dickinson is unclear, as Taylor never explained why he chose as the heroine of his first novel an advocate of women's rights. In a striking parallel, more than twenty years later James, also returning from an extended stay abroad, again found the subject of his "very *American* tale" in "the situation of women." One critic even proposes a continuing significance for Anna Dickinson, suggesting that Verena Tarrant, heroine of *The Bostonians*, is modeled on Dickinson, whom James could have heard and met in the 1860s.[46]

The similarities between *Hannah Thurston* and the better-known *Bostonians* are remarkable, enough to suggest that James, who mentions Taylor's translation of *Faust* in *The Bostonians*, probably read the earlier novel when it appeared. As Taylor says in a letter of April 1866, "whatever may be the faults [of *Hannah Thurston*] . . . the booksellers tell me that it already has the character of a standard work. Now, two and a half years after publication, there is a steady, permanent demand for it." The book was warmly praised by Hawthorne.[47]

Hannah Thurston is set in 1852, in the midst of the abolition period. The heroine, who speaks for women's rights, lives in a small, upstate New York town, Ptolemy, where reform movements from temperance to religious communitarianism flourish. Hannah, who is nearly thirty, is assumed by many in the town to be a typical women's rights woman—unmarried, unmarriageable, and hostile to men; yet the narrator describes her as "a woman to sit at a king's right hand, in thunder-storms."[48] It is apparent that no man within her limited circle is worthy to make her yield her independence.

To Ptolemy comes Maxwell Woodbury, like Taylor returning to the United States after many years abroad. He first notices Hannah when she sings at a meeting of the "Sewing Union," which brings together those working for a variety of causes: missions, abolition, and sectarian religion. Intrigued, he attends the women's rights meeting she addresses in the town hall. Most of the novel is taken up with their gradual discovery of each other's strengths: Maxwell is not so contemptuous of women as Hannah thought, and she, at the end, is revealed as a true woman, begging him to "teach me to deserve your magnanimity" (429).

The moral is driven home by a series of parallel plots in which women discover their "true nature" by yielding to men and becoming happy. The little seamstress who has rejected her worthy farmer-suitor because she nourishes foolish dreams of marrying a reformer finds, in her lover's illness, her true vocation as nurse and helpmate. An older woman, deeply depressed by the death of her children, is persuaded to elope with a charlatan reformer and is only saved by the combined efforts of Hannah, Maxwell, and other better-balanced members of the community. Yet once her husband reasserts his "rightful influence over her" (210), Mrs. Merryfield becomes happy and forgets her "jealous demand for her 'rights' " (258).

Maxwell Woodbury is the voice of reason in this novel. More sophisticated and worldly than the insular inhabitants of Ptolemy, he easily recognizes charlatanism and excess. Similarly, he intuits that under Hannah's apparent rigidity, emphasized by her Quaker background and dress, is a passionate woman waiting to be awakened. He advocates private as well as public respect for women, but does not believe in the call for "rights" and finds the "idea of an independent strength, existing side by side with his, yet without requiring its support . . . unnatural and repulsive" (62). His basic belief is that "it is not a question of superiority, but of radical and necessary difference of nature" (254).

Since Taylor is less complex and opaque than James, there is no uncertainty that Woodbury speaks for the author and is intended to persuade readers. Woodbury's position is reinforced by the most admirable women in the novel. Hannah's own mother has told her that she is mistaken in her attitude: "We cannot be wholly independent of the men: we need their help and companionship: we acknowledge their power even while we resist it" (161). Woodbury's friend Mrs. Blake, who speaks from the experience of marriage, tells Hannah that "there is no true woman but longs, in her secret soul, for a man's breast to lay her head on" (331). And indeed Hannah herself nourishes a "hopeless dream" of "the man whom every pulse of her being claimed and called upon, the man who never came!" (152, 154).

Taylor concedes some of the reformers' points. For example, when Hannah gives her first speech on women's rights, Taylor does not mock her concern with economic equality. On the other hand, he is unsympathetic to Hannah's call for marriage as a "*partnership*" (73), so the narrative voice concludes that while her speech had contained "many absolute truths," she had not touched "the profounder aspects of the subject, especially the moral distinctions of sex" (74).

By "moral distinctions of sex" Taylor means physical and emotional differences. For him the central problem in women taking direct political action is that it will bring about their intimate contact with men in public. Woodbury is certain that "woman is too finely organized for the hard, coarse business of the world." Asked by Hannah if woman would not "refine [the world] by her presence," he replies,

> Never! . . . supposing them to be equally implicated in the present machinery of politics. The first time a female candidate went into a bar-room to canvass for votes, she would see the inmates on their best behavior; but this could not last long. She would soon either be driven from the field, or brought down to the same level. Nay, she would go below it, for the rudest woman would be injured by associations through which the most refined man might pass unharmed. (254–255)

Mrs. Blake, reiterating the argument that the physical differences between the sexes are paramount, tells Hannah, "there are times when a woman has no independent life of her own—when her judgment is wavering and obscured—when her impulses are beyond her control. The business of the world must go on. . . . Congresses cannot be adjourned nor trials postponed, nor suffering patients neglected, to await her necessities" (330).

Taylor's plot bears out Woodbury's belief in woman's instinctive desire to be ruled by a man and in the absolute dichotomy between exposing the female body in public and using it properly at home. Hannah not only yields to Woodbury in marriage, but after a few months finds that "the very thought of standing where I once stood" and speaking at a new women's rights meeting makes her "faint." Instead, Woodbury agrees to go in her place, articulating the classic view of representation: "who has so good a right to be your substitute as your husband?" (449). The sense that Hannah's speaking was a sublimation of other physical satisfactions is emphasized when Maxwell returns from the meeting and she "rewards" him with the news that she is pregnant. Once this baby is born she asks him to "take back your promise of independence" (463).

Hannah Thurston articulates the antisuffragists' fear that if women take political action they will deny society their bodies. The demand for direct political participation is interpreted as an attack on the family unit. At the beginning of the novel the failure of this splendid woman to marry, apparently because of her women's rights beliefs, bears out the worst fears of the social eugenicists. From Taylor's point of view she must be forced to yield, for her own good, the good of her husband, and the good of the larger community. The choice is between independence and absolute submission. It is not accidental that Woodbury's wooing of Hannah is couched in terms of a military campaign, which ends with "the inevitable surrender" (401–404).

When James comes to write *The Bostonians* he adopts much of *Hannah Thurston*'s underlying structure, from the hero's first vision of the women's rights woman who attracts him despite her opinions, to the final meeting at which his triumph is revealed when she does not make a speech. But James makes two critical changes: he splits Hannah into Olive Chancellor and Verena Tarrant, and he obscures the extent to which the conquering hero, Basil Ransom, speaks for his author. Although these changes entail enormous consequences for the tone of the novel, the objections to the demand for suffrage are essentially the same.

The first place Basil Ransom—and the reader—see Verena Tarrant is, like Woodbury's first vision of Hannah, at a social gathering of reformers. But where Hannah must be plucked from a quiet corner to sing a touching song, Verena, who speaks with "promptness and assurance,"[49] immediately lectures on the "goodness of women, and how . . . they had been trampled under the iron heel of man" (61). Furthermore, Verena is quite literally in the hands of her father, whose type is the "detested carpetbagger" (58). From Basil's southern point of view she is politically and physically corrupted already.

The stroke of genius that elevates *The Bostonians* over *Hannah Thurston* is James's division of Taylor's heroine into two. Olive has Hannah's cultivation and literary interests; she conveys a sense of being a woman past the age of marriage, and Basil finds himself thinking of her as old, although she is younger than he (18); most important, she actually does hate "men, as a class" (22). On the other hand, it is Verena who has the capacity to speak in public, the natural attractiveness, and the secret dream of a man that will eventually lead her to realize that "she was to burn everything she had adored; she was to adore everything she had burned" (396). This split permits *The Bostonians* to be structured as a triangular "struggle for possession," [50] where *Hannah Thurston* was a straightforward battle between the hero and the heroine. The split also permits James to be more hostile and ironic about women's rights than Taylor. He can make Olive not just mistaken but perverse, since she will never yield to the masculine principle.

The great difficulty in establishing James's position in *The Bostonians* in the argument over women's rights is that so much of the judgment of Olive and Verena is made through Basil Ransom's eyes, and Basil is not, like Woodbury, simply a stand-in for his author. The plot tends to confirm Basil's judgments—Selah Tarrant, who lets Olive buy his daughter from him, is as corrupt as Basil presumes, and by yielding to Basil's love, Verena validates his assumption that this is her true desire (no matter how unhappy the marriage may prove.) Many readers, trained by the romantic novel to expect a concluding union, will agree with Basil that Olive's possession of Verena is unnatural, especially since Olive, like Tarrant, eventually displays Verena for money. Nevertheless, Basil himself is treated with ironic detachment. [51] He is particularly prone to oversimplifications on the subject of women's rights, like "the position of women is to make fools of men" (24), or "not a word" of what Verena says of female suffering is true (276), or "what balderdash he thought it—the whole idea of women's being equal to men" (325), or finally, women are quite inferior "for public, civic uses . . . perfectly weak and second-rate" (348). One of Basil's most impassioned statements, on the feminization of "our general life" and the "feminine . . . nervous, hysterical, chattering, canting age" (343), has often been assigned to James, [52] but it comes immediately after Basil himself admits that "I have been joking; I have been piling it up" (341).

The arguments Basil uses to Verena are essentially those that Woodbury made to Hannah. Each woman is told that she is made "for privacy, for him, for love" (275), and that this is her "nature." Despite the differences in tone and authorial distance, both plots confirm this masculine judgment. Hannah eventually agrees, and despite misgivings, Verena does too. As the narrative voice asserts, "it was in [Verena's] nature to be easily submissive" (337). The words Basil speaks to her about her "genuine vocation" for the "realm of family life and the domestic affections" (348) sink into her soul and ferment there until "she had come at last to believe them" (396).

When we first see Hannah she has not married because of a suspicion of men and a dearth of appropriate suitors. Verena, in contrast, gratefully accepts men's attentions, and ingenuously begs Olive to admit that "some are attractive!" (142). Therefore Olive tries to extract from Verena a promise never to marry. While some have called Olive perverse from a homophobic suspicion of her relation with Verena, a response informed by the historical and political context would focus on the social perversity of Olive's attempt to keep Verena from meeting society's need for marriages. Verena is "the first pretty girl [Basil] had seen in Boston" (45), with a "gift of expression" that, in his opinion, will be truly delightful "when [her] influence becomes really social" (402). To Basil, "real" social life, like true influence, takes place within the home.

The contrast between public and private society is continued through the portrait of Mrs. Farrinder, "the great apostle of the emancipation of women" (21). Mrs. Farrinder's style is public—she had the "air of being introduced by a few remarks" (30)—and what we learn of her married life confirms antisuffragist fears of a reversal of the male-female hierarchy. Her lecture topics portend dissension between husband and wife: "the ends she labored for were to give the ballot to every woman . . . and to take the flowing bowl from every man." (In *Hannah Thurston*, Woodbury likewise sees the temperance crusade as antimale.) The first, long description of Mrs. Farrinder concludes with the understated remark that "she had a husband, and his name was Amariah" (31). Poor Amariah only reappears once, symbolically following his wife on and off the platform. Made invisible by a public wife, it is no wonder he has a "vague" face (443).

Under Olive's tutelage Verena exemplifies both sides of the antisuffragists' image of woman. She embodies female nature and shows how easily it is corrupted. She is impulsive and excitable; she "adore[s] children" (340); she is putty in the hands of whoever manages her, whether her father, Olive, or Basil; and Basil wins because "the struggle of yielding to a will which [Verena] felt to be stronger even than Olive's was not of long duration" (337). Yet in the period when she "likes" Basil but considers his ideas "unspeakably false and horrible," Verena foreshadows the family dissension arising from differing political opinions, and belief in women's rights almost leads her to eschew marriage.

Both novels end with the women's rights heroine refusing to speak at a meeting on the subject. The conclusion of *The Bostonians* is much more dramatic, as Basil practically abducts Verena while the mob in the Boston Music Hall becomes impatient and Olive and the Tarrants try desperately to make the young girl deliver her address. This very intensity reveals why Verena, like Hannah, cannot speak to the assembled masses. A writer to the *Woman's Journal* complained of Basil's "willingness to allow others to suffer that his own ends may be attained" and found his refusal to let Verena speak proof that he cannot be "a high-minded gentleman or honorable lover."[53] But from an antisuffrage position of the 1880s it is proof of precisely the reverse. It is Verena whom he saves from suffering. Given the premises on which Basil and Malcolm Woodbury operate, for Verena to speak to the Music Hall audience is to sell herself to the crowd. No one asks a high-minded gentleman to allow his wife to prostitute herself, even just for an hour.

James's novel is more angry than Taylor's about the agitation for women's rights. Though Hannah gives up speaking, her husband urges woman's "claim to a completer trust . . . and . . . respectful consideration" (452). Ransom, on the other hand, when Verena asks what she shall do with her gift, disrespectfully responds that she can mount on the dining room table: "You won't sing in the Music Hall, but you will sing to me" (402). The increased irritability reflects heightened social tension. In 1864 Hannah is willing to "endure a little longer, to be deprived of the permission to vote and to rule" (70), if she can have equality of education and reward. By 1886 the demand for political participation was more insistent, the women more threatening. Nevertheless, the history of James criticism shows how the reader's attitude affects interpretation of this novel. Both Basil's and Olive's positions have been vigorously defended as the point of the book;[54] the historical context suggests a more guarded and balanced reading.

The Bostonians reveals many of the fears aroused by the demand for women's rights; Garland's *A Spoil of Office* (1892) presents the alternative vision. Although Garland was commissioned to write a novel about the "revolt of the farmers," [55] *A Spoil of Office* is equally about the agitation for women's rights. At this period Garland wrote frequently about the suffering of women on midwestern farms. In his autobiography, *A Son of the Middle Border,* he recounts how, as a mature man, "I no longer looked upon these toiling women with the thoughtless eyes of youth . . . I saw lovely girlhood wasting away into thin and hopeless age." [56] By 1890, he publicly supported equal rights for women. In an article in the *Standard* he visualized a world where "the liberty of man and woman is bounded only by the equal rights of others. Woman stands there as independent of man as man is independent of woman." [57] But Garland also understood the antisuffragists' argument from biology. The hero of "A Branch-Road," which appeared as the first story in *Main-Travelled Roads* in 1891, becomes enraged when he sees his girlfriend talking to another man. "It was the instinct of possession, the organic feeling of proprietorship of a woman, which rose to the surface and mastered him." [58]

In *A Spoil of Office* Garland takes up the major arguments against women's suffrage and women suffragists and refutes them. As in both of the earlier novels, women's suffrage is again associated with other reforms, in this case, the agrarian protest movement and the founding of the Populist party.[59] *A Spoil of Office* is the story of Bradley Talcott, a young farmhand from Iowa who becomes a lawyer and enters politics, first as a state legislator and then as a congressman, and Bradley's gradual awakening to the failure of "regular" party politics to respond to the suffering of the western farmers. But it is also the story of Bradley's intellectual and emotional awakening by Ida Wilbur, a Grange and women's rights lecturer.

Once again the first place the hero sees his ideal woman is at a social and political gathering, here a Grange picnic. Like Verena, Ida is speaking, but unlike Basil, Bradley is inspired rather than repelled by her words:

> As he listened, something stirred within him, a vast longing, a hopeless ambition, nameless as it was strange. . . . His eyes absorbed every detail of the girl's face and figure. There was wonder in his eyes at her girlish face, and something like awe at her powerful diction and her impersonal emotion. She stood there like an incarnation of the great dream-world that lay beyond his horizon. (14)

Bradley does not dream of possessing Ida; he dreams of being worthy of her.

Ida has the genuine connection to other women about which Olive merely fantasized. Closed in her social caste, Olive "had long been preoccupied with the romance of the people. She had an immense desire to know intimately some *very* poor girl" (35). Ida actually works for poor women; her motive is reform. Whenever she speaks, women "bent by toil above the wash-tub and the churn, shut out from all things that humanize and make living something more than a brute struggle," crowd around her. "They clung to the girl's hand, gazing at her with wistful eyes. . . . They could not bear to let her go out of their lives again. Ida greeted them smilingly, but her face was quivering with . . . sadness" (349–350).

Ida is nothing like the antisuffragist portrait of the women's rights agitator. Not impulsive or emotional, but thoughtful and educated, she can "forget her sex occasionally and become an intellect" (251). Discussing ideas with Bradley, she addresses him "precisely as one man looks at another, without the slightest false modesty or coquettishness" (148). Yet she is thoroughly feminine; while she sits "lost in philosophic thought . . . her bent head seemed incredibly beautiful" (149), and at this second encounter Bradley finds her "fuller of form and . . . more womanly" (141). There is no evidence that Ida is opposed to marriage. Like Hannah, she lives with her mother, but "she's had suitors enough" (251). When one of Bradley's colleagues in Des Moines objects that Ida "is a great woman, but . . . abnormal. . . . Look at the life she leads. On the road constantly, living at hotels. A woman can't hold herself up against such things," Bradley replies succinctly, "It depends upon the woman" (243).

The contrast is carefully drawn between the sexual constraint of Ida, who asks for, and takes, direct political action, and the sexual machinations of women engaged in indirect political action. In Iowa City Bradley encounters "one of the most dangerous and demoralizing features of each legislature," the girls who come to "cajole and flatter their way into a State House office" (219). He is sickened as he sees "those bright, pretty girls go down among those men, whose hard, peculiar, savage stare he knew" (220), and notes particularly the youth of the girls and the way they tempt married men. Ida, on the other hand, is in complete control of her sexuality. Late in the novel when Bradley and Ida travel together side by side on a wagon seat, "the pressure of his arm at her side stirred her, and she smiled at herself. Unlike Bradley, she was self-analytical; she knew what all these things meant" (376).

The experience of Bradley and Ida rebuts most of the antisuffragist arguments about politics as a cause for family division. Instead, these two are brought together by their shared goals. They agree to marry after a trip over the frozen prairie to an Alliance meeting. The meeting itself negates the claim that joint political action by men and women will encourage sexual misconduct. Nothing could be further from the minds of the audience gathered at night in an isolated schoolhouse. Bradley and Ida find "the room full of men and women—the women all on one side of the room and the men mainly on the other" (368), all there because misery has driven them to politics. These are the same women Bradley had seen at another Alliance meeting, "women with stooping shoulders, and eyes dim with toil and suffering" (340). They are desexed by poverty and oppression, not by political empowerment.

In his conclusion Garland takes the most radical position possible about the way in which political action will unite Bradley and Ida. Shortly after the meeting they marry and return together to Washington, as he completes his term as a congressman. But after a few weeks Ida tells him she must leave. She wants to return to her own work, speaking for the Alliance in the West. For an antisuffragist this would provide the final demonstration of how allowing women into politics will divide the family, but for Garland it is something else entirely. Ida is going West to "pave the way for your re-election by the people's party. . . . If you expect to do your part here, I must do my part in electing you. . . . You know how much good it does the poor wives and mothers to meet me and to hear me. Now, we mustn't be selfish, dear; you've got your work to do here, and I've got my work to do there" (384–385). Basil and Maxwell Woodbury silenced their wives, but Bradley has given his a new topic. Pure and womanly Ida will return to the platform, working both for women and for her husband.

Women in the Political Arena: Art and Life

In 1868 the Washington correspondent Emily Edson Briggs, "Olivia" to her readers, commented that "never . . . have the women performed more conspicuous parts in the national play of politics than at the present time in Washington."[60] This reality existed contemporaneously with the debate in fiction over the potential consequences of the women's rights movement. Yet the novels of the period differ greatly in their willingness to recognize how far the political mobilization of women had already come.

Novelists concerned with political corruption relied heavily on actual events and personages in order to comment on the moral nature of American women and their potential influence on government. The portraits of women lobbyists given to us by Adams, Burnett, De Forest, and Twain closely resemble those recorded by journalists and diarists of the period. Some characters and incidents, such as Twain's Laura, De Forest's Nancy Appleyard, and the Knobs University bill, have identifiable historical counterparts. The anonymous publication of *Democracy* aroused great interest in the capital because its author was obviously a Washington insider, and women like Madeleine Lee were found throughout the upper echelon of Washington society.

On the other hand, Taylor and James isolate their characters geographically and historically from the contemporary political world. *Hannah Thurston*, although published in 1864, is set in the 1850s. Ptolemy, New York, reflects national politics only through the ineffectual local reform societies; it knows nothing of Washington. The heroine speaks for economic rights for women, but makes no reference to New York's Married Women's Property Act of 1848. The conventions and petition drives for women's suffrage that took place throughout the 1850s are reduced to the generalized meeting on "reform" with which the book ends. Taylor wants to suggest that Hannah's original views are as farfetched as those of the traveling charlatan who conducts meetings indifferently on "Total Abstinence, Vegetarianism . . . Slavery, Women's Rights, or Non-Resistance" (442). Her acceptance of her role as wife and mother thus signifies a return to the values of a timeless, "real," American society.

James also minimizes the women's rights activity with which he was almost certainly familiar. He had lived in Boston from 1870 to 1872—two years "among the most active and sensational before suffrage was won"[61]—and returned from Europe in the early 1880s at a time of renewed suffrage activity. In the spring of 1881 the National Woman Suffrage Association "held a series of conventions through New England,"[62] and James's 1882 visit to Washington coincided with the beginning of congressional debate over the establishment of a House committee on woman's suffrage. Sara deSaussure Davis contends that James gathered material for the novel from his earlier days in Boston, from his knowledge of Anna Dickinson through Whitelaw Reid, and from his observations in the 1880s.[63] Yet *The Bostonians* takes place largely in the seclusion of Olive Chancellor's Boston establishment, in the drawing rooms and parlors of New York, and on the beaches of Cape Cod. This commentary on American society is played out mainly as a private love story.

In *The Bostonians* the most extensive references to a public event of the women's rights movement are the belated accounts given to Basil of the Female Convention where Verena "made an immense sensation" (241). James lessens the importance of the event by filtering the picture of the convention through first Mrs. Luna's and then Basil's hostile vision, as well as by having Verena trivialize her description of the "tremendously earnest discussions" with the comment that "we consumed quantities of ice cream" (207–209, 242–243). Mrs. Farrinder, the only representative of the national women's rights movement, is never seen making a public speech or engaging in political action. *The Bostonians* portrays the women's rights movement as a fringe group, with vague political demands; in this way James reduces as much as possible the significance of women's call for increased public power.[64]

Pro–women's rights novels, like the lobbyist novels, pay close attention to contemporary developments. Most of these novels are little more than fictionalized didactic tracts, but they exemplify the conviction that, as Elizabeth Cady Stanton comments in her preface to one of them, "the wrongs of society can be more deeply impressed on a large class of readers in the form of fiction than by essays, sermons, or the facts of science."[65] All agree that the vote, and only the vote, can ensure protection for women. Each tends to highlight one abuse that could be prevented if women had direct political power. For instance, in *Christine; or, Woman's Trials and Triumphs*, published by Laura J. Curtis (Bullard) in 1856, the heroine is tricked into a madhouse by her family, which objects to her speaking for women's rights. Christine herself concentrates on economic issues, including equal pay, and defends the need for suffrage on the basis of "no taxation without representation."[66] In *Out of Her Sphere*, written by Lizzie Boynton Harbert (1871), the heroine lectures on equal education, promising that "when women legislate, they will not tax themselves to build colleges from which they are excluded."[67] Mary H. Ford's *Which Wins? A Story of Social Conditions* (1891) details the ways in which a woman could still lose control of her fortune to her husband.[68] Helen H. Gardener's *Pray You, Sir, Whose Daughter?* (1892) centers on a proposal before the New York legislature to lower the age of consent for girls to ten, which calls forth from the heroine's father the admission that "if you or your mother, or any other respectable mother at all, were in the Legislature, no such bill would have a ghost of a chance."[69] These novels all identify the link between economic, legal, and social domination and demand political remedies.

Garland, as a prosuffragist, also closely follows contemporary actuality. The character of Ida, like the protest movement, was drawn from life. Sent west by Benjamin Flower to study the Farmer's Alliance movement,[70] Garland made the acquaintance of Mary Elizabeth Lease, a popular Grange speaker.[71] Mrs. Lease's greatest period of fame extended from 1890 to 1894 when she spoke for the Farmer's Alliance and the People's party, moving audiences with "her voice—deep, resonant, and hypnotic."[72] Like Ida, Mary Lease was renowned in midwestern politics; at the People's party convention in 1892 she seconded the nomination of General Weaver for president. But Mary Lease apparently did not speak for women's rights. In *A Spoil of Office* Garland overcomes some of the problems of the other pro–women's rights novels by intertwining the women's rights question with the demands of another oppressed group, in this case farmers, thus demonstrating how women's political action could help all the oppressed gain their political rights.

One last novel about the movement for suffrage, *Her Infinite Variety* by the popular writer Brand Whitlock (1904), takes us back to *Playing the Mischief* of thirty years earlier and shows just how much—or little—progress had been made. Once again there is a prominent contrast between a woman who asks for direct power and women who succeed through indirect influence. Once again it is a woman lawyer who asks for women's rights. The lawyer is now beautiful, ladylike, and professionally successful. Nevertheless, like Nancy Appleyard, Maria Greene is less effective than the women who use personal and sexual influence to achieve their goals.

Set in Illinois, which had granted women the right to vote in school elections in 1891, the novel traces the efforts of Morley Vernon, a state senator, to secure passage of a constitutional amendment that would give full suffrage to the women of Illinois.[73] Himself influenced by Maria Greene, Vernon gives an impassioned plea for women's rights. He is then assaulted by a brigade of older women who come down from Chicago to lobby against the bill. They are led by a matron who Vernon refers to as "General Hodge-Lathrop . . . on her way to the front to assume command."[74] Mrs. Hodge-Lathrop, a friend of Vernon's mother, demonstrates her authority by threatening the Senator with "a good spanking" (114). Though she objects that Vernon would have woman "degrade and unsex herself by going to the polls, to caucuses and conventions; you would have her . . . lobbying for and against measures in the council chamber and the legislature" (119–120), she has no hesitation in accosting legislators and persuading them to vote against the suffrage bill. Ultimately she deploys Vernon's fiancée to distract him so that he misses the crucial vote, and the bill is defeated.

The point of Whitlock's novel is Vernon's recognition of "what women are capable of, what they might do in politics" (166). Both pro- and anti-suffrage novels concede the existence of this power, regardless of formal political rights. *Her Infinite Variety* therefore suggests that the fundamental handicap of the suffrage movement at the turn of the century is the opposition of women to the demand for political rights. Whitlock is pleading men's innocence in the defeat of the proposition; if women really want suffrage, they are powerful enough to gain it.

Conclusion:
The Debate in Fiction

Two fictional characters, created less than eighty years apart, index the change that took place in American political culture between 1827 and the beginning of the twentieth century. Mrs. Romelee, wife of the Squire in Hale's *Northwood*, never speaks on political matters nor attends a political meeting, yet she plays a well-understood political role in the Republic through her influence over her family. In Whitlock's *Her Infinite Variety*, Mrs. Hodge-Lathrop, a woman of high status and impeccable character, marshals her forces to defeat proposed suffrage legislation. Leaving husband and family, Mrs. Hodge-Lathrop haunts the halls of the state house, persuading legislators to vote as she desires. Though she is unpleasantly formidable and extremely public, her actions, like Mrs. Romelee's, fall within contemporary expectations of the "traditional" woman.

The confrontation between Mrs. Hodge-Lathrop and the attorney Maria Greene reminds the reader that the proper role of women in the political system was still a matter for intense debate in 1904. Greene, although professional and successful, is sensitive to social attitudes toward female behavior, especially public speaking. She has specialized in office work rather than litigation and declines to address the senate on behalf of the suffrage bill, asking the male legislator to speak in her place. Nevertheless, when the antisuffrage ladies descend on Senator Vernon, they betray the culture's continuing suspicion of such women, accusing him of "hobnobbing with that mannish thing, that *female* lawyer!" (121). This conflict between the conservative women and the suffragists replicates a long series of such confrontations in American fiction over what active participation in the Republic should be for women.

One major cause of the controversy was the uncertain and fluctuating demarcation between the public and private spheres of life. In the early years of the Republic, most citizens lived in small communities like Northwood, where culture, rather than law, set the parameters of behavior. Although proud of their nation, as individuals Americans had few interactions with the political world. Life was, for the most part, made up of private transactions between men outside the home and between the sexes within the home. However, even in the idyllic Yankee community, this distinction was delusory; the legal system, derived from English common law, enforced women's status and economic dependence. When the nation's economic instability began to have serious consequences for families and some states revised their property laws to give married women control over their own estates, it became evident that the law could adjust the order of the home as well as the government.

As the century progressed the artificiality of the boundary between the two spheres became increasingly apparent. The Civil War brought the results of public conflict into almost every home in the United States. It also drove many women to work outside the home, where political decisions about economic regulation affected all parts of their lives. In *The Portion of Labor* Freeman depicts a familiar paradox: Ellen Brewster is forced to go to work to maintain the continuing existence of domestic life. By the time Henry Adams writes *Democracy,* Madeleine Lee's private life is completely bound up with the political life of the Republic, and in *Her Infinite Variety* the antisuffragist women use the public sphere to protect one vision of middle-class domesticity. With such fictional examples paralleling the reality of factory and legislature, it became ever more difficult to argue that public life had no place for women.

The antisuffragists' critical epithet for Maria Greene is "mannish." Throughout the century, women who attempt to gain increased political resources or to enter the public sphere are regularly attacked as either desexed or unchaste. Though these women usually claimed economic or political independence, the novels reveal that both were regarded as a cover for sexual freedom. In plot, characters, and imagery, in comments and in conspicuous reticences, novelists make manifest public fears of the female body—and fears of the female body in public. Sexlessness is ridiculed, but the specter of promiscuity is terrifying. Metaphorically the stories in which women are silenced—*The Blithedale Romance, The Lecturess, Hannah Thurston, The Bostonians*—are tales of removing women from the possibility of sexual contact with the world. The antifeminists' fears become most overt in the Gilded Age, as the actions of women lobbyists, real and fictional, apparently confirm the belief that women would use their sexual charms to gain political ends. To the conservatives, a woman's public speech—her voice—could not be separated from her body. Thus the primary concern was to maintain society's control of that body.

The feminists of the nineteenth century rejected this argument on its face. Whether they were fighting to obtain the right to control property, to speak in public, or to enter a profession, they insisted on the distinction between voice and body. From Marian Gayland through Christie Devon to Ellen

Brewster, woman's desire to speak grows out of her sense of injustice, not a desire for sexual expression outside marriage. In this positive vision of woman's public involvement, woman's voice alone is sufficient for her ends; the novels create climactic scenes in which a woman's power is revealed by and embodied in her verbal persuasiveness. The way in which an author sets the scene for a woman to speak—and an extraordinary number of nineteenth century American novels have such a scene, in public or in a smaller gathering, either directly presented or distanced—is usually a clue to the degree of personal power with which the author is willing to endow female characters.

Yet novels that take a positive view of women in the public sphere deny that giving women more political power will cause a detrimental change in the balance of power between the sexes. Women's rights sympathizers maintained that the desire of a woman to participate in the political process was unrelated to her ability to form a lasting heterosexual relationship; women, they claimed, should be independent citizens with natural rights, but they would not therefore abandon the men who had represented them. Because feminists were defensive about the charge of being unwomanly, feminist heroines tend to be beautiful and endowed with conventional domestic virtues. They almost always marry, and when they do not, extensive justifications are offered. To sustain belief in the possibility of these relationships, authors struggled to create "new men," such as Waldo Yorke in *Dr. Zay* or the reformed Harold Skidmore in *Helen Brent, M.D.* Garland twice constructs novels around the relations of strong men and strong women who have interdependent personal relations along with independent political participation.

Nineteenth-century novels make clear that the debate within the political culture over the role of women was indeed a struggle over power. In a series of "declarations of independence," from *Hope Leslie* through *The Crux*, novelists proposed ways in which women might gain and exercise power over themselves, over their communities, and over the men in their lives. Objections came from Cooper and Howells on economic grounds, from James and Taylor on biological grounds, from De Forest and Twain on moral grounds. In the prosuffrage novels, the issue of woman's power is confronted directly: these novelists asserted that the political gains women had achieved through a century of such declarations could only be protected by the vote.

The fiction we have examined sits on a continuum from conservative to radical, with the conservative end occupied largely by canonical male authors. Cooper, Howells, James, Hawthorne, Taylor, even De Forest, all present diffident or hostile pictures of the consequences of granting women increased political independence. Correspondingly, the radical end is largely female, though Garland is a conspicuous exception. Phelps, Alcott, Gilman,

and the minor suffrage writers defend different aspects of the claim for inde
pendence, but they all recognize its political resonance. The change in the
United States over the eight decades we have examined is probably best
traced in the novelists who fall in the middle of the spectrum. These authors,
appearing as early as Sedgwick and including among others Stowe, Southworth, Freeman, Jewett, and Burnett, all see the need for women to have
more protection, more opportunities, and somewhat more control over
their own lives. They are moderates, but the progression shows how such
moderates, or even a conservative like Hale, gradually exhibited more and
more sympathy for the political liberty of women.

It is not possible to measure the final impact of fiction on the public
debate, partly because it is not possible to measure the extent to which a
reader's ideological position affected—and still affects—his or her evalua-
tion of this fiction. The novels were intended to persuade, and reviews and
responses indicate that their purpose was understood. But their success
would always have been affected by the predisposition of the reader. A case
in point is found in the paired novels *Dr. Breen's Practice* and *Dr. Zay*. The
two are fundamentally similar: brief, focused on a central figure who undertakes a medical career, concerned with the failure or success of that career,
and concluding with a marriage satisfactory within the premises of the
story. Even though Howells denied any design on the reader's attitudes,
claiming to write a study of a purely individual error in life choice, a contemporary reader eager for the entrance of women into the professions
would surely have seen Grace Breen as an argument for woman's unfitness.
Phelps, who made no secret of her designs on the reader, set out to answer
Howells. But the picture with which *Dr. Zay* concludes, of the successful
female physician expanding her life to include a husband, could serve a
sympathetic reader as a model of fulfillment or an unsympathetic one as an
example of utopian unreality. Similarly, interpretations of the end of *A Spoil
of Office* depend on the reader's willingness to accept the separation of
husband and wife as part of modern marriage. Today, feminist readings of
Dr. Zay, A Spoil of Office, and *The Portion of Labor* are predisposed toward the activist heroines and find the novels correspondingly satisfactory,
but the disappearance of these novels from the canon until recently suggests
the extent to which ideology affects literary judgment.

The cultural debate between the supporters of women's rights and their
opponents grows out of the fundamental tension between liberty and order
that characterizes American democracy. This tension is already evident in
Northwood and *Hope Leslie*. Hale's vision of the perfect democratic republic values order in the community over the risk of too much liberty. Order in
the family is a metaphor for order in the nation. Sedgwick's portrait of the
Puritan moment also emphatically depicts a community order, which Hope
and Magawisca question through actions taken in the name of higher

values. In the context of the century-long debate over female power, these actions are early and significant recognitions that for the disenfranchised—women among them—the only way to experience liberty may be to challenge the lawful order of the community.

The tension between liberty and order is explored over and over again in the fictional debate over female rights. Mary Monson, a woman whose control of property has freed her from societal restraints, is Cooper's dire warning to his readers that granting independence to women will undermine the political order. Zenobia, with her mysterious past and provocative sensuality, is another "free woman" who threatens the stability of the community. Alcott and Taylor articulate two different but both profoundly American visions of community order. Christie, who has established her independence at great cost, rejects the old order and is last seen building a separatist utopia for free and equal women. In contrast Hannah Thurston, who has claimed independence and suffered under it, surrenders her liberty in marriage, becoming part of the natural order of husband and wife within a harmonized community. The moderates seek a middle ground between the patriarchal order and feminist calls for liberty and independence. Writers like Hale, Southworth, Stowe, and Burnett acknowledge woman's need for enough independence to protect herself, her children, and her property. Yet these authors believe that a true woman would never put her own desire for liberty over the bonds of love. The political order, in their view, is safe because for women, power, which can be tempting, will always give way to love.

It is in their participation in the debate between liberty and order that many of these novels seem most alive today. The conflicts over reproductive rights, over maternity leave and public support for day care for children, and over the feminization of poverty are all extensions of debates that were raised in the nineteenth century. In each case, the fundamental question is whether the individual has the right to make independent life-choices or whether the community will foreclose some choices in the interest of maintaining the social order. The novels of the nineteenth century do not only outline the contours of the debate; they are most powerful when they unmask the fears that motivate the opponents of women's rights. The same fears surface today: provision of day care may encourage women to leave the home and certainly weakens woman's role as nurturer of children; ascension to positions of economic or political power may demand a dedication to career that makes family commitments almost impossible; and granting women the right to make reproductive choices would effectively end male control of women's bodies. The feminist resolution of these issues would result in liberty for individual women or, in some visions, a new order for all. Those in American society who fear such change oppose these women's demands in the name of preservation of community. Most Americans today, like their forebears, seek the path of moderation, slowly adjusting to new cultural ideas about women's place in the political community while hoping to retain the American ideal of marriage and family for both sexes.

Notes

Introduction

1. Harriet Beecher Stowe, *My Wife and I* (Boston and New York: Houghton Mifflin, 1899), 184.

2. For a discussion of Stowe's evolving views on the woman question, see Jeanne Boydston, Mary Kelley, and Anne Margolis, *The Limits of Sisterhood: The Beecher Sisters on Women's Rights and Woman's Sphere* (Chapel Hill: University of North Carolina Press, 1988). After the Civil War, Stowe published a series of articles in the *Atlantic Monthly* entitled "The Woman Question. or What Will You Do with Her?" portions of which are reproduced in *Limits of Sisterhood.*

3. See Philip S. Foner, ed., *We, the Other People* (Urbana: University of Illinois Press, 1976), for a collection of such declarations by laborers, political groups, farmers, and women.

4. Ibid., 78–79.

5. Elizabeth Cady Stanton, Susan B. Anthony, and Matilda Joslyn Gage, eds., *History of Woman Suffrage* (New York: Arno Press and New York Times Press, 1969), 1:595.

6. James Fenimore Cooper, *The Ways of the Hour* (New York: G. P. Putnam, 1850; rpt., Upper Saddle River, N.J.: Gregg Press, 1968), 308.

7. Linda K. Kerber, *Women of the Republic: Intellect and Ideology in Revolutionary America* (Chapel Hill: University of North Carolina Press, 1980), 228–229.

8. Hannah Webster Foster, *The Coquette*, ed. Cathy N. Davidson (New York and Oxford: Oxford University Press, 1986), 44.

9. Cathy N. Davidson, *Revolution and the Word: The Rise of the Novel in America* (New York and Oxford: Oxford University Press, 1986), 147. See Walter P. Wenska, Jr., "*The Coquette* and the American Dream of Freedom," *Early American Literature* 12 (1977/1978): 243–255, for a discussion of the novel's political implications that does not isolate their significance for women.

10. Cited in Nina Baym, *Novels, Readers, and Reviewers: Responses to Fiction in Antebellum America* (Ithaca, N.Y.: Cornell University Press, 1984), 214.

11. Sacvan Bercovitch, "The Problem of Ideology in American Literary History," *Critical Inquiry* 12 (1986): 642.

12. Lennard J. Davis, *Resisting Novels: Ideology and Fiction* (New York and London: Methuen, 1987), 224.

13. Fredric Jameson, in *The Political Unconscious: Narrative as a Socially Symbolic Act* (Ithaca, N.Y.: Cornell University Press, 1981), makes the strongest case for the political interpretation of the text, arguing that only Marxism provides a "philosophically coherent and ideologically compelling resolution to the dilemma of historicism" (19), permitting the interpreter to "rewrite the individual text, the individual cultural artifact, in terms of the antagonistic dialogue of class voices" (85).

14. Terry Eagleton, *Marxism and Literary Criticism* (Berkeley: University of California Press, 1976), 19.

15. Bercovitch, "Ideology in American Literary History," 635.

16. Janet Todd, *Feminist Literary History* (New York: Routledge, 1988), 86.

17. Bercovitch, "Ideology in American Literary History," 635. The concept of emergent and residual cultures is indebted to the work of Raymond Williams.

18. Todd, *Feminist Literary History*, 15.

19. Cited in Baym, *Novels, Readers, and Reviewers*, 214.

20. Ibid., 170.

21. Davis, *Resisting Novels*, 232.

22. Nathaniel Hawthorne, *The Blithedale Romance* (New York: Library of America, 1983), 737.

23. Sandra M. Gilbert and Susan Gubar, *No Man's Land: The Place of the Woman Writer in the Twentieth Century* (New Haven, Conn.: Yale University Press, 1988), 1:xiii–xiv.

24. In contrast to Eagleton's view that the text's relation to the "real history of its time" may be mediated by a number of elements, including the author's class and economic position, the techniques of literary production, contemporary aesthetic theory, and the author's own self-conscious ideology (*Marxism and Literary Criticism*, 16), we suggest that the author's own emotions, cognitions, and moral beliefs as well as his or her life experiences can have an effect on the text independent of the pervading influence of the dominant ideology.

25. Although we do not analyze novels on the basis of their popularity among readers, we agree with Nina Baym's view of the standards by which they were judged. Readers and reviewers evaluated books by their views on the moral questions of life, by the degree to which the plot and characters stirred interest, and by the artistic execution of the work. Although reviewers tried to guide the public toward the reading of "better" novels, Baym finds that "reviewers in the mid-nineteenth century, though speaking for a reading elite, were much more hospitable than their counterparts in our own day to a wide range of fiction and believed that the first test of any novel was its ability to create an unforced interest" (*Novels, Readers, and Reviewers*, 60–61).

26. Judith Fryer, *The Faces of Eve: Women in the Nineteenth-Century American Novel* (Oxford: Oxford University Press, 1976).

27. Mary Suzanne Schriber, *Gender and the Writer's Imagination: From Cooper to Wharton* (Lexington: University of Kentucky Press, 1987). Judith Fetterley, *The Resisting Reader: A Feminist Approach to American Fiction* (Bloomington: Indiana University Press, 1978).

28. Joyce W. Warren, *The American Narcissus: Individualism and Women in Nineteenth-Century American Fiction* (New Brunswick, N.J.: Rutgers University Press, 1984).

29. Nina Baym, *Woman's Fiction: A Guide to Novels by or about Women in America, 1820–1870* (Ithaca, N.Y.: Cornell University Press, 1978).

30. Baym, *Novels, Readers, and Reviewers*, 35.

31. Baym, *Woman's Fiction*, 11, 12.

32. Jane Tompkins, in *Sensational Designs: The Cultural Work of American Fiction, 1790–1860* (New York: Oxford University Press, 1985), 126–127, refers to it as a sentimental novel, but it can hardly be reduced to Baym's basic plot.

33. Baym, *Woman's Fiction*, 16–21.

34. Tompkins, *Sensational Designs*, 126, 139.

35. In *Alternative Americas: A Reading of Antebellum Political Culture* (Chicago: University of Chicago Press, 1986), Anne Norton contrasts the northern Puritan culture that she interprets as masculine with the agricultural, "feminine" culture of the South. In her view, "Northern political culture thus retained not only the Puritan covenantal and familial paradigms, which demanded selflessness, temperance, and submission to authority, but also elements of that Revolutionary tradition which affirmed the primacy of popular authority and invested men with a conviction of their natural rights and independent worth" (62–63). Norton proposes that as the northern economy industrialized, it became more important for women to accept a subordinate role. Denied their legal, constitutional rights to equality, women reverted to using the natural rights position, "employing the rhetoric and paradigms of political action established in the Revolution" (53).

36. For examples of this fiction, see Henry L. Gates, Jr., ed., *The Schomberg Library of Nineteenth-Century Black Women Writers* (Oxford: Oxford University Press, 1988).

37. The strong reaction that the presentation of the woman's body provoked in the nineteenth century presaged the use of the woman as an object of men's gaze in the cinema of the twentieth century. These speaking women, who were subjects, not objects, violate, as Laura Mulvey puts it, "the principles of the ruling ideology," wherein "the determining male gaze projects its phantasy on to the female figure which is styled accordingly. In their traditional exhibitionist role, women are simultaneously looked at and displayed, with their appearance coded for strong visual and erotic impact." See Mulvey's essay "Visual Pleasure and Narrative Cinema," in Constance Penley, ed., *Feminism and Film Theory* (New York: Routledge, 1988), 62, 63, as well as the discussion of pornography in Annette Kuhn, *The Power of the Image: Essays on Representation and Sexuality* (London: Routledge and Kegan Paul, 1985).

38. Henry James, *The Bostonians* (New York: Modern Library, 1956), 275, 455.

39. Scholars who find the roots of nineteenth-century feminism in the abolition movement include Aileen Kraditor, ed., *Up from the Pedestal: Selected Writings in*

the History of American Feminism (New York: Quadrangle Books, 1975), 14; Eleanor Flexner, *Century of Struggle: The Woman's Rights Movement in the United States*, rev. ed. (Cambridge: Belknap Press of Harvard University Press, 1975), 41; and Blanche Glassman Hersh, *The Slavery of Sex: Feminist-Abolitionists in America* (Urbana: University of Illinois Press, 1978). Others who believe that early female reform societies taught women how to organize and work for public reform include Barbara J. Berg, *The Remembered Gate: Origins of American Feminism* (Oxford: Oxford University Press, 1978), and Keith E. Melder, *Beginnings of Sisterhood: The American Woman's Rights Movement, 1800–1850* (New York: Schocken Books, 1977).

Chapter 1. Two Visions of the Republic

1. Sarah Josepha Hale, *Northwood* (Boston: Bowles and Dearborn, 1827), 1:187–188. Unless noted, all citations are to the first edition, which varies in many small details, including names, from the second (1852). All further citations to the first edition are found in the text.

2. No precise circulation figures exist, and Nina Baym, in *Woman's Fiction: A Guide to Novels by and about Women in America, 1820–1870* (Ithaca, N.Y.: Cornell University Press, 1978), 300–301, has warned against trusting statements about sales and popularity. Nevertheless, the *Boston Spectator and Ladies Album* for April 28, 1827, reports that "Northwood is selling faster than any similar work, which has been for some years published in this city" (135), and Hale herself points out in the preface to the second edition that the book "was republished in London— at that time a very remarkable compliment to an American book" (*Northwood; or, Life North and South*, 2d ed. [New York: H. Long and Brother, 1852], iii). According to one source, this was its fifth U.S. edition (read printing) (Carol Dick Buell, "Sarah Josepha Hale, the Editor of *Godey's Lady's Book*," M.A. thesis, University of Chicago Graduate Library School, 1976, p. 17). There is more information about Sedgwick's success. Mary Kelley, in *Private Woman, Public Stage: Literary Domesticity in Nineteenth-Century America* (New York: Oxford University Press, 1984), writes that Sedgwick did "splendidly"; *Hope Leslie* brought her $1,100 for a first printing of two thousand copies (12–13). In *The Woman's Record*, 3d ed. rev. (New York: Harper and Brothers, 1872), 777, Sarah Hale wrote that *Hope Leslie* was Sedgwick's "most popular tale; and, indeed, no novel written by an American, except, perhaps, the early works of Cooper, ever met with such success."

3. Linda K. Kerber, *Women of the Republic: Intellect and Ideology in Revolutionary America* (Chapel Hill: University of North Carolina Press, 1980), 239–248, gives numerous examples of these criticisms. In a letter to a friend, Thomas Jefferson gives similar advice on the reading suitable for young women: "A great obstacle to good education is the inordinate passion prevalent for novels. . . . When this poison infects the mind, it destroys its tone and revolts it against wholesome reading. . . . This mass of trash, however, is not without some distinction; some few modelling their narratives, although fictitious, on the incidents of real life, have been able to make them interesting and useful vehicles of a sound morality." Letter to N.

Burwell, Esq., March 14, 1818, in *The Writings of Thomas Jefferson*, ed. H. A. Washington (New York: Riker, Thorne, 1854), 7:102.

4. *Boston Spectator and Ladies Album*, February 24, 1827, 57.

5. For discussion of the political socialization of adults as well as children, see W. Lance Bennett, *Public Opinion in American Politics* (New York: Harcourt, Brace, Jovanovich, 1980); Doris Graber, *Mass Media and American Politics* (Washington, D.C.: Congressional Quarterly Press, 1980); and M. Kent Jennings and Richard G. Niemi, *The Political Character of Adolescence: The Influence of Families and School* (Princeton: Princeton University Press, 1974).

6. As Cathy Davidson puts it in *Revolution and the Word: The Rise of the Novel in America* (Oxford: Oxford University Press, 1986), "the novel served as a major locus of republican education" (70).

7. Typical was the call of Sedgwick's friend William Ellery Channing in his remarks "On National Literature" (1830) for a literary Declaration of Independence. See Benjamin T. Spencer, *The Quest for Nationality: An American Literary Campaign* (Syracuse: Syracuse University Press, 1957), for a full discussion.

8. Cooper's attitudes can be seen most clearly in his social novels, particularly *Home as Found* (1838). See also the discussion of *The Ways of the Hour* in chap. 3, below. For Tocqueville, see *Democracy in America*, trans. George Lawrence, ed. J. P. Mayer and Max Lerner (New York: Harper and Row, 1966), 638–639.

9. Paula Baker, "The Domestication of Politics: Women and American Political Society, 1780–1920," *American Historical Review* 89 (1984): 620–647. Baker describes the development of the Jacksonian party system in terms of its social functions for the male citizens. As the vast majority of men gained the franchise during the 1820s, political participation became a "fraternal" and social practice.

10. Marvin Meyers, *The Jacksonian Persuasian: Politics and Belief* (Stanford, Calif.: Stanford University Press, 1957).

11. Ibid., 31.

12. Gordon S. Wood, *The Creation of the American Republic, 1776–1787* (Chapel Hill: University of North Carolina Press, 1969), 55.

13. Ibid., 52.

14. Davidson, *Revolution and the Word*, 62.

15. Emma Willard, "Plan for Improving Female Education," in Willystine Goodsell, ed., *Pioneers of Women's Education in the United States* (New York: AMS Press, 1970), 58.

16. Mary Beth Norton, *Liberty's Daughters: The Revolutionary Experience of American Women, 1750–1800* (Boston: Little, Brown, 1980), esp. chap. 6, 155–194.

17. Kerber, *Women of the Republic*, 12.

18. *Godey's Lady's Book* 44 (1852): 293.

19. Hale carefully reveals the limits of these duties: the Romelee women work only in the house, and the poorest farmer insists on hurrying home because "he feared his wife would work too hard, and women had never ought to do any thing out of doors" (2:224). Alexis de Tocqueville confirms that "you will never find American women in charge of the external relations of the family, managing a business, or interfering in politics; but they are also never obliged to undertake rough laborer's work or any task requiring hard physical exertion. . . . If the American

woman is never allowed to leave the quiet sphere of domestic duties, she is also never forced to do so" (*Democracy in America*, 601).

20. William R. Taylor claims, in *Cavalier and Yankee: The Old South and American National Character* (New York: George Braziller, 1961), that "the South which Sarah Hale created as an antipode to her North is less a place than a moral climate: an expression of what the North lacked and what the emergent Yankee needed" (123). According to Anne Norton, *Alternative Americas: A Reading of Antebellum Political Culture* (Chicago: University of Chicago Press, 1986), southerners defined themselves with a different set of cultural beliefs. As she contrasts the two regions, "While New Englanders were rocking in the bosom of Jesus, neither fed nor coddled, but rather weaned and selfless, Southerners were suckled by nature. Raised in a balmy climate, they were accustomed to regard nature as an indulgent and beneficent mother. . . . Puritan families were characterized by the absolute and arbitrary authority of the father. . . . Southern families, conversely, were characterized by indulgent and affectionate care of children" (106). Thus Norton sees southern culture as maternal, close to nature, and more self-expressive than the northern culture.

21. See Norton, *Liberty's Daughters*, 62, for a discussion of how husbands advised wives on behavior and growth.

22. Catharine Maria Sedgwick, *Hope Leslie*, ed. Mary Kelley (New Brunswick, N.J.: Rutgers University Press, 1987), 161–162. All further citations are found in the text.

23. "The Novels of Miss Sedgwick," *American Monthly Magazine*, n.s., 1 (1836): 20–21.

24. Ibid.

25. Mary Kelley, "Introduction," in Sedgwick, *Hope Leslie*, xxviii. Kelley details the ways in which Sedgwick, using historical sources, uncovered an "alternative past." Sandra A. Zagarell, in "Expanding 'America': Lydia Sigourney's *Sketch of Connecticut*, Catharine Sedgwick's *Hope Leslie*," *Tulsa Studies in Women's Literature* 6 (1987): 233, also examines the novel's treatment of Puritan oppression of American Indians, and shows how "*Hope Leslie* casts light on the collusion between established narrative structures and racist, patriarchal definitions of the nation."

26. *North American Review* 26 (1828): 420.

27. *American Ladies Magazine* 8 (1835): 661.

28. *Western Monthly Review* 1 (1827–1828): 289.

29. *American Ladies Magazine* 8 (1835): 661–662.

30. Edward Halsey Foster attributes Sedgwick's attitude toward American Indians both to the abolitionist beliefs of Sedgwick's family and to the legend of Eunice Williams, a relative of Sedgwick's, who had been carried off by Indians in 1704 and remained with them for the rest of her life. Foster points out that in allowing the marriage of Faith Leslie to Oneco, Sedgwick reverses the attitude taken by Cooper in *The Last of the Mohicans*, in which the heroine Cora must die rather than enter a marriage of miscegenation (*Catharine Maria Sedgwick* [New York: Twayne, 1974], 72–93). Kelley calls Magawisca "the only Indian woman in early American fiction invested with substance and strength" ("Introduction," xxvi).

31. Michael Bell also notes that this speech explains how to "read" Hope's desire to have her own way. For Bell, Hope's rebellious spirit is the spirit of democ-

racy, "the spirit of American history. She is liberty, she is progress. In her, above all, Catharine Sedgwick embodied her view of the essential movement of American history." This movement Bell sees going from the artificial toward the natural. Although Bell rightly notes that in this system the women have symbolic value, he does not consider what it means to embody the spirit of American history in a woman who breaks laws. By dismissing the plot as confusing, he ignores its significance. Michael Davitt Bell, "History and Romance Convention in Catharine Sedgwick's *Hope Leslie*," *American Quarterly* 22 (1970): 221.

32. Catharine Maria Sedgwick, *The Linwoods, or "Sixty Years Since" in America* (New York: Harper and Brothers, 1835), 2:232, 238.

33. Catharine Maria Sedgwick, *Redwood; A Tale* (New York: E. Bliss and E. White, 1824), 2:64. Further references are found in the text.

34. Nina Baym suggests that this pattern extends into another of Sedgwick's novels, *Clarence* (1830). Here the heroine, Gertrude Clarence, assists her friend Emilie Layton in eloping with the right man, thus escaping the villain whom her parents have been attempting to force upon her. In a slight exaggeration, Baym writes that Gertrude acts "by literally abducting the girl away from him at a masked ball. As in *Redwood*, the conventionally male prerogative of rescue is given to a woman" (*Woman's Fiction*, 60).

35. Mary Beth Norton, "The Evolution of White Women's Experience in Early America," *American Historical Review* 89 (1984): 617.

36. Ruth E. Finley, *The Lady of Godey's: Sarah Josepha Hale* (Philadelphia: J. B. Lippincott, 1931), 27.

37. Mary E. Dewey, ed., *Life and Letters of Catharine M. Sedgwick* (New York: Harper and Brothers, 1871), 43.

38. Ibid., 34.

39. Finley, *Lady of Godey's*, 36.

40. Buell, "Sarah Joseph Hale," 16.

41. Kelley, *Private Woman, Public Stage*, 66–67.

42. Dewey, *Life and Letters*, 80, 91.

43. Kelley, *Private Woman, Public Stage*, 241–243. See also Mary Kelley, "A Woman Alone: Catharine Maria Sedgwick's Spinsterhood in Nineteenth-Century America," *New England Quarterly* 51 (1978): 209–225.

44. Kelley, *Private Woman, Public Stage*, 243.

45. Dewey, *Life and Letters*, 21, 195.

46. Hale, *Northwood* (1852), iii.

47. Joseph Dorfman, "Theodore Sedgwick: From Federalism to Jacksonianism," in Introduction to Theodore Sedgwick, *Public and Private Economy* (Clifton, N.J.: August M. Kelley, 1974), 13–15. See also Meyers, *Jacksonian Persuasion*, 163–184.

48. Dewey, *Life and Letters*, 248.

49. "Catharine Maria Sedgwick," in Edward T. James, Janet Wilson James, and Paul S. Boyer, eds., *Notable American Women* (Cambridge: Harvard University Press, 1971), 3:257.

50. Dewey, *Life and Letters*, 292–293.

51. Kelley, *Private Woman, Public Stage*, 296.

52. Hale, *Northwood* (1852), 392, 402.

53. Ibid., 369, 390, 392.

54. Catharine Maria Sedgwick, *Married or Single?* (New York: Harper and Brothers, 1857), 1:viii. Further references are found in the text.

Chapter 2. Finding a Voice to Answer the Moral Call

1. Not only did the number of secondary schools and academies double in the fifty years after 1829, but the curriculum changed. Between 1749 and 1829, only 15 percent of the schools for women offered algebra, while 36 percent offered moral philosophy. In the period between 1830 and 1871, 83 percent offered algebra, and 80 percent included moral philosophy. Robert E. Potter, *The Stream of American Education* (New York: American Book, 1967), 249–250.

2. One of the leading figures of the Second Great Awakening was the revivalist Charles Grandison Finney. Finney, along with other theologians, emphasized the importance of achieving salvation through the individual's acceptance of God's grace. Every person who attained this state was committed to helping others through efforts not confined to religious work. Finney expressly endorsed work for temperance, Bible societies, aid to missionaries, and abolition. See *Lectures on Revivals of Religion by Charles Grandison Finney,* ed. William G. McLoughlin (Cambridge: Belknap Press of Harvard University Press, 1960), 297–306. Finney also encouraged women to participate in planning revivals and was much criticized for allowing women to pray out loud in mixed meetings. Clergy feared that women might also want to preach or become Bible teachers, according to Barbara Brown Zikmund, in "The Struggle for the Right to Preach," in Rosemary Radford Ruether and Rosemary Skinner Keller, eds., *Women and Religion in America* (San Francisco: Harper and Row, 1981), 1:194.

3. For an extensive discussion of women's work in associations see Carroll Smith-Rosenberg, "Beauty, the Beast, and the Militant Woman," in *Disorderly Conduct: Visions of Gender in Victorian America* (New York: Oxford University Press, 1985), 109–128; Keith E. Melder, *Beginnings of Sisterhood: The American Woman's Rights Movement, 1800–1850* (New York: Schocken Books, 1977), 37–43; and Barbara J. Berg, *The Remembered Gate: The Origins of American Feminism* (Oxford: Oxford University Press, 1978), 145–155.

4. Smith-Rosenberg, "Beauty, the Beast, and the Militant Woman"; and Berg, *Remembered Gate,* 177–190.

5. Melder, *Beginnings of Sisterhood,* 54.

6. Reprinted in Harriet Beecher Stowe, *Stories, Sketches and Studies* (New York: AMS Press, 1967), 165, 167. Further page references are given in the text.

7. Mary Kelley's *Private Woman, Public Stage: Literary Domesticity in Nineteenth-Century America* (New York and Oxford: Oxford University Press, 1984) is a full study of twelve of these women writers. Of these, only Catharine Sedgwick was publishing in the 1820s, and Caroline Howard Gilman in the 1830s.

8. Isabella Webb Entrikin, *Sarah Josepha Hale and Godey's Lady's Book* (Philadelphia: University of Pennsylvania Press, 1946), 40.

9. Sarah Josepha Hale, *Sixth Annual Report of the Managers of the Seaman's Aid Society* (Boston: James B. Dow, 1839), 15.

10. *Ladies Magazine* 9 (1836): 218.

11. Quoted in Marie B. Hecht, *John Quincy Adams: A Personal History of an Independent Man* (New York: Macmillan, 1972), 559, 560.

12. It was reported that in the same debate, Senator Benton attacked abolitionists generally as "incendiaries and agitators, with diabolical ends in view, to be accomplished by wicked and deplorable means. . . . Declamations against slavery, publications in gazettes, pictures, petitions to the constituent assembly, were the mode of proceeding; and the fish-women of Paris—he said it with humiliation, because American females had signed the petitions now before us—the fishwomen of Paris, the very poissardes from the quays of the Seine, became the obstreperous champions of West India emancipation" (*Congressional Globe*, January 7, 1837, 79). The comparison of American female petitioners with French market women was probably intended to imply that such females would be as licentious and immoral as the French females were thought to be.

13. Aileen S. Kraditor, *Means and Ends in American Abolitionism: Garrison and His Critics on Strategy and Tactics, 1834–1850* (New York: Pantheon Books, 1967), 18.

14. Nina Baym, *Woman's Fiction: A Guide to Novels by and about Women in America, 1820–1870* (Ithaca, N.Y.: Cornell University Press, 1978), 75.

15. *The Lecturess or Woman's Sphere* (Boston: Whipple and Damrell, 1839), 5. All further page references are found in the text.

16. "Frances Wright," in Edward T. James, Janet Wilson James, and Paul S. Boyer, eds., *Notable American Women*, (Cambridge: Belknap Press of Harvard University Press, 1971), 3:677.

17. Frances Wright D'Arusmont, *Life, Letters and Lectures, 1834–44* (New York: Arno Press, 1972), 31–32.

18. William Randall Waterman, *Frances Wright* (New York: Columbia University Press, 1924), 239. Eckhardt's more recent biography of Wright gives no evidence that her return to lecturing in London in 1834 caused a break with Phiquepal. Soon after the trip to England Fanny and Phiquepal returned to the United States, leaving their daughter in France with friends for a period of two years. By 1836, Eckhardt suggests, they "no longer counted on each other's company," and in that year Phiquepal returned to France alone to take care of Silva. Celia Morris Eckhardt, *Fanny Wright Rebel in America* (Cambridge: Harvard University Press, 1984), 255.

19. It is clear that her personal life must have encouraged speculation if it was not common knowledge. The *Morning Herald* for October 22, 1838, recounts a shouting match between her and a heckler, referred to as "Loafer," which concludes:

Fanny: I really do conceive, friends—
Loafer: No you dont, now, Fanny; it's a little too late in the day for that. You did once under werry queer circumstances.
Here there was such a tremendous row that Fanny announced the conclusion of her lecture for a future day.

20. Elizabeth Cady Stanton, Susan B. Anthony, and Matilda Gage, eds., *History of Woman Suffrage* (New York: Fowler and Wells, 1881), 1:81.

21. *Letters of Theodore Dwight Weld, Angelina Grimké Weld, and Sarah Grimké, 1822–1844*, ed. Gilbert H. Barnes and Dwight L. Dumond (New York and London: D. Appleton-Century, 1934), 1:416.

22. *Letters of Weld and Grimkés*, 2:637, 648–649.

23. Gerda Lerner, *The Grimké Sisters from South Carolina: Rebels against Slavery* (Boston: Houghton Mifflin, 1967), 255, 276–278, 282–293.

24. *Morning Herald*, May 19, 1838.

25. *Letters of Weld and Grimkés*, 2:921.

26. [Anne Wales Abbot], "Female Authors," *North American Review* 72 (1851): 151–152.

27. Paula Blanchard, *Margaret Fuller: From Transcendentalism to Revolution* (New York: Delacorte Press, 1978), 146–153.

28. *History of Woman Suffrage*, 1:460.

29. Ibid., 476.

30. Ibid., 522.

31. Thomas F. Gossett, *Uncle Tom's Cabin and American Culture* (Dallas: Southern Methodist University Press, 1985), 23.

32. Ibid., 36.

33. Catharine E. Beecher, *An Essay on Slavery and Abolitionism, with Reference to the Duty of American Females* (Philadelphia: Henry Perkins, 1837), 5. Further page references are found in the text. According to Kathryn Kish Sklar, in *Catharine Beecher: A Study in American Domesticity* (New Haven and London: Yale University Press, 1973), the debate between Angelina Grimké and Catharine Beecher at the end of the 1830s reflected fundamentally different visions of what the political and social function of American women was to be. Beecher "challenged Angelina Grimké's leadership and defined her own counterproposal for the role of women in American society. . . . The Grimké sisters linked the cause of women's rights with that of abolitionism, and Catharine Beecher urged the unification of American culture around a new image of politically transcendent womanhood"(132).

34. Sklar, *Catharine Beecher*, 233.

35. Letter to Mary Dutton, December 1838, reprinted in Jeanne Boydston, Mary Kelley, and Anne Margolis, *The Limits of Sisterhood: The Beecher Sisters on Women's Rights and Woman's Sphere* (Chapel Hill: University of North Carolina Press, 1988), 67.

36. Forrest Wilson, *Crusader in Crinoline: The Life of Harriet Beecher Stowe* (Philadelphia: J. B. Lippincott, 1941), 252.

37. Harriet Beecher Stowe, *Uncle Tom's Cabin* (New York: Library of America, 1982), 47. Further page references are found in the text.

38. For two very different discussions of Eva's relation to Christ, see Ann Douglas, *The Feminization of American Culture* (New York: Avon, 1977), 1–13, and Jane Tompkins, *Sensational Designs: The Cultural Work of American Fiction, 1790–1860* (New York and Oxford: Oxford University Press, 1985), 124–139.

39. Sandra M. Gilbert and Susan Gubar, *The Madwoman in the Attic: The*

Woman Writer and the Nineteenth-Century Literary Imagination (New Haven: Yale University Press, 1979), 533–535.

40. Tompkins, *Sensational Designs*, 142.

41. The "Appeal" is reprinted in Boydston, Kelley, and Margolis, *Limits of Sisterhood*, 180–183.

42. Beecher, *An Essay*, 116, 129.

43. Wilson, *Crusader in Crinoline*, 295.

44. Reprinted in Harriet Beecher Stowe, *Uncle Tom's Cabin* (New York: Harper and Row, 1965), xix.

45. Cited by Oscar Cargill, "Nemesis and Nathaniel Hawthorne," *PMLA* 52 (1937): 851.

46. *Letters of Hawthorne to William D. Ticknor, 1851–1864* (Newark: Carteret Book Club, 1910), 1:78, 2:50, 2:56.

47. Nathaniel Hawthorne, *The Blithedale Romance* (New York: Library of America, 1983), 646. Further page references are found in the text.

48. Nina Baym, *The Shape of Hawthorne's Career* (Ithaca, N.Y.: Cornell University Press, 1976), 196; Alan Lefcowitz and Barbara Lefcowitz, "Some Rents in the Veil: New Light on Priscilla and Zenobia in *The Blithedale Romance*," *Nineteenth-Century Fiction* 21 (1966): 263–275.

49. Many have noted that since *Blithedale* is narrated by the unreliable Coverdale, the reader is constantly forced to draw conclusions from insufficient information. Most recently Louise DeSalvo, in *Nathaniel Hawthorne* (Brighton, Sussex: Harvester, 1987), comments that "for the feminist reader the experience of reading *The Blithedale Romance* is terrifying because the psychopathology of the narrator's misogyny becomes the 'normal' way of viewing women within the novel." DeSalvo suggests that Coverdale may have murdered Zenobia (99, 110–113).

50. *Letters to Ticknor*, January 19, 1855, 1:75.

51. David Leverenz, "Mrs. Hawthorne's Headache: Reading *The Scarlet Letter*," *Nineteenth-Century Fiction* 37 (1983): 555. Leverenz concludes that "what starts as a feminist revolt against punitive patriarchal authority ends in a muddle of sympathetic pity for ambiguous victims" (553).

52. Margaret Higonnet, in "Speaking Silences: Women's Suicide," in *The Female Body in Western Culture*, ed. Susan Rubin Suleiman (Cambridge: Harvard University Press, 1986), 71–76, discusses the way in which the "nineteenth-century reorientation of suicide toward love, passive self-surrender, and illness" feminized suicide. Her analysis of Hedda Gabler and Emma Bovary also fits Zenobia: "In the nineteenth century the theme of female identity comes to focus on the disparity between individual aspiration and social actuality. The death of the heroine may be attributed to the deficiencies of social institutions: she attacks her own body, having introjected society's hostility to her deviance." For Higonnet, drowning as a method is "linked to dissolution of the self, fragmentation to flow."

53. The progressive silencing of Priscilla suggests that she functions in the text as a sign similar to the females found in modern motion pictures. Pam Cook and Claire Johnston, in "Woman in the Cinema of Raoul Walsh," in Constance Penley, ed., *Feminism and Film Theory* (New York: Routledge, 1988), suggest that a woman in one of Walsh's films "is not only a sign in a system of exchange, but an

empty sign" (27). The woman cannot control her own destiny, she is only a "signifier. . . . She remains 'spoken': she does not speak" (33).

54. Baym, *Shape of Hawthorne's Career*, 194–195.

55. Nathaniel Hawthorne, *The Scarlet Letter* (New York: Library of America, 1983), 344.

56. Baym, *Shape of Hawthorne's Career*, 199 and n. 7; T. Walter Herbert, Jr., "Nathaniel Hawthorne, Una Hawthorne, and *The Scarlet Letter*: Interactive Selfhoods and the Cultural Construction of Gender" *PMLA* 103 (1988): 285.

57. Caroline Chesebro', *Isa, A Pilgrimage* (Clinton Hall, N.Y.: Redfield, 1852), 29. Further citations are found in the text.

58. Nina Baym, who thinks Chesebro's presentation of Isa is consistently favorable, suggests that while "Isa's way is not for every woman," it is "the way of a woman of genius and perhaps all women of the future. Isa may not be a 'role-model' but she is an augur" (*Woman's Fiction*, 211).

59. *American Whig Review* 16 (1852): 95.

Chapter 3. Women and Property Rights

1. Norma Basch, *In the Eyes of the Law: Women, Marriage, and Property in Nineteenth-Century New York* (Ithaca, N.Y.: Cornell University Press, 1982), 48.

2. See Alan Macfarlane, "Economic Arrangements at Marriage," in *Marriage and Love in England: Modes of Reproduction, 1300–1840* (Oxford: Basil Blackwell, 1986), 263–290.

3. For a full discussion of the status of married women under common law see Elizabeth Bowles Warbasse, *The Changing Legal Rights of Married Women, 1800–1861* (New York: Garland Publishing, 1987), 5–29.

4. The equity courts developed from the English chancery court, where cases seeking compensation or actions other than money damages were heard. Over the centuries, the chancery or equity courts became a separate set of courts in England. In the United States, some states, with New York as the leading example, adopted the equity system, while others administered justice without these special courts. One of the major functions of the equity courts in New York in the early nineteenth century was the regulation of trusts, including those set up for married women, and the enforcement of prenuptial agreements. See Lawrence M. Friedman, *A History of American Law*, 2d ed. (New York: Simon and Schuster, 1985), 26–27, for a brief summary of the origin of the equity courts in England, and Basch, *In the Eyes of the Law*, 70–112, for an extended discussion of the court's treatment of women's property in New York.

5. Catharine Maria Sedgwick, *Clarence; or, a Tale of Our Own Times* (New York: George P. Putnam, 1849), 361. Subsequent references to this edition appear in the text.

6. Catharine Maria Sedgwick, *Redwood; A Tale* (New York: E. Bliss and E. White, 1824), 2:267. Subsequent references appear in the text.

7. John P. McWilliams, Jr., *Political Justice in a Republic: James Fenimore Cooper's America* (Berkeley: University of California Press, 1972), 107.

8. James Fenimore Cooper, *The Pioneers, or The Sources of the Susquehanna; A Descriptive Tale*, Historical Introduction by James Franklin Beard, text established by Lance Schachterle and Kenneth M. Andersen, Jr. (Albany: State University of New York Press, 1980), 443–444. Subsequent references appear in the text.

9. Nina Baym, "The Women of Cooper's Leatherstocking Tales," *American Quarterly* 23 (1971): 698.

10. James Fenimore Cooper, *Home as Found* (Boston: Dana Estes, 1908), 470. Subsequent references appear in the text.

11. James Fenimore Cooper, *The Redskins or Indian and Injin* (Chicago: Belford, Clarke, 1885), 439. Subsequent references appear in the text.

12. Warbasse, *Changing Legal Rights,* 137.

13. Elizabeth Brown, in "Memorandum on the Mississippi Woman's Law of 1839," *Michigan Law Review* 42 (1944): 1110–1121, gives a detailed account of the supposed origins of the bill, but Warbasse, in *Changing Legal Rights,* 138–139, doubts that the earlier anecdotal version can be supported by historical evidence.

14. Richard H. Chused documents the economic conditions that prevailed, in "Married Women's Property Law," *Georgetown Law Journal* 71 (1983): 1400–1403.

15. Warbasse, *Changing Legal Rights,* 152–155.

16. Ibid., 157.

17. *Laws made and passed by the General Assembly of the State of Maryland, 1842–1843,* chap. 293, "An act to regulate conjugal rights as they regard property," March 10, 1843.

18. Warbasse, *Changing Legal Rights,* 167.

19. Between 1839 and 1852, laws protecting married women's property were passed by twenty-two states. However, the wording of the laws varied greatly. Mississippi (1839), Maryland (1843), Kentucky (1846), and Arkansas (1846) also exempted a married woman's slaves from her husband's debts. Provisions that protected only a woman's real estate from the husband's debts were passed by Maryland (1842), Connecticut (1845), Iowa (1846), Kentucky (1846), Indiana (1847), Vermont (1845), North Carolina (1849), and Tennessee (1850). States that passed laws protecting both personal and real property included Michigan (1844), Maine (1844), Massachusetts (1845), Alabama (1846), Florida (1845), Ohio (1846), New Hampshire (1846), New York (1848), Pennsylvania (1848), Missouri (1849), Wisconsin (1850), and New Jersey (1852). For detailed discussions of the variations in these laws see Warbasse, *Changing Legal Rights,* and Chused, "Married Women's Property Laws," 1398–1400.

20. Quoted in Warbasse, *Changing Legal Rights,* 189.

21. Timothy Walker, *Introduction to American Law,* 9th ed., rev. Clement Bates (Boston: Little, Brown, 1887), 255.

22. Ibid., 272.

23. Elizabeth Cady Stanton, Susan B. Anthony, and Matilda Joslyn Gage, eds., *History of Woman Suffrage* (New York: Fowler and Wells, 1891), 1:172–173.

24. Quoted in Warbasse, *Changing Legal Rights,* 232.

25. Sarah Josepha Hale, ed., "Ought a Married Woman to Hold Property?" *Godey's Lady's Book* 45 (1852): 544.

26. Ibid., 542n.

27. Yuri Suhl, *Ernestine L. Rose and the Battle for Human Rights* (New York: Reynal, 1959), 51. Notice that Cooper's reference to the Married Women's Property Act as the "cup and saucer" law is thus an error.

28. Thomas Herttell, *Remarks comprising . . . Judge Herttell's Argument in the House of Assembly of the State of New-York, in the Session of 1837, in Support of the Bill to Restore to Married Women "The Right of Property"* (New York: Henry Durell, 1839).

29. Ibid., 82–83.

30. *History of Woman Suffrage*, 1:99; Suhl, *Ernestine L. Rose*, 59.

31. Elizabeth Cady Stanton, *Eighty Years and More* (New York: Schocken Books, 1971), 135, and Elizabeth Griffith, *In Her Own Right: The Life of Elizabeth Cady Stanton* (New York: Oxford University Press, 1984), 43.

32. *History of Women's Suffrage*, 1:66–67.

33. Peggy A. Rabkin, *Fathers to Daughters: The Legal Foundations of Female Emancipation* (Westport, Conn.: Greenwood Press, 1980), 12.

34. Friedman, *History of American Law*, 391–411; Rabkin, *Fathers to Daughters*, 52–58.

35. Rabkin, *Fathers to Daughters*, 21–22.

36. Ibid., 78.

37. Ibid., 95.

38. *History of Woman Suffrage*, 1:64.

39. Cooper himself, in the preface to *The Ways of the Hour* (New York: G. P. Putnam, 1850; rpt., Upper Saddle River, N.J.: Gregg Press, 1968) v, singles out juries among the social evils "that beset us." All subsequent references to the book are found in the text.

40. The first important notice appeared anonymously in the *North American Review* 71 (1850): 121–129; it called the novel "a lame and impotent caricature of that author's manner, exhibiting and exaggerating all his faults, but showing none of his excellencies"; the characters are "coarse and spiteful caricatures, not relieved by a single ray of wit or fancy"; the style is "prosy and diffuse"; the plot "awkward and improbable." Modern criticism continues in the same vein: Thomas R. Lounsbury, *James Fenimore Cooper* (Boston: Houghton Mifflin, 1882), 254, 260; Henry Walcott Boynton, *James Fenimore Cooper* (New York: Century, 1931), 394; Robert E. Spiller, *Fenimore Cooper: Critic of His Times* (New York: Minton, Balch, 1931), 299–300; James Grossman, *James Fenimore Cooper* (New York: William Sloane, 1949), 243; and George Dekker, *James Fenimore Cooper the Novelist* (London: Routledge and Kegan Paul, 1967), 246.

41. McWilliams, in *Political Justice in a Republic*, 389, n. 7, implies that only Dunscomb talks about women's roles and claims that his "attitudes cannot be attributed to Cooper," but see below for contrary evidence.

42. Rabkin, *Fathers to Daughters*, 80.

43. Friedman, *History of American Law*, 404.

44. Marvin Meyers, *The Jacksonian Persuasion: Politics and Belief* (Stanford: Stanford University Press, 1960), 59, 98, 99.

45. Mrs. Goodwin, once in possession of her house and money, takes an itinerant female laborer to sleep with her; their death is caused by the fall of a plough,

surely representing the land and probably the revenge of the missing male. Jane Marcus suggested to us that these overtones reveal Cooper's unconscious anger and fear of the powerful woman without a controlling husband.

46. Baym, "Women in Cooper," 703, 698.

47. Emma D.E.N. Southworth, *The Discarded Daughter*, also known as *The Children of the Isle* (Philadelphia: T. B. Peterson and Bros., 1855), 30. All subsequent references are found in the text.

48. Fanny Fern, *Ruth Hall and Other Writings*, ed. Joyce W. Warren (New Brunswick, N.J.: Rutgers University Press, 1986), 76, 78.

49. Fanny Fern, *Rose Clark* (New York: Mason Brothers, 1856), 251. All subsequent references are found in the text.

50. Mary Kelley, *Private Woman, Public Stage: Literary Domesticity in Nineteenth-Century America* (New York: Oxford University Press, 1984), 138–139, 153–158, 264–265.

51. *The Letters and Journals of James Fenimore Cooper*, ed. James Franklin Beard (Cambridge: Belknap Press of Harvard University Press, 1960–1968), 1:86–89 and notes.

52. Grossman, *Cooper*, 16.

53. Mary Bodine, a woman involved in the 1844 murder case that Grossman suggests is the basis of Mary Monson's story, is never mentioned in the journals and letters. See Grossman, *Cooper*, 240–41; the details are not very similar.

54. Angus Davidson, *Miss Douglas of New York* (New York: Viking, 1953), 46.

55. *Letters and Journals of Cooper*, 6:87.

56. Ibid., 6:32, 5:405, 6:190, 6:87.

57. Davidson, *Miss Douglas*, 212.

58. Kelley, *Private Woman, Public Stage*, 159.

59. "Emma Southworth," in Edward T. James, Janet Wilson James, and Paul S. Boyer, eds., *Notable American Women* (Cambridge: Belknap Press of Harvard University Press, 1971), 3:327.

60. Kelley, *Private Woman, Public Stage*, 238.

61. Regis Louise Boyle, *Mrs. E.D.E.N. Southworth, Novelist* (Washington, D.C.: Catholic University of America Press, 1939), 7.

62. "Southworth," *Notable American Women*, 3:327.

63. Boyle, *Southworth*, 7.

64. See the conclusions of Kay Ellen Thurman, "The Married Women's Property Acts," M.Ll. thesis, University of Wisconsin, 1966, 50; and Friedman, *History of American Law*, 211.

Chapter 4. Capitalism, Sex, and Sisterhood

1. Louisa May Alcott, *Work*, Introduction by Sarah Elbert (New York: Schocken, 1977), 1–2. Further references are found in the text.

2. As Sarah Elbert points out in the introduction to *Work* (xxii), Christie's occupations parallel the list of the seven available to women given by Harriet Martineau in 1836.

3. Kathryn Kish Sklar, *Catharine Beecher: A Study in American Domesticity* (New Haven and London: Yale University Press, 1973), 171.

4. In "From *Success* to *Experience*: Louisa May Alcott's *Work*," *Massachusetts Review* 21 (1980): 527–539, Jean Fagan Yellin contends that Alcott's omission of industrial work is fundamental to *Work*'s failure as a novel, and suggests that in not sending Christie into the mill Alcott may have been influenced by nativist bias: in this period immigrant women replaced the New England women who had been mill hands in her youth. Yellin maintains that since Christie "seems unable to conceive of identifying with women engaged in the industrial production which is redefining the nature of work in America," her isolation and suicide attempt are "almost inevitable" (537).

5. Louisa May Alcott, *Alternative Alcott*, ed. Elaine Showalter (New Brunswick, N.J.: Rutgers University Press, 1988), xxxi, xxxiv.

6. Jacqueline Jones, *Labor of Love, Labor of Sorrow: Black Women, Work, and the Family from Slavery to the Present* (New York: Basic Books, 1985), 127.

7. Charles Strickland, *Victorian Domesticity: Families in the Life and Art of Louisa May Alcott* (University, Ala.: University of Alabama Press, 1985), 86–87.

8. William Graham Sumner, *What Social Classes Owe to Each Other* (New York: Harper and Bros., 1883), 163, 113.

9. See, for a classic statement, Charles Edward Merriam, *American Political Ideas* (Chicago: University of Chicago Press, 1920; rpt., New York: Augustus M. Kelley, 1969), 325.

10. Elizabeth Stuart Phelps, *The Silent Partner*, with an afterword by Mari Jo Buhle and Florence Howe (Boston: J. R. Osgood, 1871; rpt., New York: Feminist Press, 1983), 8. All further citations are found in the text.

11. Sumner, *What the Social Classes Owe to Each Other*, 26.

12. After the Civil War, many states passed hours laws to limit the hours of workers in various occupations. By the late nineteenth century, most of these laws were under attack in the courts for violating the right to contract. Judith A. Baer in *The Chains of Protection: The Judicial Response to Women's Labor Legislation* (Westport, Conn.: Greenwood Press, 1978), 46, explains that the courts "ruled that the states' police power did enable them to protect the citizens' health, safety, welfare, or morals, but not at the expense of this fundamental right [to contract freely with respect to labor]." One of the best examples of these cases was *Lochner v. New York* (198 U.S. 145), which was decided in 1905.

13. Alice Kessler-Harris, *Out to Work: A History of Wage-Earning Women in the United States* (Oxford: Oxford University Press, 1982), 81.

14. *Mueller v. Oregon*, 208 U.S. 421 (1908).

15. See the discussion of protective legislation in Nancy E. McGlen and Karen O'Connor, *Women's Rights: The Struggle for Equality in the Nineteenth and Twentieth Centuries* (New York: Praeger, 1983), 158–159.

16. See the account of Mrs. John van Vorst and Marie van Vorst, *The Woman Who Toils: Being the Experiences of Two Gentlewomen as Factory Girls* (New York: Doubleday, Page, 1903), 160–161.

17. Lillian B. Chace Wyman, "Girls in a Factory Valley," *Atlantic Monthly* 78 (1896): 391–403, 504–517; and idem, "Studies of Factory Life," *Atlantic Monthly* 62 (1888): 16–29, 315–321, 605–612, and *Atlantic Monthly* 63 (1889): 69–79.

18. "Women As Breadwinners: A Natural Phenomenon?" *American Federationist* 4 (October 1897): 186–187, quoted in W. Elliott Brownlee and Mary M. Brownlee, eds., *Women in the American Economy: A Documentary History, 1675 to 1929* (New Haven, Conn.: Yale University Press, 1976), 213–214.

19. Julia Ward Howe, "Introduction," in Annie Nathan Meyer, ed., *Woman's Work in America* (New York: Henry Holt, 1891), 1.

20. Margaret Gibbons Wilson, *The American Woman in Transition: The Urban Influence, 1870–1920* (Westport, Conn.: Greenwood Press, 1979), 76.

21. *The Household* (1882), 290, quoted in Harvey Green, *The Light of Home* (New York: Pantheon Books, 1983), 27–28.

22. Gail Hamilton [Mary Abigail Dodge], "Self-Support," *Independent*, March 2, 1871.

23. Elizabeth Stuart Phelps, "Unhappy Girls," *Independent*, July 27, 1871.

24. Elizabeth Stuart Phelps, "What They Are Doing," *Independent*, August 17, 1871; Gail Hamilton, "Exemption or Imposition," *Independent*, September 7, 1871.

25. Frances Willard, "A Speciman 'Girl of the Period,'" *Independent*, May 25, 1871.

26. Cf. Green, *Light of Home*, for the details of home life, health, etc

27. Merriam, *American Political Ideas*, 366.

28. Helen E. Starrett, "Two Types of Women," *Woman's Magazine* 9 (1885): 106–107.

29. Charlotte S. Hilbourne, *Effie and I; or, Seven Years in a Cotton Mill* (Cambridge, Mass: Allen and Farnham, 1863), 6. Further references are found in the text.

30. Philip Foner describes the rise of protests against working conditions in the Lowell mills in 1845 in *The Factory Girls* (Urbana: University of Illinois Press, 1977), 57–60; Thomas Dublin details the rise and fall of the Ten Hour Movement in the Lowell mills and the replacement of native-born workers by immigrant women operatives in *Women at Work: The Transformation of Work and Community in Lowell, Massachusetts, 1826–1860* (New York: Columbia University Press, 1979).

31. Thomas Dublin's collection of letters written by mill workers and their families between 1830 and 1860 testifies to the essentially nonthreatening nature of mill work. These letters, exchanged between family members and their unmarried daughters and sisters who worked in the mill, exhibit no fear that such work would hurt the girls' chances to marry. The letters do reveal, however, that work in the mills appealed to the women's desire for personal and economic independence. See Thomas Dublin, ed., *Farm to Factory: Women's Letters, 1830–1860* (New York: Columbia University Press, 1981).

32. Merriam, *American Political Ideas*, 316.

33. Litere [Lillian E. Sommers], *For Her Daily Bread*, with a preface by Col. Robert G. Ingersoll (Chicago: Rand, McNally, 1887), 43. Further page references are found in the text.

34. Ingersoll, who received his military title in the Civil War, was a lawyer, attorney general of Illinois, and a well-known platform lecturer on agnosticism. See *Dictionary of American Biography*, ed. Dumas Malone (New York: Chas. Scribner's Sons, 1932), 9: 469–470.

35. Sumner, *What Social Classes Owe to Each Other*, 17.

36. This is Walter Fuller Taylor's term in discussing what he also calls "adventure" novels of the industrial age. He notes that the "romance of business struggle delivers no criticism, proposes no reform; its conservatism lies in an acceptance rather than an explicit defense of the industrial *status quo.*" Taylor, *The Economic Novel in America* (Chapel Hill: University of North Carolina Press, 1942), 111–112. Taylor gives a full list of novels in his bibliography, pp. 346–365.

37. Taylor, in *The Economic Novel*, concludes that the sentiment of most late nineteenth-century novels "inclined rather toward liberal reform than toward radicalism, and even the radicalism of the age was of the middle class, not of the proletariat." Virtually no novels espoused a radical class-based perspective, nor were any on the extreme right. In Taylor's view, most of the American authors seemed to write "quite without benefit of the European example" (61).

38. Phelps, *The Silent Partner*, 57–61.

39. Judith Fetterley, " 'Checkmate': Elizabeth Stuart Phelps's *The Silent Partner*," *Legacy* 3 (1986): 27.

40. William D. Howells, *A Woman's Reason* (Boston and New York: Houghton Mifflin, 1882), 137. Further references are found in the text.

41. See Howells's depiction of this situation in *Dr. Breen's Practice*, discussed in the next chapter.

42. Sarah Elbert interprets Alcott's conclusion as a complete rejection of the ideology of individualism ("Introduction" to *Work*, xxxiii). We agree that Alcott embraces sisterhood and cooperation, but Elbert's statement indicates a much stronger condemnation of nineteenth-century liberalism than the novel will support. At no time does Alcott condemn marriage or conventional social relationships. One of the strongest characters in the book is Mrs. Wilkins, who has learned obedience to her husband and yet kept her spirit of womanhood. Nor does Alcott really attack capitalism through any of Christie's experiences.

43. Henry George, a social critic of the post–Civil War era, proposed that a single tax, on property, would lead to a natural redistribution of land and thus to the end of poverty in the United States. His treatise, *Progress and Poverty,* published in 1880, made him an international figure. The influence of his ideas is discussed by Arthur Nichols Young, *The Single Tax Movement in the United States* (Princeton: Princeton University Press, 1916). Lawrence Gronlund's *The Cooperative Commonwealth* (Boston, 1884) influenced the work of Bellamy and Howells. (See Taylor, *Economic Novel*, 190–191.) Gronlund's proposal was more closely aligned with European socialism than were the Scottish cooperatives originally founded on the ideas of Robert Owen.

44. Beverley Ellison Warner, *Troubled Waters. A Problem of Today* (Philadelphia: J. B. Lippincott, 1885), 39. Further references are found in the text.

45. Ann Douglas, *The Feminization of American Culture* (New York: Avon, 1977).

46. Edward Bellamy, *Looking Backward, 2000–1887* (Cambridge: Belknap Press of Harvard University Press, 1967), 151. Further references are found in the text.

47. Edward Foster, *Mary E. Wilkins Freeman* (New York: Hendricks House, 1956), 155; Perry D. Westbrook, *Mary Wilkins Freeman* (New York: Twayne, 1967), 129. In 1915 Fred Lewis Pattee, in *A History of American Literature since 1870* (New York: D. Appleton-Century, 1915), expressed no opinion on the book's

political position, referring to it simply as a "problem novel . . . long and sprawling and ineffective" (240).

48. *Harper's Weekly*, 47 (November 21, 1903): 1880.

49. Mary E. Wilkins (Freeman), *The Portion of Labor* (New York: Harper and Bros., 1901), 192–194. Further references are found in the text.

50. For an analysis of the party realignment in 1896, see James L. Sundquist, *Dynamics of the Party System: Alignment and Realignment of Political Parties in the United States*, rev. ed. (Washington, D.C.: Brookings Institution, 1983), 159–165.

51. Grace H. Dodge, "Glimpses into Working Girls' Club Life and Principles," *American Federationist* 1 (1894): 69.

52. See Fetterley, "Checkmate," 17.

53. In Nancy Schrom Dye's study of the Women's Trade Union League of New York at the turn of the twentieth century, *As Equals and as Sisters: Feminism, the Labor Movement, and the Women's Trade Union League of New York* (Columbia: University of Missouri Press, 1980), she finds that the league's members believed that "women could . . . surmount social and ethnic differences and unite on the basis of their femininity. . . . A conviction that women could relate to one another across class lines in the spirit of sisterhood and an emphasis on the special qualities that women shared linked the league to the larger woman movement. . . . League members used the term *sisterhood* to convey the idea that class was less important than gender for understanding women's status" (45–46).

54. Dodge, "Glimpses," 68.

55. "Editor's Literary Record," *Harper's New Monthly Magazine* 43 (July 1871): 300–301.

56. In their afterword to *The Silent Partner*, Howe and Buhle note that Sip and Perley move "with conviction and without self-righteousness . . . to the independence of their own employment" (378).

57. Lori Duin Kelly says, in *The Life and Works of Elizabeth Stuart Phelps, Victorian Feminist Writer* (Troy, N.Y.: Whitston, 1983), that "here . . . the antagonist to a woman's development is clearly identified as male society which . . . forcibly endeavors to debar women from entering any fields outside their supposedly natural ones" (83).

58. See Cathy N. Davidson's discussion of *The Power of Sympathy* in *Revolution and the Word: The Rise of the Novel in America* (New York and Oxford: Oxford University Press, 1986), 98–109.

59. Martha Louise Rayne, *What Can a Woman Do? or Her Position in the Business and Literary World* (Petersburgh, N.Y.: Eagle Publishing, 1893; rpt., New York: Arno Press, 1974).

60. M. L. Rayne, *Against Fate. A True Story* (Chicago: W. B. Keen, Cooke, 1876), 83. Further references are found in the text.

61. Dublin notes that one of the mill girls whose letters appear in *Farm to Factory* evidently became involved in an affair with a married man who was a co-worker in the mill (135). The family's letters to Delia Page exhort her to be cautious and to reject this man. She finally does break off the relationship, much to their relief.

62. Leslie Woodcock Tentler, in *Wage-Earning Women: Industrial Work and Family Life in the United States, 1900–1930* (New York and Oxford: Oxford University Press, 1979), analyzes the romanticized atmosphere of the work environment

of young girls in a slightly later period. According to Tentler, "contemporary testimony is virtually unanimous that young working women looked forward to marriage as a desired rite of passage to adult freedom" (73). She also notes the conflict between young girls and their parents over evening social life (109–114).

63. Josephine Donovan, *New England Local Color Literature: A Women's Tradition* (New York: Frederick Ungar, 1983), 125.

64. In the case of the strike, as so often in analysis of *The Portion of Labor*, Freeman's novel has been made less radical by critics. Taylor, in *Economic Novel*, says that Ellen "leads out the factory girls" (311), but in fact she leads both men and women out to strike, and Freeman emphasizes her persuasion of the men. By 1901, women had led strikes of other women, but it is difficult to find any evidence of women leading a mixed strike before the early 1900s. See Philip S. Foner, *Women and the American Labor Movement* (New York: Free Press, 1979) for detailed accounts of many strikes, and Susan Levine, *Labor's True Woman: Carpet Weavers, Industrialization, and Labor Reform in the Gilded Age* (Philadelphia: Temple University Press, 1984), 63–101, for an account of the carpet weavers' strike of 1885.

65. Foster, *Freeman*, 154–155; Westbrook, *Freeman*, 127–129.

66. Levine, *Labor's True Woman*, 92, 113.

67. Taylor, *Economic Novel*, 311.

68. For an annotated list of novels that focus on labor unrest and strikes, see Fay M. Blake, *The Strike in the American Novel* (Metuchen, N.J.: Scarecrow Press, 1972), 207–275.

69. [John Hay], *The Bread-Winners: A Social Study* (New York: Harper and Bros., 1883), 241. Hay wrote the novel between government appointments. Serving as Lincoln's private secretary from 1861 until 1865, Hay later held various government posts, including secretary of state in the administration of President William McKinley.

Chapter 5. The Power of Professionalism

1. Harriet Beecher Stowe, *My Wife and I, or, Harry Henderson's History* (Boston and New York: Houghton Mifflin, 1899), ix, xii. Further references are found in the text.

2. In actuality Ruth Bolton's story is almost entirely by Warner. He wrote every chapter in which she appears: volume 1, chapters 14, 15, 21, 22, 31; volume 2, chapters 10, 17, 19, and 32. Twain was, however, responsible for some sections of the book dealing with her lover, Philip Sterling. See Albert Bigelow Paine, "Introduction," in Mark Twain and Charles Dudley Warner, *The Gilded Age: A Tale of Today* (New York: Gabriel Wells, 1922), xvi, n. 1. All further references appear in the text.

3. A summary of the college's early history can be found in Regina Markell Morantz-Sanchez, *Sympathy and Science: Women Physicians in American Medicine* (New York and Oxford: Oxford University Press, 1985), 76–79.

4. For a discussion of the reaction of female physicians to Clarke's thesis, see Morantz-Sanchez, *Sympathy and Science*, 54–56.

5. For a discussion of the early licensing provisions, see William G. Rothstein, *American Physicians in the Nineteenth Century: From Sects to Science* (Baltimore and London: Johns Hopkins University Press, 1972), 72–79.

6. Joseph F. Kett, *The Formation of the American Medical Profession: The Role of Institutions, 1780–1860* (New Haven and London: Yale University Press, 1968), 110–111.

7. Ibid., 123.

8. Ibid., 119.

9. Paul Starr, *The Social Transformation of American Medicine* (New York: Basic Books, 1982), 52.

10. Martin Kaufman, *Homeopathy in America: The Rise and Fall of a Medical Heresy* (Baltimore and London: Johns Hopkins Press, 1971), 29. The four fundamental principles of homeopathy were: the rule of similars which held that diseases should be treated by drugs that produced the same symptoms as the disease; prescription of the appropriate drugs in very small quantities; the belief that all chronic disease was caused by the itch; and experimentation by testing drugs on healthy persons in order to determine their effects.

11. Ibid., 53. Kaufman holds that the primary motivation for the formation of the AMA was the desire to improve medical education and that the concern with excluding homeopaths intensified only in later years. However, Oliver Wendell Holmes attacked homeopathy in a series of public lectures in 1842, and the pamphlet that reprinted those lectures was widely circulated in the 1840s. See Kaufman, *Homeopathy in America*, 34–40.

12. A short novel of 1886, *Love and Medicine* by Dr. Charles F. Gilliam (Washington D.C.: Gray and Clarkson), paints an appalling picture of the conditions of medical education in the guise of a warning from a medical preceptor to his apprentice, who is about to start medical school in Cincinnati. When the student asks why such poor conditions—cheating, cutting classes, general negligence—are tolerated, the older doctor explains that there are "so many medical colleges . . . there is a great rivalry between them to see which can secure the largest classes and turn out the most graduates. . . . Many of these colleges are organized for the purpose of advertising the doctors who compose the faculties. . . . Another reason is that the income from most of the colleges is divided among the faculties *pro rata*" (221).

13. Mary Roth Walsh, *"Doctors Wanted: No Women Need Apply": Sexual Barriers in the Medical Profession, 1835–1975* (New Haven, Conn., and London: Yale University Press, 1977), 186.

14. Morantz-Sanchez, *Sympathy and Science*, 31–32.

15. Ibid., 4.

16. The phrases are John Ware's, quoted in Morantz-Sanchez, *Sympathy and Science*, 52.

17. Ibid., 53. On pp. 51–55 Morantz-Sanchez summarizes the chief arguments of those opposed to women in medicine, including the "menstruation" thesis maintained by Dr. Edward H. Clarke of the Harvard Medical School in *Sex in Education: or, A Fair Chance for Girls* (1873).

18. The most extreme example of the tension between the physicians and the politicians occurred in Michigan, where the state legislature mandated the addition

of homeopathic doctors to the teaching faculty of the University of Michigan Medical College. The faculty refused to comply, and the legislature threatened to withhold appropriations for the school. After a protracted struggle, the faculty agreed to let homeopaths teach several of their own courses and to note attendance in the homeopathic division on diplomas. See Kaufman, *Homeopathy in America*, 93–109.

19. Ibid., 79–86.

20. See Walsh, *"Doctors Wanted,"* 147–162, and tables on pp. 185 and 186.

21. These were not the only novels to participate in the debate, though they were undoubtedly the best. In 1881 Howells visited one young woman with the proofs of *Dr. Breen's Practice* to prove that he had not stolen her plot, and later he encountered a "pretty young doctress who had written out her own adventures!" See Jean Carwile Masteller, "The Women Doctors of Howells, Phelps, and Jewett: The Conflict of Marriage and Career," in Gwen L. Nagel, ed., *Critical Essays on Sarah Orne Jewett* (Boston: G. K. Hall, 1984), 146, n. 4. Neither of these novels is probably the same as Sara E. Hervey's *The Esty Family* (Onset, Mass.: Published by the author, 1889), in which a young woman whose beloved has died decides to become a doctor. In short order she receives medical education in Philadelphia, opens an office in New York, keeps a betrayed girl from "committing foeticide," ushers three consumptives into the next world with proper religious assistance, and becomes physician to one of the most prominent male doctors in the city. Poorly as the novel is written, Esty understands that becoming a physician is a means to achieving independent power within the community.

22. See Ellen Moers, "A Note on Mark Twain and Harriet Beecher Stowe," in *Harriet Beecher Stowe and American Literature* (Hartford, Conn.: Stowe-Day Foundation, 1978), 39.

23. *Sarah Orne Jewett Letters*, enlarged and rev. ed., ed. Richard Cary (Waterville, Maine: Colby College Press, 1967), 27, n. 13.

24. Ibid., 40–41, 81–82, 84–85.

25. W. D. Howells, *Selected Letters, Volume 2: 1873–1881*, ed. George Arms, Christoph K. Lohmann, and Jerry Herron (Boston: Twayne, 1979), 258, n. 2.

26. Masteller, "Women Doctors," 135.

27. William D. Howells, *Dr. Breen's Practice* (Westport, Conn.: Greenwood, 1969; rpt. of 1881 ed.), 44. All further references are found in the text.

28. Elizabeth Stuart Phelps, *Dr. Zay*, with an afterword by Michael Sartisky (New York: Feminist Press, 1987; rpt. of 1882 ed.), 63. In fact, it is the hero who drives badly and has a serious accident. All further references are found in the text.

29. Kaufman, *Homeopathy in America*, 90.

30. Howells, *Selected Letters*, 2:77 (Nov. 29, 1874); 90, n. 4 (Jan. 31, 1875); 296 (Sept. 11, 1881); 302 and n. 1 (Dec. 15, 1881).

31. Kaufman, *Homeopathy in America*, 126. Following this action the New York Medical Society was expelled from the American Medical Association and a more conservative faction from New York was seated in its place. The same debate took place in many states, and within a decade the consultation clause was rarely used.

32. In his depiction of Dr. Mulbridge as the ideal physician, particularly for the female patient, Howells shows his own deference to medical authority. Here he may be revealing his feelings of dependence and helplessness before the physicians who were treating his daughter.

33. Elizabeth Stuart Phelps, *Chapters from a Life* (Boston and New York: Houghton Mifflin, 1897), 261–265. After pointing out that divergent schools of literature agree that it is "the province of the literary artist to tell the truth about the world he lives in," Phelps objects to Howells's statement that the novels of the "great New Englanders" were marred by "intense ethicism." Instead, she maintains, it is "a radically defective view of art which would preclude from it the ruling constituents of life. Moral character is to human life what air is to the natural world. . . . Strike 'Ethicism' out of life . . . before you shake it out of story!" (259–262). Howells in turn faulted Phelps "for vagueness, obscurity, and 'a certain feminine desire to get yet one sigh or one gasp more out of expression,'" though he found some of her work "very simple, powerful, and affecting." Alfred Habegger, *Gender, Fantasy, and Realism in American Literature* (New York: Columbia University Press, 1982), 312, n. 1.

34. "Recent Fiction," *Lippincott's* 34 (1884): 318.

35. Mary Putnam Jacobi, "Woman in Medicine," in Annie Nathan Meyer, ed., *Woman's Work in America* (New York: Henry Holt, 1891), 200.

36. See Michael Sartisky, "Afterword," in Phelps, *Dr. Zay*, 296–299. Sartisky's suggestion that Yorke's mother's lameness is a reference to Hephaestus is highly dubious. It is more likely that Phelps was explaining why Mrs. Yorke would have opinions about medical practice.

37. Phelps, *Chapters from a Life*, 250–252.

38. Rachel Bodley, Valedictory Address, "The College Story," quoted in Gulielma Fell Alsop, *History of the Woman's Medical College, Philadelphia, Pennsylvania, 1850–1950* (Philadelphia, London, and Montreal: J. B. Lippincott, 1950), 132–133.

39. "Medical Coeducation," *Woman's Medical Journal* 3 (1894): 99. Morantz-Sanchez says that "married women who ceased to practice medicine remained distinctly in the minority. . . . Available data suggests that the marriage rate for women physicians was disproportionately high in the nineteenth and twentieth centuries. . . . Between one-fifth and one-third of women physicians married in the nineteenth century, and by 1900 their marriage rate was twice that of all employed women and four times the rate among professional women" (*Sympathy and Science*, 135).

40. Masteller, "Women Doctors," 138–140. This was also pointed out in the review of "Recent Novels" in *The Nation* 39 (1884): 97.

41. "Recent Fiction," *Lippincott's* 34 (1884): 318.

42. "Recent Novels," *The Nation* 39 (1884): 96–97.

43. Jewett was both the daughter and granddaughter of doctors. Her grandfather was trained at Harvard Medical School, her father at the Jefferson Medical College in Philadelphia. Dr. Leslie in *A Country Doctor* is a portrait of her father, Dr. Theodore Herman Jewett. Much of Nan's early life, traveling through the countryside in Dr. Leslie's buggy, is autobiography on Jewett's part. Jewett herself contemplated a medical career for part of her girlhood. See Richard Cary, *Sarah Orne Jewett* (New York: Twayne, 1962), 12, 20–22, 138–141, and Margaret Farrand Thorp, *Sarah Orne Jewett*, University of Minnesota Pamphlets on American Writers, no. 41 (Minneapolis: University of Minnesota Press, 1966), 14–16.

44. Sarah Orne Jewett, *A Country Doctor* (Boston: Houghton Mifflin, 1884), 27. All further references are given in the text.

45. Dr. Jewett "often made journeys to Boston to talk with colleagues and inform himself on the newest practices in his art," and Thorp says that the portrait of him in *A Country Doctor* "may be accepted as accurate" (*Sarah Orne Jewett*, 15).

46. Summaries of the school's history can be found in Morantz-Sanchez, *Sympathy and Science*, 81–84, and, in fuller detail, in Walsh, *"Doctors Wanted,"* 35–75.

47. Morantz-Sanchez, *Sympathy and Science*, 81.

48. Ibid., 71.

49. Cited by Irving Howe in the "Introduction" to Henry James, *The Bostonians* (New York: Modern Library, 1956), xi. All further references are found in the text.

50. See Howard M. Feinstein, *Becoming William James* (Ithaca, N.Y., and London: Cornell University Press, 1984), 203, and the *Henry James Letters*, ed. Leon Edel (Cambridge: Belknap Press of Harvard University Press, 1974–1984), passim.

51. Morantz-Sanchez, *Sympathy and Science*, 192.

52. Putnam Jacobi, "Woman in Medicine," 177.

53. Annie Nathan Meyer, *Helen Brent, M.D.* (New York: Cassell, 1892), 13. Further page references are given in the text.

54. Rothstein, *American Physicians in the Nineteenth Century*, 290.

55. See Meyer's autobiographical work, *Barnard Beginnings* (Boston and New York: Houghton Mifflin, 1935), for a complete account of her efforts.

56. Ibid., 158.

57. Meyer became even more dubious with time that professional activity could be combined with marriage. In *The Dominant Sex*, a play she published in 1911, the heroine neglects her children as she runs for the presidency of the Federation of Women's Clubs, and her secretary, a widow, is forced by economic necessity to be away from her little boy while he is ill.

58. Critics were very negative about *Rose of Dutcher's Coolly*, not because of the idealized portraits of Rose or Dr. Herrick, but due to Garland's frank discussion of the sexual awakening of Rose and her companions. Comparing his work to that of Zola, the *Critic* complained, "Mr. Garland's word 'sex maniac' is barbarous enough; but the continual dwelling on (we had almost said gloating over) the thing is far worse." Garland's friend and patron, Howells, found the work flawed by Rose's ability to overcome her youthful sexual indiscretions. Cited in Jean Holloway, *Hamlin Garland, A Biography* (Austin: University of Texas Press, 1960), 121–122.

59. Hamlin Garland, *Rose of Dutcher's Coolly* (Chicago: Stone and Kimball, 1895), 287. All further references are given in the text.

60. Starr, *Social Transformation of American Medicine*, 69–70.

61. Putnam Jacobi believed that motherhood made for better doctors. She argued that "the increased vigor and vitality accruing to healthy women from the bearing and possession of children, a good deal more than compensates for the difficulties involved in caring for them, when professional duties replace the more usual ones." Cited in Morantz-Sanchez, *Sympathy and Science*, 59.

62. See chapter 6 for discussion of Garland's feminist views.

63. Charlotte Perkins Gilman, *The Crux* (New York: Charlton, 1911), 59. All further references are given in the text.

64. Vivian's grandmother tells her that "things are changing very fast now, since the general airing began. Dr. Prince Morrow in New York, with that society of

his—(I can never remember the name—makes me think of tooth-brushes) has done much; and the popular magazines have taken it up" (244–245). The society was called the New York Society of Sanitary and Moral Prophylaxis; see David J. Pivar, *Purity Crusade, Sexual Morality, and Social Control, 1868–1900* (Westport, Conn.: Greenwood, 1973), 243–245.

65. After a women's suffrage amendment was defeated in Colorado in 1877, local suffrage clubs formed to work on a new campaign. The male voters of Colorado approved a referendum granting woman suffrage in 1893. The campaign's success was attributed to the rise of the Populist party in that state. Susan B. Anthony and Ida Husted Harper, eds., *History of Woman Suffrage* (1902; rpt., New York: Arno and New York Times Press, 1969), 4:509–518.

Chapter 6. Political Power, Direct and Indirect

1. Mary Clemmer Ames, *Ten Years in Washington Life and Scenes in the National Capital as a Woman Sees Them* (Hartford, Conn.: A. D. Worthington, 1874), 125–126.

2. Francis Parkman, "The Woman Question," *North American Review* 129 (1879): 312.

3. Elizabeth Cady Stanton, Susan B. Anthony, and Matilda Joslyn Gage, eds., *History of Woman Suffrage* (New York: Arno Press, 1969), 2:145.

4. Ibid., 2:101.

5. George William Curtis, "The Right of Suffrage," presented at the New York Constitutional Convention, July 19, 1867, reprinted in *Orations and Addresses of George William Curtis,* ed. Charles Eliot Norton (New York: Harper and Bros., 1894), 1:187, 189.

6. *History of Woman Suffrage,* 2:126.

7. Susan B. Anthony and Ida Husted Harper, eds., *History of Woman Suffrage* (New York: Arno Press, 1969), 4:84.

8. For an extended discussion of the split in the movement, see *History of Woman Suffrage,* vol. 2; Eleanor Flexner, *Century of Struggle: The Woman's Rights Movement in the United States* (New York: Atheneum, 1974); Carrie Chapman Catt and Nettie Rogers Shuler, *Woman Suffrage and Politics: The Inner Story of the Suffrage Movement* (New York: Charles Scribners Sons, 1926); and Israel Kugler, *From Ladies to Women: The Organized Struggle for Woman's Rights in the Reconstruction Era* (New York: Greenwood Press, 1987).

9. For an excellent discussion of the politics of the suffrage movement, see Catt and Shuler, *Women Suffrage and Politics.*

10. *History of Woman Suffrage,* 4:107.

11. Edward Winslow Martin [J. D. McCabe], *Behind the Scenes in Washington. Being a Complete and Graphic Account of the Credit Mobilier Investigation . . . Workings of the Lobbies* (N.p.: Continental Publishing, 1873), 221, 231.

12. One of the best summaries of the positions for and against women's suffrage was provided by a series of articles in *North American Review* 129 (1879): 303–321, 413–447; and 130 (1880): 16–30. Francis Parkman explicated the negative position, and "The Other Side of the Woman Question" was argued in separate

replies by Julia Ward Howe, Thomas Wentworth Higginson, Lucy Stone, Elizabeth Cady Stanton, and Wendell Phillips. Another selection of comments on women in England and the United States in the period is contained in the three-volume set *The Woman Question: Society and Literature in Britain and America, 1837–1883*, by Elizabeth K. Helsinger, Robin Lauterbach Sheets, and William Veeder (New York and London: Garland, 1983).

13. See, for example, Gordon Milne, *The American Political Novel* (Norman: University of Oklahoma Press, 1966), which discusses Twain, De Forest, and Adams, or Joseph Blotner, *The Modern American Political Novel, 1900–1960* (Austin: University of Texas Press, 1966), which mentions the books of Burnett, Adams, and De Forest as forerunners of the political novel with a female protagonist (173–175). *Through One Administration* was compared to *Democracy* in *The Nation*, June 28, 1883, 552, and in *Athenaeum*, May 12, 1883, 600; *Playing the Mischief* was compared to *The Gilded Age* in *Appleton's*, August 14, 1875, 215.

14. See chap. 5, n. 2, for the breakdown of the authorship of *The Gilded Age*.

15. Mark Twain and Charles Dudley Warner, *The Gilded Age: A Tale of Today* (New York: Gabriel Wells, 1922), 2:33–34. All further references are found in the text.

16. Bryant Morey French, *Mark Twain and "The Gilded Age"* (Dallas: Southern Methodist University Press, 1965), 104.

17. Louis J. Budd, in *Mark Twain, Social Philosopher* (Bloomington: Indiana University Press, 1962), writes that "as late as 1871 he had planned to amuse the lyceums with 'An Appeal in Behalf of Extended Suffrage to Boys'—a satire on the 'general tendency of the times,' meaning especially the rise of the suffragettes"(55). There are discussions of Mark Twain's attitudes toward women in Edward Wagenknecht, *Mark Twain the Man and His Work*, 3rd ed. (Norman: University of Oklahoma Press, 1967), 125–127, and in Joyce W. Warren, *The American Narcissus: Individualism and Women in Nineteenth-Century American Fiction* (New Brunswick, N. J.: Rutgers University Press, 1984), 149–185.

18. Mark Twain, *Europe and Elsewhere* (New York: Harper and Bros., 1923), 27, 29.

19. Martin, *Behind the Scenes*, 225.

20. J[ohn] W. De Forest, *Playing the Mischief* (New York: Harper and Bros., 1875), 59. All further references are found in the text.

21. See James F. Light, *John William De Forest* (New York: Twayne, 1965), 145, or Joseph Jay Rubin, "Introduction to *Playing the Mischief*," rpt. in James W. Gargano, ed., *Critical Essays on John William De Forest* (Boston: G. K. Hall, 1981), 123.

22. "Mary Edwards Walker," in Edward T. James, Janet Wilson James, and Paul S. Boyer, eds., *Notable American Women* (Cambridge: Harvard University Press, 1971), 3:533.

23. Ibid., 2:414, 3:532.

24. "Recent Literature," *Atlantic Monthly* 37 (February 1876): 238–239.

25. Martin, *Behind the Scenes*, 240.

26. Henry Adams, *Novels, Mont Saint Michel, The Education* (New York: Library of America, 1983), 8. All further references to *Democracy: An American Novel* are found in the text.

27. George Hochfield, however, in *Henry Adams: An Introduction and Interpretation* (New York: Holt, Rinehart, and Winston, 1962), sees in Madeleine's final self-evaluation "an absolute condemnation by Adams of the desire for power" (31).

28. Ernest Samuels, *Henry Adams: The Middle Years* (Cambridge: Belknap Press of Harvard University Press, 1958), 69–70.

29. "Marian Hooper Adams," in *Notable American Women*, 1:15, including James quote.

30. As a historian Adams took a long view of the place of women in political society. In 1876 he had delivered a Lowell lecture titled "Primitive Rights of Women," examining the history of the subordination of women and concluding that women had had considerable social and political rights before the advent of Christianity. *Historical Essays* (New York: Chas. Scribner's Sons, 1891), 1–41.

31. Mary Clay made the argument forcefully at the Senate hearing in 1884: "You need woman's presence and counsel in legislation as much as she needs yours in the home . . . you need her sense of justice and moral courage to execute the laws; you need her for all that is just, merciful and good in government" (*History of Woman Suffrage*, 4:45).

32. Robert Lee White, "Introduction," in Frances Hodgson Burnett, *Through One Administration* (New York and London: Johnson Reprint Corp., 1969), xiii. All further references are found in the text. The novelists were generally familiar with each other's work, although Ernest Samuels writes that Henry Adams "apparently did not read or was unimpressed by Mark Twain's (and C. D. Warner's) *Gilded Age*" (*Henry Adams*, 442, n. 46). After *Democracy* was published anonymously, Howells and Warner guessed that the book was the work of De Forest, and Adams, replying to an inquiry made of his publisher by Edmund Stedman, who was including an excerpt in *A Library of American Literature*, writes that the author "is not in his list in that connection, even if he or she is a professional, like Harry James or Mrs. Burnett." *The Letters of Henry Adams*, ed. J. C. Levenson, Ernest Samuels, Charles Vandersee, Viola Hopkins Winner (Cambridge: Belknap Press of Harvard University Press, 1982) 2:472, 3:192. Samuels points out that one reason Adams was anxious to keep his authorship secret was so that he could continue to frequent Washington society: "Frances Burnett was 'sneered at behind her back' for her *Through One Administration*" (*Henry Adams*, 100).

33. The pattern was borne out in Burnett's own life, where both her marriages failed but her love for her sons sustained her. See Phyllis Bixler, *Frances Hodgson Burnett* (Boston: Twayne, 1984), 6–10 and passim, and Ann Thwaite, *Waiting for the Party: The Life of Frances Hodgson Burnett, 1849–1924* (London: Secker and Warburg, 1974).

34. *The Nation* 36 (June 1883): 552.

35. *History of Woman Suffrage*, 4:107.

36. Parkman, "The Woman Question," 315–316.

37. Minority Report by Sens. Brown and Cockrell, presented on January 25, 1887, reprinted in *History of Woman Suffrage*, 4:99.

38. Horace Bushnell, *Women's Suffrage: The Reform against Nature* (New York: Charles Scribner and Co., 1869), 155–156.

39. *History of Woman Suffrage*, 4:106.

40. Ibid., 4:100, 99.

41. Parkman, "The Woman Question," 307, 319.

42. *History of Woman Suffrage*, 4:98.

43. Bushnell, *Women's Suffrage*, 149.

44. Ernest Earnest, *The American Eve in Fact and Fiction, 1775–1914* (Urbana: University of Illinois Press, 1974), 127.

45. *Life and Letters of Bayard Taylor*, ed. Marie Hansen-Taylor and Horace E. Scudder (Boston: Houghton Mifflin, 1895), 1:343–365.

46. Sara deSaussure Davis, "Feminist Sources in *The Bostonians*," *American Literature* 50 (1979): 571–573. Davis proposes a full historical reading of *The Bostonians*, with Olive, Verena, and Basil Ransom based on Susan B. Anthony, Anna Dickinson, and Whitelaw Reid, but she admits these parallels were not noticed when the novel was published.

47. *Life of Taylor*, 2:453, 417.

48. Bayard Taylor, *Hannah Thurston: A Story of American Life* (Boston: G. P. Putnam, 1864; rpt., Upper Saddle River, N.J.: Gregg Press, 1968), 58. All further references are found in the text.

49. Henry James, *The Bostonians*, with an introduction by Irving Howe (New York: Modern Library, 1956), 53. All further references are found in the text.

50. Leon Edel, *Henry James, The Middle Years: 1882–1895* (New York: Avon Books, 1962), 139. This point is reiterated by many later James critics, e.g., Judith Fryer, *The Faces of Eve: Women in the Nineteenth-Century American Novel* (Oxford: Oxford University Press, 1976), 149. Howe summarizes the triangular structure thus: "the struggle between Ransom and Olive over Verena is a struggle between competing ideologies over a passive agent of the natural and the human" (*Bostonians*, xxvii).

51. Much of the criticism of Basil replies to Lionel Trilling's analysis in *The Opposing Self* (New York: Viking, 1955), which found the novel suffused with "apprehension of the loss of manhood," a story of "the sacred fathers endangered" (113, 117). See the discussion in Judith Fetterley, *The Resisting Reader: A Feminist Approach to American Fiction* (Bloomington and London: Indiana University Press, 1978), 101–115. Howe replies that "if Ransom is expressing James's views at all, it is in a style so deliberately inflated as to carry the heaviest ironic stress" (*Bostonians*, xvi). Fetterley points out numerous ways in which "James's irony plays . . . over Ransom's self-serving simplifications" (128). Most recently, however, Sandra Gilbert and Susan Gubar have returned to the view that "Basil's aesthetic is an essentially Jamesian one" and that "Basil's rescue of Verena from the diseased clutches of Olive and her band of fanatical acolytes reflects James's desire to tell women that 'Woman has failed you utterly—try Man.'" *No Man's Land: The Place of the Woman Writer in the Twentieth Century, Volume I: The War of the Words* (New Haven and London: Yale University Press, 1988), 26–27.

52. Edel, *Henry James*, 140, followed by Fryer, *Faces of Eve*, 148–149, Gilbert and Gubar, *No Man's Land*, 26, 133–135.

53. *Woman's Journal*, March 13, 1886, 83.

54. The strongest supporter of Olive is Judith Fetterley, who carefully analyzes the biases of earlier James criticism (*Resisting Reader*, 101–153).

55. Eberhard Alsen, "Introduction," in Hamlin Garland, *A Spoil of Office* (Arena Publishing, 1892; rpt., New York: Johnson Reprint Corp., 1969), v. All further references appear in the text.

56. Hamlin Garland, *A Son of the Middle Border* (New York: Macmillan, 1924), 366, 365.

57. Hamlin Garland, "Women and Their Organization," *Standard*, October 8, 1890, 5, quoted in Donald Pizer, *Hamlin Garland's Early Work and Career* (Berkeley: University of California Press, 1960), 72.

58. Hamlin Garland, *Main-Travelled Roads: Six Mississippi Valley Stories*, with an introduction by Thomas A. Bledsoe (New York: Rinehart, 1954), 13. The Arena Press, which sent Garland west to gather information about the farmer's revolt, also published books about women's suffrage.

59. In reaction to the desperate conditions of farm life in the 1880s and the collapse of farm prices, the Farmer's Alliances were organized throughout the southern and western states. Begun as quasi-secret fraternal organizations in the South, the Alliances developed into educational organizations that shared information on agricultural practices among farmers, as well as alerting their members to the abuses perpetrated by business interests. Although some of the state Alliances were able to win local elections, the national organization was not successful politically. In 1891, the Populist party organized to provide a cohesive voice for the farmer's demands, and in 1892 they nominated General James Weaver for president. For an account of the Alliances, see Carleton Beals, *The Great Revolt and Its Leaders: The History of Popular American Uprisings in the 1890s* (New York: Abelard-Shuman, 1968.) Garland himself, like his hero Bradley Talcott, began his political life as a Democrat but converted to the Populist movement in 1891 and campaigned for the party in Iowa that year.

60. Emily Edson Briggs, *The Olivia letters, Being Some History of Washington City for Forty years as Told by the Letters of a Newspaper Correspondent* (New York and Washington: Neale, 1906), 52.

61. Davis, "Feminist Sources," 574.

62. Elizabeth Cady Stanton, Susan B. Anthony, and Matilda Joslyn Gage, eds., *History of Woman Suffrage* (Rochester, N.Y.: Susan B. Anthony, 1886), 3:192. A list is given on p. 197.

63. Davis, "Feminist Sources," 570–580. See also Ruth Evelyn Quebe, "*The Bostonians*: Some Historical Sources and Their Implications," *Centennial Review* 25 (1981): 80–100.

64. There is considerable disagreement about the extent to which James was trying to paint a realistic portrait of the women's rights movement. Davis, in "Feminist Sources," notes that "James's knowledge of his subject matter . . . has been impugned or ignored since 1885" (570).

65. Elizabeth Cady Stanton, "Preface," in Helen H. Gardener, *Pray You, Sir, Whose Daughter?* (Boston: Arena Publishing, 1892), vi.

66. Laura J. Curtis [Bullard], *Christine, or, Woman's Trials and Triumphs* (New York: De Witt and Davenport, 1856), 184.

67. Lizzie Boynton Harbert, *Out of Her Sphere* (Des Moines: Mills and Co., 1871), 43.

68. Mary H. Ford, *Which Wins? A Story of Social Conditions* (Boston: Lee and Shepard, 1891).

69. Gardener, *Pray You, Sir, Whose Daughter?* 95.

70. Alsen, "Introduction," v.

71. Jean Holloway, *Hamlin Garland, a Biography* (Austin: University of Texas Press, 1960), 65.

72. "Mary Elizabeth Clyens Lease," in *Notable American Women*, 2:381.

73. The suffrage situation in Illinois was unique: in 1891, the legislature gave women the right to vote in school elections, but the bill was so poorly drafted that its implementation was subject to numerous court challenges. After four interpretations by the courts of Illinois, women were given the right to vote for school officers but not for school taxes or bond issues. Under a nondiscrimination law, however, women had the legal right to hold most local offices. The struggle to obtain municipal suffrage and the right to vote in presidential elections was carried on by the women's suffrage organizations at every session of the legislature. According to the *History of Woman Suffrage*, 4:602, most of the campaigns were managed by Catharine Waugh McColloch, a practicing lawyer from Chicago.

74. Brand Whitlock, *Her Infinite Variety* (Indianapolis: Bobbs-Merrill, 1904), 126. All further references are found in the text.

Index